ADVANCE PRAISE

Part Holocaust survival story, part coming-of-age story and intimate family portrait, *American Wolf* is a true and unforgettable account of war, escape, and immigration, told with ultimate grace and in vivid detail. The spirit and emotional force of Wolf Schwersenz's story, beginning with his boyhood during Hitler's chilling ascent, will stay with you long after you finish turning pages. A must read! – **Katie Sise, nationally bestselling author of *We Were Mothers*, *Open House*, and *The Break***

An absorbing account of the Holocaust told through the eyes of a young boy. By narrating this true story in the first person, Audrey Birnbaum deftly transports the reader to 1930s Berlin and we are at once immersed in a family drama during the rise of Hitler. *American Wolf* is a captivating Holocaust escape story that goes past the genre to tell a moving immigration narrative. This is a story of determination, survival and resistance that is as relevant today as at any time in the last three generations. – **Steve Hunegs, Executive Director Jewish Community Relations Council of Minnesota and the Dakotas**

An intimate personal account, an important contribution to the body of work reminding us that while the Holocaust altered the course of history, it is best understood for the ways it affected the lives of individuals and families. – **Diana Shaw Clark, Former Member United States Holocaust Memorial Museum Council**

Who will be left to tell the riveting and profound life stories of those who had a front row seat to the ravaging experiences of the Holocaust? We will! Through the shared specific details and intrigue gifted to us by Audrey Birnbaum, we witness the arc of an artful narrative where the truths of perseverance, tenacity and challenge unfold before us to reveal how one man's journey of survival impacts us all. – **Rabbi Elaine Zecher, Senior Rabbi, Temple Israel of Boston**

AMERICAN WOLF

FROM NAZI REFUGEE TO AMERICAN SPY.
A TRUE STORY

AUDREY BIRNBAUM

ap

ISBN 9789493322004 (ebook)

ISBN 9789493276987 (paperback)

ISBN 9789493276994 (hardcover)

Publisher: Amsterdam Publishers, The Netherlands

info@amsterdampublishers.com

American Wolf is part of the series Holocaust Survivor True Stories

Cover image: Alexander von Ness www.nessgraphica.com

CONTENTS

PART VI

For Dad

INTRODUCTION

In his last few days, my father spoke only German.

"*Vati, Vati,*" he called out from his hospital bed, over and over. *Papa. Papa.*

How strange it was to hear my father calling out for his own father. I did not know if the words had any significance or were simply the garbled gibberish of agitation and dementia; the only words I could discern in a language I barely understood. The fact that he only spoke German – his mother tongue – was something I could fathom, though. It's what always happens when you are dying.

The end came quickly after that.

I held onto the podium with one hand while I pulled my notes from my dress pocket with the other. The crinkled pages had been crossed out and annotated dozens of times. I smoothed the pages of the eulogy and steadied my voice.

This was my moment to pay tribute to my father and I had it all planned out. I would begin with an amusing anecdote and add a warm family tale. The congregants would laugh a little, maybe shed a tear or two. Then I would pause.

It would be time to share with everyone the most seminal events of my father's life: his last-minute, death-defying escape from Nazi Germany and his difficult immigration and painful transition to life in America. These experiences shaped my father's entire life. They *defined* him. His Holocaust trauma was not only a source of pain and suffering; it was also a point of pride. "Look," he would try to convey to people who heard of his hardships, "I survived this terrible thing. I am both wounded and special. My story is important. Do not let it die."

Telling his story would not be as easy as I had imagined. In the four final years of his life, as my father surrendered to the steady ravages of Alzheimer's disease, the details of his early life experiences were gradually disappearing. The many stories of Nazi Germany he had told me as a child were already fading in my own memory. I knew the skeleton of them, but not the marrow. During his steady descent to dementia, it became too late to ask for details; his mind was too addled, too unreliable.

Then I remembered "the book." Shortly after he retired, my father sat down with his manual typewriter and began to type compulsively. For weeks on end, barely stopping to eat and sleep, he typed all his indelible memories with his index fingers. Everything he could remember from the earliest days of his childhood he committed to paper and placed in a spiral binder. It was all written down. Somewhere.

I had not seen his manuscript in 12 years, but after a deep dive into my attic I eventually found the 340-page document. I thumbed through the pages. Some of the writing was rough, some of it astonishingly beautiful. It was all there, every detail, a vivid and precious memoir. He had entitled it, *The History of my Life's Struggles.* That title was uncomfortably close to *Mein Kampf.* Some editing was probably going to be needed.

Yes, I would re-read my father's story cover to cover. I would know him better and understand his struggles with the depth and perspective of an adult and a parent in my own right. I would continue to feel the essence of my father, even as his mind succumbed. And maybe, just maybe, his story would bring meaning and insight to others.

The eulogy was over; the mourners trickled out. I had one last chance to see my father before his burial. Wrapped in a *tachrichim*, the traditional plain white shroud of Jewish burial, my father's face was set in an expression of permanent serenity, his suffering smoothed away like a polished stone. *Finally at peace.* I kissed his wordless face and said goodbye.

He is not here any longer, but if you turn the page, I will resurrect him.

PROLOGUE

I thought I heard howling. It was far off in the distance and somehow, I knew it made no sense. After all, it was broad daylight, and we were in the middle of the city. And then I heard it again.

I had to investigate, so I slipped off my grandfather's lap and crawled under the dining room table. Opa Hiller was so busy fussing with his new crystal radio set, he did not even grunt. I tiptoed past the kitchen where my mother and sister were washing the dishes. They were immersed in their endless arguing again and did not even see me. I made it all the way to the living room window without being noticed and pressed my nose against the cold glass.

I could not see a thing. I took my chances and stepped out onto our balcony, certain that I would be able to see over the ledge.

The crisp spring air carried the sounds of the street up to my fourth-floor balcony. That's when I realized it wasn't howling that had drifted into our apartment. Was it singing, or chanting? A parade? I raced to the other end of the balcony, stood tall on my toes, and stretched my neck up as far as I could.

I was still too small, my view completely blocked by the balcony wall. All the while, the noise from the street was growing louder. It was the steady sound of voices, car horns, excitement. Suddenly, my father and grandfather were right behind me. I hadn't even heard them come outside, but I guess they finally noticed the noise. Then the door to the balcony swung open, and through it came my mother and my sister, Anita. My mother was scowling, as usual. "What is all this ruckus?" she barked.

Opa reached down and swooped me up onto his broad shoulders. From my high perch, I could finally see. Balconies all around me were filling up with people, with families. They were venturing out and peering down, curious about the commotion. I followed their gaze down to the street below me.

A long caravan of Army trucks was slowly winding up our block. Bursting with gaiety and excitement, bands of young, bold men in billowing brown shirts leaned out of the backs of the trucks. They were swaying and swinging as they passed, their bodies exploding with youthful and unbridled enthusiasm. With outstretched arms they waved their caps wildly in the air like victorious soldiers returning from war.

And they were all chanting in unison. Plain but passionate, the two simple words they shouted sounded just like a song.

Juden Raus!

Over and over and over.

Juden Raus! Juden Raus! Juden Raus! Jews Out! Jews Out! Jews Out!

The whole neighborhood joined in.

That was 1933, Berlin. It was the year of Hitler's rise to power in Germany. It was also the year my parents had finally clawed their way up from poverty to the middle class. It was the year my grandfather, Opa Hiller, would later die of cancer, and Oma Ernestine would move in with us in her time of mourning.

Juden raus. Jews out? Unthinkable!

My parents had just begun to make it in Berlin. It was as if they had finally arrived. How could they think of leaving? Certainly not now. They would dig in their heels – until one day we would have to run for our lives.

We would not make it out of Germany for eight more years – not until 1941, when the last of the trains heading west carried just a part of our dismembered family out of Berlin. With our visas to the US about to expire, we raced against time as we rumbled stealthily by train through an occupied, war-torn Europe. When at last we found a freighter ship that would take us out of Europe, we sailed across the Atlantic amidst death, disease, and despair only to arrive in an America that did not want us. But we were alive. We had made it. What more could we do but sew together the remnants of a fractured life?

Years later, long after the war, long after I had become a proud American, I would eventually return to Berlin. I would find my pale-yellow stucco apartment building on Schillerstrasse still standing, its balconies gone, amputated. Right next to my apartment would be an empty space, like a missing tooth, where the neighboring building had succumbed to the relentless bombing; the grocery owned by my friend Achim would have simply disappeared, as if it had never existed.

I would walk through the arched doorway to the courtyard behind my building and find a lone pear tree still standing, its branches reaching elegantly toward the sky, its white flowers just beginning to bloom. I would know that a remnant of my German childhood still lived; a time when I had looked out of my kitchen window onto that courtyard, and I had been happy.

PART I

CHILDHOOD

1

FOR RICHER OR POORER

That day in 1933 – when the Stormtroopers made their way down Schillerstrasse – will forever be frozen in my mind, for it is my very first memory. And although I was only three years old, and some would say, "It's impossible, he could never remember so many details," they would be wrong. I can recall each moment with precision; conjure up every texture, every smell, every color. Perhaps it was because the beginning of my consciousness happened to collide with the very start of Nazism as we know it. They say danger heightens your alertness. Maybe that's why every single image has remained seared in my mind for my entire life.

Memories – ones that I treasure; some that I wish were buried forever. Memories were all I brought with me to America when I finally made my way to its shores.

I can taste it now: the warm beef with gravy, the sweet and sour ruby-red cabbage, and always *Kartoffeln*, those marvelous potatoes. They're the flavors of the hearty lunch we had eaten that day at our formal dining table; the big meal we ate every Sunday afternoon, as though we had just come back from church, as if Sunday was our Sabbath. Our family customs were so German, we did not even recognize the Christian practices that had trickled into our own traditions. My parents were Jews by birth only. In all other ways, they believed they were full and equal members of Berlin society. At least, that's what they had thought until lunchtime.

After our meal, we had all stood on the balcony while Hitler's Stormtroopers came up our block, serving us their dire warning cloaked in a mantle of jubilation. Jews out!

It was over in a matter of minutes. Afterwards, we walked blankly back into our apartment, shutting the doors of the terrace, silencing the sounds from the outside, closing our minds to what we had witnessed. I could see how solemn my parents looked, even a little embarrassed, but all I felt was disappointment, for we had not participated in the cheering and exuberance outside. Why hadn't we joined in the celebration with all our neighbors, I wondered? I was too young to understand.

I still remember the quiet, despondent mood of the apartment as we walked back in, our living room furniture staring mutely at us. Our tall grandfather clock stood guard imposingly in one corner, while the upright piano waited idly across the room. The tea cart with the silver samovar sat expectantly near the dining room table. My mother's little porcelain figures that adorned the mantle above the gray-tiled heating stove, stood fixed and motionless in their various poses. Her excessively polished silver glistened on every available surface, reflecting our somber faces back to us. The inanimate objects in the apartment seemed to know our days were numbered. But we ignored their message.

My father and grandfather shut down their new crystal radio and we all sat dumbly for a while. And then gradually, my parents shook off the shock of the insult and humiliation. My mother stood up, and with a look of determination on her face, she simply said, "Let's finish the dishes, Anita." We did not know what else to do. So we decided to just keep living.

"Don't touch that!" my mother shouted. I had just picked up one of her prized porcelain figurines from the mantle. And just as quickly, I reunited it with its figurine family.

"It is *sehr teuer* [very expensive]. Put it back! And do not step on the rugs with your shoes. They are Oriental. Handmade. Never let me see your shoes on them. Do you hear me? Never!"

In those early years, I had assumed we were rich. Since everything in the apartment was cherished, breakable, handmade, and untouchable, what other conclusion could I have come to? To my parents, who had come from a state of dire poverty, every single possession *was* precious. Everything they owned, from a sock to a silver platter, was to be treated like a museum piece of rare value. After my mother's warning, I learned my lesson. I did not touch a thing.

And the apartment itself – oh, how my mother treasured it. How proud she was of our little home in this fine neighborhood of Charlottenburg, Berlin. And our specific building, 103 Schillerstrasse, was the most desirable of the entire apartment complex, with its street view and spacious balcony. Mutti [Mama] told me so all the time. "You see the other three buildings in our complex? They are so inferior. Look how they are set far back and only face the rear courtyard. And no balconies!"

How often she spoke to me about how far we had come. How she raved about our building and all our possessions and our trinkets and our rugs. Naturally, I came to believe we lived in the height of luxury. Like royalty!

Each day, I would walk into that fine apartment and proudly hold onto the gleaming wood balustrade while climbing up that elegant staircase to our marvelous apartment.

One day, I would look more attentively at our building and notice the less-deluxe details. A pleasant enough structure, it lacked a luxurious lobby or even an elevator. The majestic red carpet lining the staircase was, on closer inspection, made of cheap, scarlet-colored straw. Our beautiful apartment was an ordinary dwelling on the fourth floor of an unremarkable walk-up building in an unexceptional neighborhood in Berlin.

Eventually I would realize the apartment was not the epitome of luxury and we were not members of a royal house. But proper middle class German citizens? Yes, my parents had finally been able to enter that class. And that alone, I suppose, was something of a miracle. Because unlike a sizable number of German Jews who were already wealthy, my parents lacked any financial springboard. They had no family members in manufacturing. They did not have professional degrees. They made their way to Berlin with nothing, riding into the city without a penny to their name.

Let us rewind 14 years. It is 1919, and we find ourselves in the province of Posen (*Poznan*) in West Prussia, about 160 kilometers (100 miles) from Berlin. In these times, Prussia is part of the nation of Germany, and Berlin is its capital. The Great War – now known as World War I – has just ended with total defeat of Germany that can only be compounded by the country's further humiliation.

Over there, in the corner of that ramshackle house, stands my father, Arthur. Wait just a minute; is he standing? It is hard to tell because Arthur is tiny, just barely over 153 centimeters. Yes, that's right, only five feet tall. If people aren't falling over little Arthur, then they are tripping over his last name, Schwersenz. He is accustomed to it by now, but despite the 10 intimidating letters, it is just two syllables, *Schwer* and *senz*, pronounced phonetically. Easy.

Arthur has just returned from the front in France where he served in the cavalry fighting for the German Army. Amazingly, he managed to survive mustard gas attacks, illness, combat, and even radiation. Was it bravery that allowed him to survive? Or perhaps he was so small that he slipped right between the legs of the enemy!

At last, that monstrous war is over and Arthur has returned to his hometown of Briesen. His beloved sisters Frieda and Hedwig greet him affectionately. "Welcome home, Arthur!" they shout gleefully, while smothering him in a fleshy embrace. *Even stouter than before*, Arthur marvels as he tries to breathe, though he notes pleasantly that he is still a bit taller than his sisters (if only a centimeter or two). He extricates himself from the love-hug and turns to greet his parents, Henriette and Wolf. Alas, they look older and grayer since he went to the front. Nothing else about them has changed. In fact, they are even poorer, just eking by selling brooms and brushes and handwoven cane baskets in their small shop in town.

Arthur, now nearly 27 years old, is in a state of shock, but it is not "shellshock" from the war. Oh yes, has seen horrors there; he has lived in the trenches. No, he cannot believe he is back in this tiny village and must again live with his impoverished – let's face it – piss poor family. How suffocated he feels! The situation is untenable.

Arthur looks at his tired, worn-out mother. Lovingly, but with sadness, he understands that his uneducated mother, Henriette Wolff, did not improve her situation much when she married the thoroughly illiterate Wolf Schwersenz. He loves his father, but he thinks to himself, "*She just traded in one Wolff for another.*" He laughs, amused by his private joke. Little does he know that things will only get worse for Henriette; years from now, his father will be taken away from that little shop in an old-fashioned straitjacket with an undefined mental illness. That is his family's future. Well, it will not be *his* future. One thing Arthur knows with certainty: there is no future for him here in Briesen.

Arthur does what he can to improve his prospects. He takes a couple of business classes and manages to procure a *Diplom Kaufman,* a certificate to be a "businessman." It is only a vocational degree, however, and it requires that he do an apprenticeship. Leaving his parents and sisters behind, Arthur heads to the nearby town of Thorn. This is his one chance. He must figure out a way to do better than his family. He must try to make something of himself.

Roughly 60 kilometers (40 miles) west of Thorn, my mother, Grete Jacob, is living with her parents in the town of Lobsenz. Although the Great War has ended, she is certainly not at peace. Her very own younger brother, Siegfried, returned from the war injured – an amputee. In the last few years, it's like the whole world has gone mad.

Grete is 26 already and she is overwhelmed by anxiety. Her own mother, my Oma Ernestine, has been contributing to her daily feelings of impending doom. "You must marry soon, or you will be a spinster and end up caring for *us* all your life!" spews Ernestine. Every. Single. Day.

Grete is keenly aware that she should marry; she needs no regular reminders, thank you very much. For she has been asking herself the same question every day. *Why am I not married yet*?

"Why, I have completed the highest education one can get in Lobsenz – middle school – I can read and write in English, and I am a talented dressmaker. That should be worth a great deal," she says to herself with pride (and a bit of arrogance). And Grete is fine-looking enough (true, she has a bit of a robust, angular nose) with full and rosy cheeks (that help to soften the nose).

None of these things matters, she finally realizes. The bottom line is, she has no dowry. And another thing: there are simply no men. The few men that have survived the Great War have been snatched up by every unmarried woman around. The war practically decimated the entire population of eligible young men.

If only Grete had a different kind of mother, one who would have offered her some consolation. A mother who might have said, "I'm so sorry Grete, that we cannot provide you with a dowry. You know that although your father is a fine master tailor, we have the burden of caring for your grandparents, Pauline and Salomon, and with the war having just ended money is very tight. But I am sure with your talents and intellect, charm and good looks, you will find a kind and suitable husband. Just be patient, dear."

If only Grete's doting father, Hiller, would have said something – anything at all! He could have lit his pipe, stroked his salt and pepper beard, and offered, encouragingly, "Grete, my dearest, I am sorry we have no money for your dowry, but at least I have taught you everything I know about tailoring and dressmaking. These skills should be useful so that you can make your own living. Married or not, you have nothing to fear." Instead, frightened of his own wife Ernestine, Hiller did what came naturally: he kept his mouth shut.

How such conversations would have assuaged my mother's anxiety and built her confidence. But Ernestine was too neurotic, and Hiller too meek, for comforting words to be spoken.

The truth is, Ernestine was busy battling her own demons. Left behind in the shadows of her six siblings' various successes, Ernestine was riddled with jealousy. "All my brothers and sisters are better off than I am!" she regularly lamented to her daughter. "Louis is a doctor, Moritz and Joseph are successful businessmen, and Abraham sailed off to America to make his fortune. And my lucky sisters, Bertha and Rosa, both married wealthy furriers! And now they have all left me behind to take care of our aging parents. Now do you understand, Grete? It is so unfair!

"And now their children – your cousins – have already had such advantages. They had money; they could go to university. Take Louis' three children: Paula is a dentist, Arthur a doctor, and Sigfried a lawyer. And my brother Abraham who went to America – his son Ellis inherited a successful shoe business in New York. Then there is your cousin Clara who is married to the famous actor Fritz Plischke. And your cousin Ella – well, she is not even married, but so what – she is living in a fancy apartment in Berlin, paid for by a Turkish pasha, no less! Let's face it, we are the poor relations. We don't even have money for your dowry. Goodness, Grete, how will you ever get married!"

Not surprisingly, Grete is swimming in a sea of uncertainty; she is drowning in self-doubt, and she is consumed by envy. It is an inherited condition.

Arthur enters the picture right in the middle of Grete's predicament. When he sees Grete, he is immediately entranced. Grete looks sophisticated. Fashionably dressed, tall, and slender, she sports a black wool coat with a fur-lined collar. A charming hat rests askew on her head. It is a lovely, delicate head framed by a dark blonde bob. Bright blue eyes brimming with intelligence meet Arthur's unwavering gaze.

Arthur could never have imagined that those stunning dresses she wears are all home-made. Grete has copied the up-to-date patterns and crafted the fit and style to perfection. She looks elegant, and at 26 her skin is still smooth and glows with the last vestiges of youth. How refined she looks. Haughty, even. He does not yet know that insecurity floats right under the surface of my mother's thinly assumed arrogance.

Arthur, from the poor town of Briesen. A year older, a half foot shorter, with no money or education to speak of. Thoroughly impressed and enamored of the clever, industrious Grete. *I have found quite a woman*, he thinks. *She has no dowry, but darn, she is a talented seamstress!*

Grete looks around and sees no one else. Not a single suitable suitor. Only Arthur with the unpronounceable last name. She does a quick calculation... and then she marries, quite literally, beneath her.

From then on, my mother lorded her superiority (and height) over my father and did so for the rest of their life together. But whether he was always an embarrassment and disappointment to her, I will never know. In those early days, I can only imagine that she was charmed by his kind heart, his twinkling blue eyes and what seemed like eternal optimism. A dreamer, he was, with an impish grin on his compact, triangular-shaped face, a small pink radiation scar on his pale left cheek, and no hint of his own father's mental illness lurking about, waiting patiently for the right time to emerge.

With no time to lose, they "tied the knot." It was 1920, and just a year later they had a baby girl. They named her Anita.

One morning, about four weeks after Anita's birth, Arthur heard a shriek. He came running in from outside and found Grete looking distraught and holding some papers. "What on earth is the matter?" he asked, all out of breath. "Is the baby all right?"

"She's fine, Arthur. It's not the baby; it's the mail. A terrible mistake has been made. Anita's birth certificate came today and it is riddled with errors!"

Arthur mopped his brow with relief. "What is wrong with it?"

"For one thing, it does not say 'Anita.'"

"What do you mean? What does it say?" Arthur inquired, his heart still racing from Grete's earlier scream.

"It says *Annietta.*"

Arthur pulled the registration papers out of Grete's hands and gave them a once over. "Oh, I see, Grete. Not to worry, my dear. Someone has just written the Polish version of her name. A bureaucrat must have changed *Anita* to *Annietta,*" Arthur hastily concluded, as he knew a few words of Polish.

"What do you mean, 'don't worry.' This is an outrage, Arthur! We must find out what has happened!"

While my mother continued her rant, my father realized she had raised a valid question. Why this little spelling correction? And did it matter? What difference did those few letters really make, anyway? But that little typographical alteration that negated my parents' and sister's ethnicity would later be of *vital* significance. It would call to question *where* in fact my parents came from and symbolize our family's uncertain future at the very start of their lives. And eventually, it would delay and deny our escape from Germany in the years to come.

My parents soon learned that the very German area of West Prussia, and with it, the province of Posen, was about to be annexed to the new nation of Poland. Amongst a long list of humiliating war reparations, Germany was being stripped of many of its territories and ceding land to other nations as part of the Treaty of Versailles.

And now, just one year into their marriage, my parents found themselves caught in a geographical dilemma. They were suddenly about to lose their national identity. If they stayed in Posen, they would become citizens of Poland. However, their only alternative was to pack up and leave the safety of their homeland.

"What do you think we should we do, Grete? Should we stay here and become Polish citizens?"

"It is not an option, Arthur. I do not speak a word of Polish, and you speak only a few. And let us not forget the most important thing. We are Jews. Jews are not welcome in Poland."

"What do you mean? There is an enormous population of Polish Jews. Millions, even."

"Yes, Arthur, but the Jews that live out in the country are Orthodox, and live in the old ways in *shtetls*, as if it is still the year 1600. They are isolated in their little villages. And in the big cities, most Jews are blue collar workers without any education."

"But that's us, Grete! You are describing *us*."

"Nonsense. Don't you want an integrated life, Arthur; one that is modern and secular? A better life and a future for our children? I've already decided. Our best option is to emigrate to Germany. We have no choice. We must go west."

West. The concept was not new. Jews had been heading west from Eastern Europe since the early 1800s. Most had come west as a matter of survival, escaping waves of pogroms – organized massacres or purges – over the prior century.

They came from regions where they had no rights, no citizenship, and in some cases, not even a last name. Inventing names, they used their occupations, like Fleischmann (butcher) or Kaufmann (shopkeeper), or took the names of trees, like Birnbaum (pear tree). Nostalgic Jews borrowed the names of their hometowns.[1] They settled in Germany, which seemed to be the most welcoming, with Berlin its profoundly liberal center. In Germany, even Jews could attain citizenship, pursue higher professions, or enter civil service. Yes, *even Jews*. And they were coming to Germany in droves.

In 1921, Arthur and Grete, mismatched in height, temperament, and education, but full of optimism for their future, decide they must emigrate to Berlin.

They travel in a horse drawn carriage, with all their possessions, empty wallets, and their new baby Anita wrapped safely in a blanket. It will take them five days to get to Berlin. They are young and hopeful, ready to begin their new and prosperous life.

"Bicycles. I will sell bicycles, Grete. Everyone needs a bicycle for either transportation or leisure. I cannot fail." That was my father's plan once they arrived in Berlin.

I have a fantasy that at this point in their lives my parents were joyful and in love, excited and optimistic, in a way that I never got to witness. But if it was not exactly love, then at the very least, they had an understanding about their union, and still had the energy and zeal of the newly married.

They started out in the east end of the city, in a storefront apartment on Emdener Strasse. My father was a glib salesman and the bicycles practically sold themselves. My mother opened a tailor shop in the front of the apartment, and they both shared a room with baby Anita in the rear. While hard work and humble conditions never daunted my mother, she had no intention of staying in this working-class neighborhood, living below the poverty line. She had a grand plan. *Save money. Keep moving west. Move up the food chain.* Onward and upward.

Over the next few years, our entire extended family made its way out of the provinces and into the city. My father's stout sisters settled in the eastern part of Berlin near my parents, but my mother's wealthy cousins were scattered throughout the posher districts. This created a new dilemma. How would my mother ever catch up to her cousins? She was so far behind. She must work harder. Save more. Sew faster.

As the extended family grew in Berlin, my parents tried to grow their nuclear family as well. Four years after they moved to the city, they finally had another child. A son! No, it was not me, for I have not entered this drama yet. It was their son Manfred. He was the boy I never knew, a child rarely mentioned, dead of diphtheria and buried at the Weissensee cemetery at just four months of age.

It took an entire decade after my parents had been married for me to make my auspicious appearance. Why the late arrival? Were they waiting for financial security? Maybe I was never a part of my mother's plan and I was just a "happy accident." They never did say. I arrived anyway, bald, and skinny with great big ears that resembled giant cup handles. It was 1930.

I looked into my father's eyes. He was beaming with pride. *I have just had a son,* he thought. *What a handsome bugger!*

I looked into my mother's eyes. She looked riddled with worry. *Will this one survive,* she wondered? *And what's with those ears?*

I looked into my sister's eyes. She was scowling with annoyance. *I am nine years old already,* she sighed. *What use are you to me*?

I ignored them all and howled liked a healthy, helpless newborn.

Naturally, they named me *Wolf.* Wolf Schwersenz. Named after my now deceased paternal grandfather – the one who went mad.

By the time I was born, my mother and father were already 37 and 38 years old and steeped in the marital discontent and disappointment of long-time companionship. But regardless of the strife that had steadily seeped into their marriage, my parents were still chugging along, working toward their goal. They believed wholeheartedly in the German dream, that they could work hard, prosper, and be treated as equals despite being Jews.

And it seems that my parents had saved just enough money to move to Lothringerstrasse, in the working-class Mitte [center] section of Berlin. They had managed to inch their way further west, into the heart of Berlin, near the famed Brandenburg gate. With the move to this new apartment, we gained a tiny bedroom, which Anita and I shared, while my parents slept in the living room. And we all shared a hallway bathroom with our neighbors. This was not uncommon; one simply had to be grateful for indoor plumbing, and if one was lucky, toilet paper.

"Arthur, we are four people now. If we are going to make it to the middle class, it is high time you look for better employment."

Is this how my mother "gently persuaded" my father to leave the bicycle business? Of course not. More likely, she phrased it like this: "What did you think, Arthur! That you were going to sell bicycles for the rest of your life? Don't you have any ambition? How did you think you were going to feed your family?" Mutti was always very encouraging.

But a salesman was all my father was cut out to be. Besides his pleasant personality, he had no specific skills with which to climb the ladder of success. That was the reality my mother had to accept. Then my father found a position at a large men's clothing store – Paul Klein's – and our fortunes took a positive turn.

The store was located on a triangular-shaped corner on Wilmersdorfer Strasse, right in the heart of the shopping district. It was a respectable business in a respectable location, which was a point of pride for my mother. My father's one skill – his amiability – served him well. His natural loquaciousness found its audience in the male customers, and the more he connected with the patrons, the more indispensable he became to the eponymous Mr. Klein. Within just a year or two my father advanced from salesman to manager. He started to bring home a decent living wage, and we moved one notch closer to my mother's middle-class dream.

And behind the scenes, slowly, steadily, secretly, my mother was scrimping and saving, scrimping and saving. Somehow, within three years of my father landing the job at Paul Klein's, my parents had miraculously saved 40,000 Deutschmarks. That was the equivalent of 10,000 dollars. We were not rich, not by a long shot, but we had enough money to finally make another improvement in our living situation. Pushing even further west, we moved once again, this time to the fine Charlottenburg section of Berlin.

We had done it! We had arrived! It was 1933, and *finally* we had made it to the middle class.

We had risen up in Germany, right along with Hitler.

2

SCHILLERSTRASSE, CHARLOTTENBURG

"Lazy... slovenly... ungrateful... spoiled... unappreciative." The new set of vocabulary words emanating from my mother's mouth drifted down to my imaginary fort underneath the kitchen table. All the colorful adjectives were directed towards my sister, Anita. Surrounded by the security of the kitchen chairs, I played in relative safety while my sister and mother played out their daily routine of fighting bitterly in the more perilous space above me.

"Mutti, my bedroom is freezing," complained Anita. "I feel like I am sleeping outside. I can even see my breath. And can you explain to me why my room is the only room in the apartment without a heating stove?" My sullen 12-year-old sister sat directly above me at the small rectangular kitchen table, shelling peas with my mother and unsuccessfully debating the thermodynamics of her room. While they pared, prepped, cooked, and quarreled, I smelled the buttery aroma of warm pound cake wafting down to me as it baked on top of the stove in a *Draluma*, a metal contraption that functioned as a feeble stand-in for a non-existent oven.

Every day I heard their arguments, and every day my mother prevailed. By then, I had been convinced that Anita was an incorrigible daughter. There seemed to be so many issues. Her grades were poor. She didn't practice the piano. She showed no respect. I drowned out their combat with the apocalyptic sounds of my own imaginary battles. My Army soldiers had their own wars to fight, and they were very, very busy.

We had moved into 103 Schillerstrasse in the early spring of 1933, when the northern air was still chilly, the daylight too short, and bright yellow crocuses were just beginning to bloom.

In the morning I woke up with the light of day. Anita's icy bedroom – a converted maid's room – was just across the hall from me. As I shuffled past, a blast of arctic air gusted out her room and seemed to attack me. Anita had been right. Her room, or any room for that matter, without a heating stove really *was* freezing.

On I trotted, needing to make urgent use of the tiny bathroom. It was just past Anita's room and although it was compact, it was our very own private bathroom; thus, it was a prized part of our apartment. Squeezing through the narrow entrance, I sat down on the toilet which was hopelessly wedged into a miniscule space between the sink and the claw-footed bathtub. As I "did my business," I nervously peered up to the ceiling. As always, the small hot water heater perched above me teetered at a precarious angle. Worried that it was about to fall on my head, I wondered if I should avoid defecating entirely. But I made myself relax by humming a jaunty tune and continued sitting on the toilet until I was finished.

"Mutti, I'm done!" I called out to my mother. Mutti came in now to evaluate the product of my efforts. Our German toilet was brilliantly engineered for this purpose, with a "landing pad" at the rear of the bowl, built solely for fecal inspection. "Good color, good consistency. No parasites," Mutti announced. "You can flush now."

We could flush the stool away, but the neuroses, it seemed, were permanent residents.

I ambled into the kitchen and pulled myself onto the kitchen chair. Once settled, my eyes turned to Mutti's face, and I tried to gauge her mood. It was often inscrutable, but I could usually tell if she was angry. Lips pursed or frowning, brow furrowed, an angry look would mean a difficult day for me. Today as I waited for breakfast, she just looked tense; and that was a typical day, as good or as bad as any other. Mutti left the kitchen while I waited at the table. Her pace picked up as she ran to each of the rooms, lighting the wood heating stoves that had gone out during the night. She returned to the kitchen, still scurrying about, as she prepared a simple breakfast for the four of us. This morning we were having buttered rolls; tomorrow we might have rolls again, or warm oatmeal. I would have to wait until Sunday to get my one egg for the week.

When I had finished breakfast, I slipped below the table to play in my fort. Peeking out I could only see legs. A sea of legs. Legs of the table, of Anita, of Mutti. Suddenly, Mutti's legs were on the move again, zooming from room to room like a bee, zigzagging into the kitchen, out of the kitchen, running in and out, back and forth. She had pulled the thick down comforters, nuzzled tightly in their cotton duvets, off all the beds, and was now hanging them on lines in the kitchen to air out.

It was exhausting just to watch her frenetic morning routine. I pulled out my Army men and quietly busied myself with the serene activity of playing war.

"Time to go, Wolf. Hurry," called my mother.

Playtime was over. I quickly packed away my few Army men and emerged from the safety of my fort, for it was time to make our daily shopping trip. Mutti handed me our empty milk container, and together we climbed down the steep staircase of our building, the painted white milk can clanking back and forth noisily against its handle. We started up the street, but after we had only gone a block, I found that I was already falling behind.

"Slow down, Mutti, my legs are tired!" I said these words, but only in my mind, as I would not dare let such thoughts pass through my lips. My mother held my hand firmly, but when she pulled at my arm, I realized that affectionate grasp was just an effort to keep me from falling behind.

In time, I was nearly jogging just to keep up. Fortunately, a much-needed break would be coming up soon, as our shopping rounds were about to begin throughout the neighborhood. Our first stop was at the grocer's. We refilled the container with fresh milk, then picked out fresh eggs and "candled" them ourselves. Holding each egg up to the flame until we could see through the translucent shell, we rejected the ones with "blood spots," a sign that the egg might be fertilized. Further up the block we stopped at the butcher to get a freshly plucked chicken, and a *Braten* – a beef roast. We rounded the corner and came to a street lined by uneven rows of produce stands covered by cheap green awnings. The produce stands were manned by "gypsies" [Romas] and they called out to us from every stand, "The fruit, it's sweet!" We stepped up to one of the booths, sniffed the fruit and squeezed the vegetables. Then we waited while the Romas wrapped our tomatoes and produce in old newspaper pages. Now we came up another block, completing a broad circle. We stepped into the fragrant *Bäckerei*. The warm bakery, smelling of yeast and earth, was my favorite stop on our journey and would be our last. We picked out some freshly baked *Brötchen*, the small rolls that might be used either for sandwiches or for tomorrow's breakfast.

When we finally returned home, we gradually unloaded our groceries, placing the perishables in a cool hollow nook underneath the window that had a ventilated opening to the outside. Exhausted, with aching feet from all the trudging around, I dragged myself into my protective fort to play and relax. while Mutti stayed in motion. She finished unpacking and then immediately began making a hot lunch for the four of us.

Lunch was the main meal of the day, and all the stores and schools shut down for two hours so everyone could be together for the main family meal. I prayed that my Papa – "Vati" – would come home for lunch. But too often Vati remained at the store, in which case I would not get to see him until suppertime.

Today Vati did not come home. Anita delivered his hot lunch to the store, and when she returned, the three of us ate together. Without Vati, lunch was boring and solemn. The tension between Anita and my mother was palpable, and we ate our meal in near-total silence.

Anita returned to school, and Mutti at once began her daily housecleaning. She cleaned and dusted the entire apartment and fluffed and remade the beds with their freshly aired-out linens and blankets. Then Mutti spent the rest of the day on her afternoon cleaning project. Today she boiled our soiled clothes and linens in massive kettles on top of the stove. She stirred them slowly with a wooden spoon while the kitchen gradually became steamy and warm; once they had cooled, she wrung them with her hands and hung them to dry. Later in the afternoon Mutti would heat an iron on the stove and iron all the laundry before starting to work on our supper.

Sometime in the late afternoon, before supper, I stepped out of my fort and spied my mother sitting under the light of the kitchen window. It was the first time the whole day I had not seen her in motion. Her head was slumped at the neck and a large blanket was covering her lap; it looked as though she was resting. I tiptoed past her, afraid to disturb her peace, but suddenly her right hand darted up and out to the side, pulling something invisible with it. A quick tug, then back it went into her lap and out again, following the identical path. In and out, stopping short just before her arm was fully outstretched and free. A flash of light glinted; there was something metallic between her closed thumb and forefinger, and I saw that she was holding a needle, and it was pulling an unseen thread. On closer look it was not a blanket warming her lap; it was in fact a tablecloth that she was embroidering.

How many times I had seen my mother in this chair, holding some garment in her lap – a sock she was darning or pants that needed hemming. Or sometimes she would be knitting some intricately designed sweater. And if she were not here in the kitchen chair by the light of the window, she would be in the living room, leaning quietly over her sewing machine. Her foot would be pressing the pedal up and down rhythmically, as if pushing the pedals of a piano. And her hands would be guiding the fabric through the machine with a gentleness I rarely knew. Gentle hands, knowing hands. She would be making clothes for us, or creating beautiful draperies and dresses and blouses for clients, because this was her actual career beyond her housekeeping. She sold these artisanal items privately from our home to upper class German women. It was how she supplemented our income, and how we managed to afford our apartment on Schillerstrasse.

No, of course my mother was not napping in a chair. She was as relaxed as I had ever seen her, but she was not resting. She was working, always working.

"Come quickly, Wolf! Anita called. "Over here, by the window."

On an early Saturday morning, before the city had awakened, my sister beckoned me to the kitchen window that faced the rear courtyard and the surrounding buildings. Anita – almost 13, and nine years my senior – was never going to be my playmate, but she was more than a sister to me. Something more protective, more maternal. I scampered onto a chair, rested my pale, thin arm on her shoulder and peered outside.

That early morning, Anita's twinkling blue eyes assured me of amusement. I stuck my head out of the kitchen window and felt the cool and crisp spring air that carried a hint of latent warmth. A single, silent pear tree stood gracefully in the center of the empty courtyard, its white flowers just beginning to blossom on its upturned branches. The courtyard was otherwise completely empty.

"But I don't *see* anything," I said, with exaggerated disappointment.

"Shh. Just wait. Listen," instructed Anita.

This time when I put my head out of the window, I heard the faint echoes of simple organ music. It was coming from the arched entrance to the courtyard, built for a horse and carriage from another era. An old organ grinder had just entered the courtyard;

he was making his weekly rounds. Mustachioed and rumpled, he wore a short-brimmed hat and threadbare jacket. Behind him trailed a small-faced, long-tailed monkey, dressed in a miniature jacket and a tiny hat. As the organ grinder moved deeper into the courtyard and his music grew louder, the windows of the surrounding buildings started to open. One by one, the neighbors stuck out their heads and waved. *"Guten Morgen!* [Good morning!]" they called out.

The old man lifted his hat off his head and waved back with it; then he put his hat upside down on the ground. He continued to play his organ grinder, while the whole courtyard and all the building inhabitants slowly woke up to the joyful music and opened their windows. The sound of whistling birds joined in as if they had also just awakened. And then, as if on cue, the building residents began simultaneously throwing things out of their windows. Anita began delicately wrapping coins in paper and handing them to me, and I started throwing them out the window as far as I could. The old man's clever little monkey scampered around the courtyard gathering up the hailstorm of paper-wrapped coins as they landed, and placing them in the hat. When the coin shower ended and all the coins had disappeared from the ground, the organ grinder picked up his heavy hat and ambled out of the courtyard, followed by his little monkey.

Gradually, each of the neighbors began lowering their windows. A boy about my age across the courtyard was looking out his window. Another coin thrower, like me – a mirror image. He waved and waved to me, until a pair of sweater-clad arms reached over his head and pulled his window shut.

From then on, every Saturday morning I would wake up early. Climbing onto a chair, I would wait for the organ grinder by the kitchen window, throw my paper-wrapped coins to the clever monkey, and wave to the mystery boy across the courtyard.

Oma Ernestine moved in with us that first year, shortly after Opa Hiller died of lung cancer. She furnished the second bedroom with a simple bed and couch. On the wall above the bed, she hung a colored tapestry, woven with strangely upsetting unicorns and fearsome mythical beasts that seemed to threaten my very existence. Each night I raced past her door with my eyes shut until I reached my parents' room. I stood by my little four-poster bed, waiting for my mother to come tuck me in, for this is where I slept too. My junior bed was painted in white enamel and still had safety rails attached. Mutti lowered the rail with one hand, and with the other she lifted me onto the mattress. Then she sat down next to me, and we both recited our traditional German nighttime prayer:

Müde bin ich, geh' zur Ruh',
Schliesse beide Äuglein zu.
Vater lass die Augen dein
Über meinem Bettschen sein

[I am weary, I go to rest,
I close both of my little eyes,
Father, let Thy eyes
Keep watch over my bed.]

These were one of the few moments of quiet affection I remember having with my mother. This simple traditional German prayer was one my Oma had told to my mother and now she told to me. I had only ever heard it spoken, and so, I always assumed *Vater* [Father] meant *my* father. But it was not until I was much older, when I happened to see the prayer written down, that I realized we had been saying a Christian nighttime prayer all along. Suddenly I realized it was a capitalized Father! The *holy* Father. Oh, Lord!

Mutti tucked me in tightly, kissed me and left, shutting the light, but I did not close my little eyes as the prayer instructed. In the dark I looked around my parents' simple room with its twin beds and plain wardrobe, and its defiantly bold, burgundy-colored wallpaper.

Hanging from the center of the ceiling was the only ornate object in the room, a crystal chandelier, its glass shaking ever so slightly from the footsteps just above us. I watched as the light from the crystal cast a parade of eerie shadows on the ceiling; and I conjured up visions of mythical tapestry monsters as I lay staring from my little white bed.

Those brief years of my early childhood – before the Nazis influenced and infiltrated every aspect of my life – were filled with the innocence of youth, the freedom of childhood, the simplicity of springtime. And yet, I am also lying. My early childhood was far from idyllic. It was simply better than the years that followed. It was sweet and nostalgic, because despite my parents' flaws – my mother's severity and my father's follies – I felt loved. I did not have a conscience yet and I was not burdened by responsibilities, worries, or moral dilemmas. Life was still full of possibility and its colors were bright. I had not fully uncovered the fallibility of my parents, and the only things I was afraid of besides that ugly tapestry, were the monsters I conjured in the dark.

Had times been normal, I would have eventually recognized that my mother was a difficult woman. She was hard angles and pursed lips. She was Food! Shelter! Behavior! Education! Discipline! But either because of, or despite her neuroses, she was also determined. It was that determination which ultimately saved our lives.

My mother's strictness was entirely at odds with my father's easy-going nature. Vati would have made a wonderful clown. As a young child, I saw him as jocular and friendly, warm, sensitive and kind. I suppose he was not particularly ambitious, at least not enough for my mother. "If it were up to you, Arthur, you would be satisfied selling bicycles your whole life..." My mother pushed him. And pushed him and pushed him.

While the contrast in their temperaments made for good counterbalance for my childhood psyche, it did not lead to a harmonious home. What rage my mother seemed to have! How much frustration! Bitter fighting between my parents and my mother's arguments with Anita made the inside of our apartment loud and tumultuous. But *outside* our apartment was another story all together. Outside was relief.

Just four flights down the red carpeted staircase (or a slide down the banister if no one was looking), the quiet, tree-lined street of Schillerstrasse stood beckoning in front of my apartment. During the day, only the occasional car or delivery truck – either motorized or horse drawn – would pass along the quiet side street. Scattered bicyclists might pedal through, or an occasional pedestrian would head to the grocery, but that was the extent of the traffic. In the summer, this wide, calm street was like a perfect, giant, peaceful playground for innocent, spirited boys to entertain themselves.

As soon as the weather warmed, I temporarily abandoned my kitchen fort and went out to the street hoping to find playmates. I stood on the sidelines, ogling the older boys with envy as they rode their bikes and played in the quiet road. I was still too young to ride, and I was too small to join the other street games. I just stood there and stared, too shy to assert myself, while I fantasized fruitlessly that someone would just ask me to join a game. How awkward and self-conscious I felt until I noticed another boy my size also standing on the sidewalk. I recognized him as the coin thrower in the window across our courtyard and immediately sidled over to him. Together we watched the older boys show off their bike riding skills and felt a bit less conscious of our inferiority.

One by one, the boys proudly passed us – one riding with no hands, another hoisting up on his rear wheel. Yet another boy balanced on his spinning wheels without moving. They were putting on a show for us younger kids while they simultaneously displayed their dominance to the other boys. We looked on wide-eyed at what seemed to be the impossible and felt braver in the safety of each other's company.

My new friend's tight buzz haircut earned him the permanent

nickname *Glatze* [Baldy]. In our effort to act indifferent and not just gawk at the bigger boys, we busied ourselves with younger childhood games, playing hide and seek, tag, and hopscotch. One warm day, sweaty and bored, we moseyed further down the block and came upon a group of kids who had chalked up a mock Grand Prix racetrack full of twists, turns, and angles. They boys had each brought their own hand-made, colorfully painted wooden boxcars for the competition, and they were taking it very seriously, for Grand Prix racing was a favorite of Hitler's and it had become a national pastime.

We strolled past the mock racetrack and came upon a tall, skinny, angry boy who was standing on the sidelines. On closer look, we saw that he was not just standing, but stomping, his fine yellow hair flying up like corn silk each time his foot hit the ground. His face flamed so red with anger, that his light eyebrows and lashes looked nearly white against his crimson skin.

"*Das ist so unfair*," he was protesting to anyone around who would listen.

"What happened?" said the outgoing Glatze.

"They eliminated me from the race. They say my boxcar went out of bounds, but it's not true. They're lying!"

The glib Glatze immediately knew just what to say. "*Ja, ja*, we saw, your car wasn't out of bounds," Glatze lied. "That was a bad call."

Achim Anders was a good two years older and at least three inches taller than us. Under ordinary circumstances he would never have given us the time of day. But Glatze had somehow managed to stroke his ego, and right now, we were the nearest available playmates.

And just like that we became a trio. What an unlikely threesome we were: Glatze, Achim and me. We had nothing in common other than living in the same apartment complex. Glatze's father was a mailman and Achim's father owned a small grocery store next to our building. Achim was the blond and blue-eyed German ideal, and by the time his beet red, angry face had faded to a normal skin tone, his eyebrows and lashes had become a rabbit-invisible, colorless color. Glatze was a tiny bit shorter than me; his big square, closely buzzed head sat on a wide short neck and stocky body from which sprouted solid muscular limbs. And I was pale all over, with pale skinny legs, pale blue eyes, and pale brown hair, as if I were allergic to the sun.

Yes, we were as different in appearance as was humanly possible. And my new friends were Christian, as was nearly everyone in my building complex. But who cared back then if we were Jewish or Christian, tall or short, blond or brown-haired, ugly or handsome? Certainly not us. We were boys, boys who just wanted to play, at a time when all that mattered was how fast you could run and whether you could throw a ball straight.

The Berlin summer days seemed endless, and our threesome played for as long as the sunlight would allow. After dusk, a silence would descend, and the only sound disrupting the peace was the low hum of a generator that kept the streetlamps lit. At the end of a long day, I came inside, dusty, chalky, and sweaty, with a thin film of dirt concealing my normal pallor. Mutti looked at me and declared "*Ach.*" Shaking her head with disappointment, she marched me into the bathroom and pulled my undershirt roughly over my head while she simultaneously began to fill the claw-footed tub with warm water. A few briquettes of coal in the small water heater perched perilously on the ceiling would heat just enough water to fill the tub.

Mutti scrubbed me raw with the harsh efficiency I had come to expect. Only when my skin was the light pink color of a newborn pig, and the bathtub water had taken on the dull gray-brown color of my hitherto dirty skin was I finished. Wrapping me efficiently in a towel, she quickly hustled me out of the bathroom. "Anita!" she called.

"What, Mutti?" Anita barked back.

"Come. Hurry! Time to take a bath."

Anita reluctantly approached, knowing that her only opportunity for a hot bath was to soak in the remains of my dirty tub water. "Coal is expensive," Mutti always said.

We scrubbed ourselves clean in the shared murky water twice a week.

During one week of our first summer on Schillerstrasse, my mother seemed even more fraught than usual. She snapped at us more often, and she was in an intense cleaning frenzy, polishing as all the silver flatware and every silver trinket in the living room to a mirrored shine. Our pace during our daily grocery walks accelerated from a jog to a near sprint as we went from store to store. I could not fathom the reason for my involuntary increase in aerobic exercise. At the end of the week, I saw that my mother was painstakingly preparing an ambitious meal for Sunday. In the kitchen, lounging peacefully in a tub of tinted water, was a huge beef roast.

"Is the meat getting a bath, Mutti?" I asked my mother, innocently.

"No, Wolf, don't be silly. I am making a *Sauerbraten*, and that is not a bath; it is a special brine," she explained. "The roast must spend three days pickling in vinegar, onions, juniper berries and spices. Then I will cook it on Sunday and serve it with *Spätzle*."

How I loved *Spätzle,* the soft, boiled dumpling made from a batter of flour, milk, and eggs. Uncooked, it looked vaguely like thick glue; but the batter transformed to a glistening, loosely S-shaped noodle/dumpling hybrid in a boiled metamorphosis. *Spätzle,* and a three-day roast? This was no ordinary meal. Someone important must be coming over.

I waited impatiently until Sunday finally arrived. Mutti had carefully picked out our clothes: a fine handmade sweater for me, and a silk floral dress for Anita. We listened dutifully while Mutti reviewed important directions. "Wolf. Anita. Now listen to me carefully. We have a special visitor coming today. My cousin Paula is coming over for lunch. I have not seen her in years, and I expect you both to be on your best behavior."

"Come now, Mutti," Anita chortled, sarcastically. "Do you really think you need to give us these instructions? Don't you think you have already drilled into us how to be good German children? Shall we review the rules, Wolf?"

Anita elbowed me and we quickly began to recite Mutti's regulations, alternating between each other:

Anita: "Be polite."

Me: "Bow or curtsy when greeting an adult."

Anita: "Take only one cookie when offered a plate of treats."

Me: "Refuse another cookie, even if offered." (I had trouble saying that one!)

Anita: "Never put your fingers on a glass table or counter."

Me: "Always give up your seat on the bus for an elder."

We knew the rules and we had them memorized. And when we did not behave, we were certain to be properly punished. "Yes, Mutti," we chimed in unison. We will be good for Cousin Paula."

I had no way of understanding the significance of this visit. Apparently, our guest was not just any cousin, this was Paula Kahnemann (née Arndt), one of the fabled well-to-do cousins from the "old country." So much preparation! Such a fancy lunch! I could not help but be excited. But Paula was running late, and I could sense my mother becoming increasingly anxious. Finally, the doorbell rang, and my mother ran to open it.

The woman standing in the doorway was plain-looking and stout. She looked like a typical middle-aged woman, although it seemed as though we had been preparing for a visit from a queen. Only after she stepped across the threshold into the foyer did I notice how elegantly Paula was dressed. The jewelry, the fur, the hat! I had only ever seen people dress like that for the High Holy Days at synagogue. Paula carefully removed her fur stole and handed it to my mother, displaying a dazzling array of diamonds on her fingers as she did so.

"May I take your hat?" asked Mutti. A black hat shaped like an upside-down shallow soup bowl sat tilted at a precariously sharp angle on Paula's head. It was tufted with ornate feathers and beads on one side. Mutti reached for the elaborate headpiece.

"No, dear. I will keep it on," declared Paula. We did not realize that keeping her hat on meant something significant.

I bowed, and Anita curtsied, just as we had been taught, treating Paula like an honored guest. "How chaaarming," Paula drawled, saying it just the way I imagined a queen would.

We were all ushered into the living room. As we passed the dining room table, I saw that my mother had, with no attempt at subtlety, displayed multiple layers of her own hand-embroidered tablecloths and napkins on the dining room table. "Such '*goldeneh hande!*'" Paula exclaimed.

Mutti gave her "golden hands" a self-satisfied look, but then she shook her head as if to deny the polite compliment. "Oh this?" My mother pointed to the tablecloths and then waved her hands from side to side in a gesture of false modesty. "It's nothing."

Paula took a seat on the couch. "What a lovely little apartment, Grete. "My, oh my, the room is so very beige," she commented, giving a little snort, and raising up one lip in a half smile. It had not sounded like a compliment.

It was certainly true. My mother had a penchant for beige, and it was everywhere: on the couch, on the upholstered chairs, even splashed onto the fabric chandelier over the dining room table. Only the Persian rugs, in shades of blue and red, broke the monochromatic beige tones of the room.

The grownups proceeded to have coffee. I ate precisely one cookie, then sat and waited patiently while they chatted stiffly about matters of which I cared little and understood less. "And how are your girls?" Mutti inquired, referencing Paula's daughters, who were already grown young women.

"Oh, they are doing marvelously!" exclaimed Paula, suddenly animated. "Always an adventure! Meta is planning to travel to Africa during her school break, and Ilse is dating a handsome and brilliant young man." There was a pause. My mother was oddly quiet. Paula took a sip of coffee. "And how about your Anita?" Paula asked, looking up from the gold-rimmed porcelain cup and nodding toward my tuned-out sister. "Will she be continuing her studies in high school, or will you be sending her to a school for household management?"

Anita choked slightly and suddenly looked up from studying her fingernails. She *had* been listening. Her eyes widened so much, I thought they were going to detach from her head and roll onto the Oriental rug. I suddenly recalled something. Hadn't Anita and my mother been arguing about this very issue all week? I had been playing in the kitchen, and my mother had shouted, "You had better improve your grades, Anita, or you will be going to a school for household management!" And my sister – always ready to engage in a fight – had said, "You would deny your own child a real education and send her to a school where all she learns is the art of dusting and silver polishing? Oh, that is rich, Mutti." Now I could understand Anita's giant bouncing eyeballs. Why was Cousin Paula bringing up this sensitive topic?

"Well, we are still discussing it," Mutti hoarsely answered Paula, after a pause. "Maybe Anita could study a little harder."

What happened to my Mutti, I wondered? I had never heard her sound so meek!

Paula shook her head and clucked with sympathy. "Too bad," she shrugged. "Young people! Well, you know my house is in Flatow, outside Berlin. If you would like Anita to pick up some household skills, she is always welcome to spend the summer with us."

"Oh, thank you," said the mild-mannered woman who was impersonating my Mutti.

Just then, Paula stood up. "I really must be going now!" she remarked abruptly. "How the time has flown! Thank you so much for the coffee, Grete."

My mother looked stunned. We were all surprised. What had happened to our marvelous meal? My stomach growled loudly as we all walked to the foyer. Paula took her fur stole, gave my mother an air kiss in the general vicinity of both cheeks, adjusted the hat that had never left her head, and walked out the door. She had been there less than an hour, and her perfunctory visit to my mother was over. There would be no lunch. There was never going to be a lunch, as far as Paula was concerned.

As soon as the door closed, I saw my mother's mood darken. She pivoted to Anita and me and began to speak, the anger in her tone laced with a note of desperation. "Wolf, how rude you were, staring off into space like an imbecile! Anita, you embarrassed me, picking at your nails like a child and not making any useful conversation." Her vocal pitch was rising fast now. "And where is your father? At the pub, no doubt, telling his war stories to anyone who will listen. Never where he is supposed to be. *Wasting* our money. Useless man! It's no wonder Paula left so early. What a horrible reception she received!" Mutti was yelling by now, hurling insults and blaming us, Vati, and the world, for the ruined day.

Lunch had slipped away completely. No matter, for the rumblings in my stomach were supplanted by humiliation and fear. It was not the first time Anita and I had witnessed this mood. Anita had seen many more years of it, as she was older and had more time to accumulate real or imagined infractions.

Mutti left the room, and for a moment, I thought the tirade was over, but soon she returned. In her hands was an old "friend." It was a cat-o-nine tails – which thankfully, after years "disciplining" Anita, had long ago worn down to only three tails.

Later that evening I lay in my bed, beaten and bruised. It was not just my bottom that hurt, but my pride. The injustice seemed worse than my mother's outburst itself because there was no way to avoid the next eruption; it could spew at any time. I could be good, I could be better, I could even be best – but another episode of manic rage would eventually make its appearance again, and all I would do is cower powerlessly in a corner until it was over.

And I was angry at Vati too, who had not yet returned. Where had he been all day? Where was he now? Why hadn't he rescued me? He had sidestepped the whole day, quite possibly on purpose. Just a little trip to the pub – and somehow one Pilsner turned into two, then three, and he lost all track of time. That is what Mutti had told us and so it must be true.

Now I heard the front door open. Vati had finally returned

home, and a few minutes later, he came into my room. He pulled down the side rail of my little white bed and sat down next to me. I forgave him immediately even as I inhaled the yeasty, slightly sour smell of beer on his breath. He leaned over, his usually combed-over, thin hair falling over his clear blue eyes and landing just above the pale pink radiation scar on his cheek. He pulled my shuddering shoulders into his chest and listened patiently as I explained the day's events.

"It was unfair... we were good... we missed lunch... Paula was mean... Mutti was angry..." An explosion of words poured out of me between staccato breaths. Vati squeezed me tightly and chuckled sympathetically, trying to assuage my hunger and hurt. I threw my arms around his neck, and my legs around his slight body, as he lifted me out of bed and carried me into the kitchen, where the remnants of the neglected lunch were still waiting patiently on the cold stove.

The *Spätzle* had lost their luster; the little dumplings now sat in clumps as if held together by the glue they once resembled. Vati sat me right on top of the table. He sliced the *Sauerbraten* thinly and spooned some fragrant gravy over the cold meat. He gracefully glided around the small kitchen in silence while he made a plate for us to share, and only then did he speak. "Ahh *mein liebes Kind,* my dear child. Well, now you have met Cousin Paula, the snob."

"Is she really a dentist, Vati? She seemed so fancy."

"Yes, Wolf, she is, although she does not practice dentistry now.[1] And her brother Sigfried Arndt is a judge, and her other brother Arthur is a doctor. And yes, it is true, they are all very well off. 'Good for them,' I say. Your mother was always the poor relation of all of her cousins. That is why she was working so hard to impress Paula. But Paula's life is not so perfect. Do not be fooled. Her daughters are rich and spoiled and always in the middle of some scandal or another."

"But aren't we rich, Vati?" I asked.

"Well, Wolf, I would not say we are rich. Then again, we have our very own toilet... What more could we possibly want?" He handed me a forkful of meat and gravy. It was cold but delicious.

"Hmm. So Paula did not even stay for lunch," he remarked. "How rude. What a snob!"

"Yes, what a snob," I repeated. "Vati, what's a snob?"

And we both started laughing.

Summer faded to fall. The air chilled and the days grew bleak and gray. By December, the daylight was already fading by 3:30 in the afternoon. It had become bitter cold, and the snow that landed on our street stopped melting entirely. The white, frozen streets finally meant the end of playing outside.

Vati hammered two nails into the bathroom doorway and hung a swing in the hopes that we could play indoors, but I was too small. With my feet unable to touch the ground, I could not direct the swing to stay straight and the wooden seat kept banging into the narrow door frame. Only Anita, springing off the ground with long-legged precision, could perfect this miraculous feat. I gave up and tried to amuse myself by looking out over the balcony; I would climb onto a chair, lean on my elbows, and watch the activity in the road below.

How dull Schillerstrasse was in the winter! Hardly any traffic, and only a rare pedestrian. Here and there, a horse-drawn delivery truck would come down the block, the rhythmic clip clopping of the horse muted by the snow.

Sometimes, the icy conditions were simply treacherous. The horses would try to make their way warily along the frozen road, their heads down, their strong, thick legs sliding and stumbling as they pulled their heavy cargo. One afternoon, while I watched the scene below, a cart horse could not make it up Schillerstrasse. The black horse pulled and heaved his load but made no progress. With his head down and his long mane flowing wildly, his hooves slid and slid until he finally lost his footing and fell in the icy street. The exhausted horse lay on his side hopelessly trying to stand. I saw him try to lift his body slightly, but the straps and the weight of his load pulled him back. As he struggled, his legs slid sideways on the snow as if he were trying to swim. A random trail of overturned cargo that looked like black cubes of coal lay scattered around him in the white snow. Two or three bystanders in the street now ran over to help. They unhitched the wagon and worked together to lift the beautiful horse and steady him back on his feet.

I watched this drama recur throughout the winter while I waited impatiently for the warm weather to return.

Early signs of spring moved in with a warming sun. Vati cleaned up the coal that he had stored on the balcony during winter. Mutti planted blue forget-me-nots in four white window boxes and hung them over the balcony wall. In earthen pots, all along the balcony floor, she planted string beans, the vines eventually blossoming into white fragrant flowers long before they would erupt into beans.

As soon as it was warm enough to venture outside, Vati and I began to take Sunday outings around Berlin. Sometimes we strolled the city streets. On beautiful, sunny days, we walked to the Bahnhof elevated train station and took a 30-minute ride to Grunewald, the "green forest" on the outskirts of Charlottenburg. We joined hikers, young parents with baby carriages, picknickers, and an endless stream of bike riders who filled the forested paths. Sometimes it seemed as if everyone in Berlin was riding their bikes through Grunewald. Everyone, that is, except me.

How was it that I – four years old since February and the son of a former bicycle salesman – did not yet own or know how to ride a two-wheeler? It was inexplicable. Vati must have finally realized this deficiency, too. One evening in early spring, he returned from work, and called out to me from our foyer, "I have a surprise for you Wolf." I came running up to Vati and tried to get past him. He tried to block me at first, but then he lifted me up and swung me around. Behind him stood a two-wheel bike, painted in a flaming orange color.

"Is this for me, Vati?" I asked in an excited, near-soprano voice.

"All yours," he replied. "Don't you love the color?"

I did like it in fact, but then I noticed a few scratches and some peeling paint. "Oh, I see it is not a new bike." My vocal pitch had already dropped with my waning exuberance. "Wait, is it a girl's bike?" I now asked in a nervous whisper. "Vati, did this bike used to be Anita's?"

Any disappointment about my not-so-new bike only lasted a few days, then melted with the last remnants of snow. Vati and I went out for our first riding lesson. I pedaled furiously while Vati held the back of the bicycle and ran with me down Schillerstrasse. I turned around just to be sure he was still there. Thank goodness, he was still there, waving to me from the front of the arched entrance of our building, becoming ever smaller as I rode further away. I lifted my hand to wave back. Predictably, I hit the curb and fell over. I lay on my side, just like the winter horses, my left foot swimming wildly in the air. My father ran to me; he lifted the bicycle off me and wiped my tears and the blood and gravel from my skinned right knee with the sleeve of his wool tweed jacket. "You're all right, little Wolf. Do you want to try again?"

Vati placed me right back on the seat. I pushed the pedals frantically, but as soon as Vati let go, the handlebars wobbled from side to side as if some unseen, contending forces were pulling them in opposing directions, dragging me down to the curb. How many times we went through the same routine! Then, the magical laws of physics applied all the appropriate forces to my rotating wheels, and I could ride upright and straight.

It was not long before I was a confident rider, and Vati and I began spending almost every Sunday riding through the enchanted green forest paths of Grunewald.

One Sunday in early spring, Vati and I got on the U-bahn underground train as usual, but this time we did not have our bikes.

"We are not riding today, Wolf," Vati yelled in my ear, his voice straining over the sound of the train. "It is too cold and rainy."

"Where are we going?" I yelled back at him. Our train ride seemed interminably long.

"Well, Wolf, now I need you to be an excellent spy. Do you think you can keep a secret?" The train stopped at a station, and Vati lowered his voice. He bent down to reach my ear and conspiratorially said, "We are going to visit my sisters, your Aunts Hede and Frieda, on Perleberger Strasse."

This was news to me. Aunts? Was it possible that I had a whole family hidden somewhere in Berlin? As hard as I tried, I could not remember ever having met my aunties. My family had always seemed so small. So rarely did guests, family friends, or relatives come over. "Why haven't my aunties ever visited us?" I asked Vati.

Vati opened his mouth, then he closed it again as if reconsidering. A few minutes later, he opened it again and with an air of finality, said, "You have to ask Mutti that question." Then his expression changed, as if he decided to share something else. "Let me tell you what happened, Wolf. A long time ago, Mutti banned my sisters from visiting us."

"But why, Vati?"

"Well, she felt they had insulted her."

"Did they?"

"Who knows. That is how Mutti saw it. But things got even worse a few years later when my elderly Aunt Auguste died. My sisters and I were Aunt Auguste's only living heirs and she left everything to the three of us. Mutti became convinced that my sisters had run to Auguste's apartment as soon as she took her last breath and had stolen all of Auguste's valuables before even notifying us that she had died."

"And was that true, Vati?"

"Of course not! Well, I doubt it. At least, I don't think so. Honestly, Wolf, I don't even know what to believe anymore. The point is, that's what Mutti believed. After that incident, she made me promise to cut off all contact with them."

"But aren't they your sisters?"

"*Ach*, you're right, my little Wolf! But according to your mother, we are not allowed to visit them."

I pondered this whole story. What terrible relatives I had. First the snobbish Cousin Paula, and now the selfish and evil thieving aunties. How could they have done these awful things to my mother? What would I say when I met them? Before I could resolve this dilemma, we had already arrived at *Tante* Hedwig and *Onkel* Arthur Jacobsohn's apartment. Evil or not, I could not suppress my excitement about meeting my relatives for the first time. However, as soon as we entered the apartment, my enthusiasm withered.

An overwhelming smell of smoke hit me as I stepped into the small, cramped apartment. The dim living room had bare wood floors, and was furnished with only a threadbare sofa and a few chairs. What little light came in through the single living room window served only to illuminate a coating of gray dust. As my eyes adjusted to the darkness, I saw that there was something in the shadowy corner of that dusty room. It was an old, weathered woman, rocking softly in an old wooden rocker.

Vati motioned to me, and we made our way over to the old woman. She was dressed entirely in black. "This your Oma Henriette. She is my mother, and your other grandmother. Say hello, Wolf," Vati commanded gently. He kissed Oma politely on her sallow, sunken cheek.

I had another Oma? This was turning into a day full of surprises. I had no recollection of ever meeting Oma Henriette. According to Vati, she had been living with Aunt Hede since my grandfather Wolf – my namesake – died many years ago. There she sat silently, rocking in her chair, still wearing her black mourning dress. An old-fashioned white cotton bonnet covered her head tightly, hiding all but a few strands of silver hair that had escaped their fabric shelter. Eager though I was to meet my Oma, I couldn't help but feel vaguely nauseated as I reached up to kiss her waxy cheek.

I turned back to the sparsely furnished living room. How drab and colorless it was. Then my eye caught one giant flash of brilliant color. How could I have missed it? In the center of the room stood a large cage which held an enormous, bright green parrot. The bird sat so perfectly still that for a moment I was not even sure he was real. Then he took a single step on his perch as if to clarify that, yes indeed, he was living and breathing. He was simply magnificent. I waited patiently for either my grandmother or the parrot to greet me hello, but no one said anything. Certain that one of them would break the silence, I waited longer, but neither of them uttered a word.

At last, the interminable silence was interrupted. A wide woman entered the living room and waddled over to me with amazing speed. She pulled me into her ample chest, wrapped me with her generous arms, and gave me a warm and hearty greeting. "I'm your Aunt Hede!" she cried loudly as she held me to her bosom. Hede was shorter than Vati, but she was built nothing like my spindly father. She was the size of a house. And she was not letting go of me. I thought I was about to run out of air, when a young girl peeked out from behind Hede's large rump. I had not even seen her hiding back there! Aunt Hede instantly released me. "Oh, come here, come here, darling," she said, turning to the child behind her and gesturing with her arm. "Wolf, my dear, may I introduce you to my daughter? This is your cousin Ilse.[2] Ilse, why don't you bring Wolf to your room. You two can go and play."

The girl, Ilse, was about a year or two older than me, with a round face and an ear-to-ear smile. I took one look at Ilse and thought, *why on earth would I want to play with a girl?* In truth, I had never played with a girl before – not even Anita, really – and lacked any real-life experience in the matter.

At that very moment, a tall, lean, handsome man, wearing an outrageously bright orange, puffy sweater, walked into the living room. Ilse scooted over to him and hid shyly behind his black-and-white checkered pants; the man was undoubtedly her father. Ilse began mindlessly twirling his insanely long watch chain around his finger. I followed the lengthy chain from its source at his belt loop, down a long path along his stunningly bold pants, reaching almost to his knee, and then looping back around until it was back in his pants pocket.

"Hallo, Arthur," gushed my father, cheerily, for this boldly dressed man was apparently named Arthur too. "What on earth are you wearing today, brother-in-law? Are you competing with your parrot for most colorful plumage?" Arthur Jacobsohn, my uncle, put his hand to his chest dramatically and acted as if he had just been stabbed. "No, don't worry, my friend," my father laughed, quickly backpedaling. "I'm just teasing you! You look as fashionable as ever. How is the window-dressing business going? Back at our store we could sure use some pointers. No one has your keen eye for design at Paul Klein's."

"Your store doesn't need me," cried Uncle Arthur. "Your country bumpkin customers are way too dull for my futuristic fashion visions."

"Without a doubt," agreed my father. "Now, Wolf," Vati added, turning to me, "why don't you run along and go play with your cousin Ilse. Leave us grown-ups to smoke and talk. Maybe have a schnapps or two. What are you pouring, Arthur?"

Ilse slowly stepped away from her father and tried to motion me toward her bedroom, but I was still reluctant to play with her; besides, I was still obsessing over the non-verbal parrot in the living room. "Can't he speak?" I asked Ilse.

"No, isn't it terrible? No one has trained him to talk," Ilse lamented.

Well, at least Ilse was talking; she had finally overcome her shyness. Still, I was thoroughly dejected. How in heaven's name would I ever get through this tedious visit with an aunt and uncle I did not know, a girl for a playmate, an elderly grandmother in mourning, and a mute parrot?

Just as I was contemplating the tiresome afternoon, there was a knock at the door, and in walked another short, square woman. She looked so much like Aunt Hede that she could have been her twin. There was no other possibility: this woman must be my other aunt, Frieda. The exceedingly tall man who entered just after Frieda was her husband, Alfred Herrmann.[3] With the same gregarious enthusiasm as her sister, Aunt Frieda stretched out her flabby arms and enveloped me in a constricting boa-like embrace. "Wooolf," she cried, "my darling." While tilting my head up for air, my eyes landed warily on Frieda's giant of a husband.

What an intimidating figure he made! Uncle Alfred bowed formally and clicked his heels together when he greeted me, just like a German soldier. Then he sat down stiffly and very erect in a plain wooden chair. Leaning over and grabbing me with his long arms, he freed me from Frieda's suffocating squeeze and lifted me swiftly onto his knee. "Call me *Onkel*," he said.

Suddenly I was sitting face to face with this forbidding-looking stranger who was presumably my uncle. Perched on his lap, I shivered despite wearing the bright-blue woolen sweater with fire-red buttons that my mother had knitted for this cold and wet spring day. Perhaps it was nerves. "And how many buttons do you have on your sweater, young man?" my uncle immediately asked me. He looked quite serious.

My counting skills were somewhat shaky, and I was uneasy, for I had not expected to be tested today. "Five?" I answered, with a hint of uncertainty.

He recounted them. *"Nein,"* he countered. "No. There are four buttons."

I counted them again. Five buttons, I was sure of it.

He counted the buttons – up this time, instead of down. "You are wrong again," he bellowed. "There are six buttons."

By now I was utterly flustered, and my lower lip was quivering. Then his stern countenance broke out into a hearty laugh, and I finally realized he was just toying with me. And when he magically pulled a *Pfennig* out of my ear minutes later, I started to laugh too.

Gradually, I began to warm to the atmosphere in this plain little apartment. A house of mirth, so unlike my own! The men joked and drank, the women laughed and embraced. Everyone seemed so relaxed, so casual. Even the dust seemed to dance in the air. Eventually, the men retired to another room to play a popular card game "Skat," and I finally stopped resisting and went to Ilse's bedroom to play doctor and nurse.

We had played for an hour or so when Ilse and I came to an impasse; I wanted to see blood and guts and Ilse wanted all the dolls to get married. Unable to broker a peace deal, we ventured back into the living room to amuse ourselves with the gorgeous viridescent parrot.

The parrot ogled us warily from within his cage, but he still did not utter a sound. It was driving us mad. Surely this parrot was here only for our own amusement. Bored and frustrated we tried every possible way to make him speak. We gave him just a little poke. No response. We shook his cage a bit. He faltered for a second, moved a talon a centimeter to his left, then righted himself. Still, not a peep. "This is no fun at all," I complained to my cousin. "Let's try something."

We proceeded to yell into the parrot's cage. "A parrot who can't speak. What use are you!" Cruelly, we walked around the parrot's cage, insulting the poor bird, intentionally trying to rile him up. "Maybe you are just dumb! You are a *Dummkopf!* A dumbhead! You should be returned to the store!" we taunted.

Suddenly the parrot let out a loud squawk. We jumped back. He squawked again, louder. And then, holy mackerel, did he begin to speak. Not just any tiresome words, but a holy tirade. That parrot began to utter a stream of consciousness of every kind of invective and expletive I had ever heard, and many I had never heard before.

Du hast den Arsch offen [You're full of s%#@]
Du Hurensohn [You son of a bitch!]
Du kannst mich mal! [f%#@ you!]
Du Lusche! [Jerk!]

All the adults came running into the room. "*Ach, mein Gott!*" Aunt Hede shrieked.

"What in heaven's name is going on?" cried Aunt Frieda. "Cover the children's ears!"

They tried to usher us innocent little ones out of the room, but Ilse and I refused to move. Squealing with delight, we stayed put. We had done it! We made the parrot speak. And we were going to learn those forbidden swear words no matter what. We were not going anywhere!

It was Uncle Arthur who started to snicker first. Then my father joined him, and then Uncle Alfred and both my aunts. Soon we were all laughing so hard that tears started streaming in rivulets down our cheeks. "So this is how you trained the parrot?" my father finally managed to sputter through his cries and laughter.

"No, I swear to God, I did not!" cried Uncle Arthur. "But I have to admit, it is possible he has been a very good listener!" With that we all began to laugh again until we had collapsed onto the hard wooden floor, sending the dust flying into the air around us.

All this time, Oma Henriette was rocking back and forth in her rocking chair, her loose strands of silver hair sliding up and down against her black mourning dress. She did not look up; she did not laugh or smile. In fact, during my whole visit, my grandmother never said a word.

We returned home from our excursion, exhausted and elated. I was bursting with excitement, itching to tell my mother all about my day, about Ilse, my aunties, and of course, the highlight: the swearing parrot. I had never really experienced such affection, such warm (if suffocating) embraces, such unbridled laughter before today. But as soon as we walked in the door, I could feel the blithe lightness of the day instantly vanish. With one glance from my mother, the joy was sucked out of me, and the air suddenly became thick and heavy. She looked livid, and I shut my mouth. Vati did the same. We were never supposed to speak about the day. It was to be our secret.

The next day, for the first time I could remember, my parents stopped speaking to each other completely. Anita and I started to really worry; the silence somehow felt more unsettling than my parents' quotidian insults and accusations. Without any information, Anita could only hypothesize what my parents were fighting about. "They always fight about the same things Wolf," she said. "Most often, it's money. Vati probably agreed to help financially support Oma Henriette. Maybe he lent his sisters money this time. Or he had the gall to take their side in this stupid family feud."

All these charges ultimately flew across the room when my parents did finally "speak" a few days later – or rather, yell –

shouting invectives and expletives just like the parrot. But I had a feeling the real transgression was that we came home extraordinarily happy. The fact that we enjoyed ourselves without my mother, in someone else's home? – well, that was a crime worth punishing.

3

THE BEGINNING OF THE END

Heil Hitler!

It was as if something had changed overnight. Our previously friendly neighbors suddenly began to greet us with this government-mandated salute as they passed us in the hallway. The more antisemitic ones did it with aggressive intent, as a small act of intimidation. It was hard not to shrink from their rigidly outstretched arms. Jews were forbidden to use the salute and this seemed to titillate our neighbors further. They wanted us to feel powerless, humiliated. We could not conceive of a way to respond.

Of course, things only seemed to have changed overnight. In actuality, the shifts in power and loss of freedom had been occurring steadily in the background throughout the entire previous year. 1933 had been the year of Hitler's rise, the consolidation of power to a single Nazi party, and the destruction of democracy. Hitler then fully established his unopposed dictatorship with the Enabling Act, allowing him to pass any law without parliament, even in opposition to the constitution. Once German democracy ended, the future of the Jews was essentially over too. It would be incremental at first, but like a runaway train, there would be no stopping it.

The *Heil Hitler* salute was the very first government-issued decree we felt directly. The salute had been around for years, but in 1934 it was mandated that every non-Jewish citizen use it or face punishment. Eventually 2,000 anti-Jewish decrees would be passed by the Nazis. The decrees to come were designed to segregate Jews from German society, strip them of their rights, prevent them from earning a living and eventually impoverish them completely. And to murder them? That was an afterthought.

In the summer of 1934, my older playmate, Achim, joined the Hitler Youth. We should have seen that coming. He proudly sported his uniform. How impressive he looked in his tan shirt and brown shorts, a leather strap slung diagonally over his shoulder and a dagger on the other side! Various patches and emblems, along with his knee-high socks, completed his outfit to perfection. He looked like a young soldier, his white-blond, swept-over bangs adding to the image of perfect German youth. I could not help but be impressed. I looked at my older friend, standing at attention, wearing his dagger and his crisp uniform, and for the first time in my life, I understood what it meant to feel jealous.

Soon after, Achim's whole family joined the Nazi party, allowing them all to participate in Nazi indoctrination. Achim met with the Hitler Youth on weekends and marched down the street in a large group. With their Nazi flags and drums, they looked like a paramilitary unit in a parade. His sister joined the BDM (*Bund Deutscher Mädel* [League of German girls]) where she was given lessons in the "virtues of German motherhood and the duty of producing children for the Fatherland." Instead of marching, the girls received gymnastics training. And the whole family participated in propaganda vacation retreats promoted and organized by the *Kraft durch Freude* [Strength through Joy] Nazi leisure organization.

How important Achim's family felt! The uneducated owners of a small grocery had become members of something larger than themselves. They walked around in uniform. Marched. Paraded.

Saluted. *Belonged.* They bonded with their neighbors while their sense of German patriotism grew. And what could fuel patriotism better than a common enemy? At every event they attended, Achim's family received a robust dose of well-orchestrated, antisemitic indoctrination, until they were absolutely confident that the Jews were the enemy of the German people.

My parents watched these events with some concern, but remained somewhat detached. Their own lives seemed to be chugging along. True, their neighbors had joined a political group. Who hadn't seen friends and neighbors join a radical political party from time to time? Sure, they also saw a rise in antisemitism. Then again, hadn't there always been antisemitism throughout history? When it wasn't overt, it was endlessly simmering just beneath the surface.

Well, if my parents could stay calm, I could too. Like Achim, I had my own retreat to look forward to. I would be heading to the country in the summer of '34, and I would not let my envy towards my friend get the better of me.

"Papers. Take out your papers everyone." The train we were riding had just ground to a halt, and the Polish police had unexpectedly boarded. "Where is your identity card?" the Polish police demanded of all the passengers.

"Where are we, Vati?" I whispered.

"We are at the *Polnischer Korrido*r [the Polish Corridor]," Vati breathed back, leaning close to me.

"Shh," scolded my mother, glaring at us both.

"This is an area that was given to Poland after the war so they would have an outlet to the Baltic Sea," Vati murmured softly.

"Do you have an identity card, Vati?"

"Of course. We must have our papers with us all the time. An identity card, and a passport with my fingerprints on it. The government always knows who I am and where I am. Everything must be in order."

The Polish police had interrupted a near-perfect day. We were heading to the northern river town of Friedland, about 350 kilometers (220 miles) from Berlin, for a vacation with my uncle, Siegfried Jacob, and his wife Irma. We had woken up to cloudless skies that morning and walked with our few bags from our apartment to the U-bahn station at Bismarckstrasse. The underground train took us to the main Berlin Bahnhof Zoo station that connected Berlin to the rest of Europe. That is where we boarded our coal-powered express train. We were now heading towards the town of Königsberg where we would transfer to a local train and complete the journey. I counted at least three trains for the journey and I could barely contain my excitement.

Now our idyllic journey was being interrupted and we all sat nervously as one by one, each rider showed their papers. Fortunately, everyone's identification was in order, and the moment passed without incident. It was just bureaucracy, borders, and bookkeeping. No one got thrown off the train and no one was arrested. This train ride, I would eventually learn, was just a dress rehearsal.

The train slowly picked up speed again. I peered through the window as it chugged through the flat farmland. Geometric fields of golden wheat glowed in the summer sun. The occasional giant moving shadow announced the presence of a sporadic cloud in an otherwise outrageously blue sky. As the sun rose higher in the sky, the vivid colors faded into a haze of bright sunshine. The farms and the shapes melted together into a blur of green and gold dots peppering the German countryside, and I did not even know that I had fallen asleep.

"Wake up, little Wolf. We're here."

We had arrived in Friedland, and my father was shaking me awake. We quickly disembarked and retrieved our suitcases while my mother peered nervously up and down the platform. "Where are Uncle Siegfried and Aunt Irma?" There was no sign of her younger brother and sister-in-law, but a grand car with a white-gloved chauffeur was waiting for us near the platform, and the driver was holding up a sign that read "Schwersenz." He took our plain luggage and placed it in the trunk of the massive car and instructed us to get in the backseat.

We drove along some country roads for a few kilometers and then turned onto a long gravel drive. Perfectly trimmed cone-shaped trees lined the gravel road at even intervals. "Oh my, it's a palace!" I heard my mother exclaim. I slid off my seat and stared out the car window just as we pulled into the circular driveway and came to a stop.

A team of servants stood at the entrance of a house that seemed gargantuan. The chauffeur brought our luggage from the luxurious car into a house whose interior was equally lavish. Cream-colored silk fabric covered the walls. Furnishings were stately but not overly ornate. There was a breezy, effortless elegance to the home that seemed totally at odds with Mutti's vigorously polished silver ornaments, her posed porcelain figurines, and her carefully positioned rugs. Mutti had said this large, lovely, country home was a palace. So now I knew what a palace looked like.

A servant showed me to my own room that was drenched in the warm glow of late afternoon sunlight. I sank into the giant milky white bed, with a mattress as soft and high as risen dough; it swallowed me whole as I slid into its middle and rested after my long journey.

When I woke up, daylight had turned to dusk and I was disoriented and alone. I was impatient to meet my Uncle Siegfried, the only person my mother ever spoke of in unconditionally glowing terms. In fact, I could not think of a single disparaging, judgmental thing she had ever said about her younger brother. Eager to find my perfect uncle, I slipped off my bed, and walked out of my room in my stocking feet.

A long hallway lay between me and the rest of the house, with dark wooden floors shined to a high-gloss slippery finish. I started carefully padding down the hall and finally caught sight of a man at the other end. "Wolf," he called to me from across the hall, "finally, you're awake. I'm your Uncle Siegfried. Come on now, why don't you take a running slide."

Seriously? He would allow this inside his home?

"Go ahead," he bellowed again, encouragingly.

Ten running steps later, I plunged into a long sideways skid. I put my arms out for balance – and found myself sliding down the hallway as if I was skating on slick ice. Suddenly Siegfried intercepted me. He wrestled me down to the floor, pinned me down by the arms, lay over me with his generous torso… and I was stuck.

My face tickled slightly as Siegfried's moustache inadvertently grazed it. Then my uncle began a lavish body tickle in earnest. He tickled me all over my belly and under my arms. I was laughing so hard, I thought I might die. He finally released me. Sitting up, he said, "Well, Wolf, that is your first wrestling hold. Don't worry, there's plenty of time, my little nephew. I'll teach you more wrestling moves later this week."

And that is how I met my Uncle Siegfried, a man who would encourage me to play in his home rather than tell me not to touch anything. Still sitting beside me, Uncle Siegfried smiled, and his rosy, round cheeks, slightly damp from our tussle, filled his countenance. He was all roundness, wearing none of the hard angles of my mother. For an instant I could see Anita's button nose and ocean-blue eyes staring back at me in his handsome, smiling face.

Then Siegfried stood up. He smoothed out his shirt and pants. He leaned over and picked up an ornate silver-handled walking stick that had been lying on the floor. And leaning weightily on his stick, he slowly limped down the hallway away from me.

Siegfried and Irma hosted a sumptuous dinner on our first night in Friedland. That evening, Siegfried ate and drank heartily, filling the plump body that suited his affluence. "Tell me, Grete, why is Anita not joining us this summer?" Siegfried queried my mother between slurps of soup.

"Well, really, Siegfried, she is 13 already! Way too old for child's play and leisure. Besides, Cousin Paula sent us a letter offering Anita a chance to go to Flatow for the summer. She suggested – and I couldn't agree more – that it was a good way for Anita to get out of the city while learning proper housekeeping and home management. Frankly, Anita is lazy. Some hard work and discipline won't hurt her."

"Oh, Grete," laughed Irma, kindly. "I hope you do realize that Paula is just using Anita as an unpaid summer maid."

As dinner went on, I was eager to learn more about my uncle. I already knew the basic story: that he was my mother's beloved younger brother, a successful businessman, and a decorated veteran of the Great War with an Iron Cross awarded for bravery. But the question I had been barely containing all evening finally escaped from my mouth. "Why do you have a limp, Uncle Siegfried?"

There was dead silence. Mutti glared at me. Vati stared at his plate uncomfortably. I knew I had been impolite, but I just had to know.

"It's okay Grete. Relax, everyone! Let the boy ask. I am not ashamed," reassured my uncle. "Wolf, young man. Here is my whole story in a nutshell. I fought proudly for Germany during the Great War. But when we got to the Russian front, it was a disaster. The German Army was unprepared for the bitter, frigid winter. It overtook many of us, and I lost part of my foot and my toes to frostbite. In the end, they had no choice but to amputate. It was the only way to prevent gangrene. Oh, come now! Don't give me that sad puppy look! Do not feel bad for me, Wolf. I am the luckiest man alive. I survived! And I have ended up with a great life. As soon as I got back from the war, I got a fine job, and not long after, I met Irma, and the rest, as they say, is history."

Now Aunt Irma interrupted. "Yes, Wolf, when I met your Uncle Siegfried, he was working as a buyer for the Hermann Tietz chain of luxury department stores.[1] It so happened that my father Theodore Petzall – he is the mayor here in Friedland – owned a department store that was in serious financial trouble. Siegfried saved the store from going bankrupt. Our marriage ended up being so helpful to my family." She looked at Siegfried with glowing admiration.

In time I would learn a couple of details that the kind and warm-hearted Irma did not mention at dinner. She did not let on that she was a woman from a very prosperous family, whose failing department store was just one of her family's numerous businesses. Irma, a plain-looking woman, did not admit how lucky she felt to have found Siegfried, a man who was handsome, dashing, and brave, and who undoubtedly loved her. And she did not point out that she loved him so madly, apparently, that she was even willing to tolerate his occasional girlfriend on the side.

After a delicious dinner, we headed back to our rooms in well-nourished, contemplative silence. All except my mother, that is. "Irma is so plain," she murmured to my father, unable to contain her opinions.

"Oh Grete, I know you think no one is good enough for Siegfried, but Irma is a lovely woman."

"Yes, but her forehead is so large, and her complexion is so sallow. And Arthur, did you see how unsightly Irma's legs are? Why, she has no ankles!"

"Well, Grete," my father said, "since Siegfried actually has no toes, they make a perfect couple!"

The brief vacation in Friedland was blissful and full of simple joys. Each activity seemed like an adventure because I was only four and had yet to experience the world.

Uncle Siegfried and Aunt Irma owned a slick, monstrously large convertible automobile. With extra fold-down seats in the back – a novelty at the time – eight people could squeeze inside. Each day we all piled in and went on a lovely day trip. We hiked and picnicked in the nearby woods. We swam in the brisk Leine river and I stayed in the water until Mutti was sure I would freeze. "You will catch pneumonia and die!" she cried out anxiously, pleading with me to get out. Wrinkled, shivering and blue, I had no choice but to comply.

My only disappointment was that my aunt and uncle had no children to play with. I yearned for more companionship. What they lacked in children, however, my aunt and uncle made up for in maids.[2] Two young women that managed the household duties for the Jacobs had been given explicit instructions to take care of my every need. I felt like a young king. A Kaiser. Kaiser Wolf!

When we were not out on our daily excursions, we lounged like I imagined royalty did, in the spacious, elegant house. It was a leisure to which I was thoroughly unaccustomed. Uncle Siegfried, as promised, taught me to wrestle each morning. Afterwards, we all ate a sumptuous breakfast together, with dense and chewy dark Westphalian bread, cheese and salami, and pickled herring. The lovely maids made me a soft-boiled egg with butter and salt, and they served it to me in a crystal egg dish. Here in Friedland, I was allowed an egg for breakfast every single day.

Towards the end of our trip, Uncle Siegfried, who fancied himself an amateur photographer, had us all gather for a lasting family photo. That day, we all dressed in sailor suits with white shorts and tops adorned with navy-blue neckties and sailor caps.

How well we had been getting along! My parents had taken a respite from their usual fighting and even my mother seemed unusually relaxed. We hiked up to the riverbed and positioned ourselves beneath the trees. I sat on a big rock, my legs swinging, the adults flanking me on both sides. Siegfried set a self-timer and quickly limped back so he could also be in the photo. Days later, we saw the developed photos. How happy we looked in our silly sailor suits. We were all smiling, except for Mutti.

My enchanted vacation eventually had to end, and we returned to our real and tedious lives. I went back to playing in my kitchen fort, with my new title of Kaiser in my bloody dramas.

On those last summer weekends, I walked all over Berlin with Vati. We had deep conversations about everything. I thought Vati was brilliant. He explained the Nazis and current events to me in simple terms I could understand; I listened with rapt attention and I was, no doubt, his best audience. My favorite moments were when he would imitate Hitler. Yelling vociferously with clipped speech, his fists clasped – sometimes almost conducting with his arms – he did it to perfection, making me howl with laughter. It was still funny, back in those early days. We walked and walked and sometimes forgot to be home for lunch on time, sending my mother into hysterics. And not the funny kind.

In the late summer evenings, I would lie in my father's lap on the canvas chair on our balcony, inhaling the sweet smell of flowers, and he would tell me stories of his war days as we gazed at the constellations.

Within weeks of our return from Friedland, having barely settled back into our routine, an unexpected visit from a relative cast a shadow over our otherwise glorious summer holiday.

"I'm afraid we have come to say our goodbyes." My mother's cousin Sigfried Arndt sat in the living room with his wife and two children, Lutz and Susi. Sigfried[3] was the younger brother of Cousin Paula, our short-lived, aborted lunch guest.

"I can't believe you would just pick up and move. Why now?" said Vati, incredulously. "This is craziness. You are a successful young judge. You have everything you want right here."

"That might have been true a year ago, but not anymore, I'm afraid," sighed my mother's cousin. "I have been let go. Dismissed, just like that. It is simply no longer possible for me to make a living here in Berlin."

"Look, Sigfried," argued my mother, as if she could change his mind with rational debate. "Think about it. You are not a low-level clerk. You are a highly educated professional. A judge. I simply don't believe that you are not employable. I am sure this is just a temporary situation. Or a fear tactic. I'm telling you," she now declared, emphatically, "if you ride it out, you will come out on the other side."

Cousin Sigfried shook his head. "No, Grete. Don't you think my wife and I have gone over it again and again? And it is not just me who is out of work. The Nazis are dismissing all Jewish civil servants from their posts. One after the other, they are receiving termination letters. The Nazis are making certain we cannot make a living here. What choice do I really have? I simply must move elsewhere."

"But where will you go?" my mother asked, unable to hide her mixed expression of horror and confusion.

Sigfried turned to his wife, Else-Lotte, who nodded back at him encouragingly. "We will all travel to Haifa in Palestine. This has been the most difficult decision – for let me tell you, I am no Zionist. We hope it is only temporary. To be completely honest, I cannot stand the climate in Palestine. I mean, the heat! It is unbearable. They say 'oh, it's dry heat' as if that makes it tolerable. Well, of course it is dry, damn it, it's a desert! And obviously, I cannot practice the law in another country. No, we have no desire to make this permanent. Our plan is to stay there for a year and return to Germany when things settle down. We only wanted to bid you a fond goodbye, with sincere hopes to see you soon."

It was quite a visit. The first of our family members was leaving Germany and no doubt it gave my parents pause. Was it all right to stay in Germany? Nobody knew for sure; but my parents had no pressing reason to go. They focused on the little morsels of optimism that had passed Sigfried's lips. *Hadn't our cousin assured us his move was temporary? Hadn't he said things would settle down?* Their hearing had become quite selective.

But as the year continued, we could not ignore stories and rumors that began to trickle down. Everyone knew about them. People were being dismissed; Jewish professionals were expelled from their posts. In no time, another cousin, Clara, was affected. Married to the well-known Berlin stage and movie actor, Fritz Plischke, she quickly began making plans to head to the United States when the unions suddenly dismissed all Jews in the performing arts.[4]

The unemployment problem spread like a virus. Journalists were next, as the Nazis took over the newspapers run by their Jewish owners. Before long, every profession seemed to be affected. Yet it was still early days, and only salaried employees bore the brunt of this new Nazi policy. Since Jewish-owned businesses continued to operate unimpeded, Paul Klein's clothing store went untouched and my father still had a job. We thought that was a blessing. And so we did not do a thing.

We smugly watched family and friends make plans for departure, pack up their things, and say their goodbyes, as the spate of unemployment caused an exodus of Jews away from Berlin. Meanwhile, a massive influx of Jews began steadily migrating *into* Berlin. They heard that the city was the safest place to be within Germany and had stories to tell that were far worse than what was happening here at home. In the outskirts of Germany, their property was being seized and they were made to feel unwelcome in their towns. They were rolling in from every corner of the country until Berlin was veritably bustling with Jews.

That clinched it for us. More proof: it was obvious that we should stay right here.

"Are you sure we are safe here, Arthur?"

"Yes, of course, Grete. Look how many Jews are in Berlin. They're coming here from all over. In the meantime, I am making good money at the store, you have all your sewing clients, and Anita – can you believe it – passed her exams and is about to start the Lesser Schule High School. We have everything we ever dreamed of here. Why in God's name would we leave?"

While we lived in our happy state of denial, the fall arrived, bringing with it cooler temperatures and the High Holy Days. These were the days when both our Judaism and our fine porcelain emerged from hibernation to honor Rosh Hashanah – the Jewish New Year – and Yom Kippur, the day of Atonement, just a week later.

I came home from playing in the street and found the silver freshly polished to a brilliant shine. My mother was in the kitchen fussing and fretting over her holiday chicken soup. There she stood, bent over the stove, rotating a whole chicken over an open flame until the last of the tiny feathers were singed to a black dust and fell off the bird.

While the chicken stock simmered on the stovetop, Mutti slapped some dough onto our small rectangular kitchen table. She rolled it in every direction until it was as thin as a sheet of tissue paper; then she cut the dough into the skinniest of strips to make noodles for the soup. Lacking adequate kitchen space to dry all the noodles, Mutti skittered from room to room, placing noodles anywhere she could find a bit of real estate. She gingerly placed them over the beds, over the clothes lines, and over the lampshades. By the time she was done, noodles hung like stalactites from every corner of the apartment. When the noodles had finally dried, she brought them back into the kitchen and threw them into a giant pot of water to boil. As a last step, she added them to the finished soup, and only then were we ready to start our Rosh Hashanah meal.

Celebration of the High Holy Days had been the sum total of my religious upbringing. My parents got tickets for services at one of the large conservative synagogues in Berlin. They dressed up in their finery like all the Jews of Berlin: the men wore black top hats and fine suits with tails and the women donned their best fashions and furs and ornately decorated soup-bowl-shaped hats. My father's top hat added a good six inches to his height and my parents gave the illusion of a well matched, handsome, happy, upper middle-class couple.

The Berlin synagogues, just like its congregants, had yielded to the influences of Christianity. The grandiose, church-like houses of worship were built with domes, stained glass, gilded ceilings, and flower-filled altars. A full choir and beautiful organ music added to the experience for those of us who knew little of daily *davening* [praying].

We took our seats on the hard, wooden pew. "Make sure you listen carefully to the sermon," Vati whispered to me between prayers. "It's the highlight of the service."

When the sermon began, even my parents were surprised that the subject this year was not spiritual. Instead, it had taken on new political urgency. I did my best to pay close attention, but it was well above my level of comprehension. I only remember the end of the sermon, when the rabbi reassured us that the current persecution of Jews was a passing phenomenon. His message to the congregation? "Be law abiding, for it will help you gain the respect of the German Christians." And his final words of hope were to remind us of the most important message: "God will come to our rescue."

So we followed the law, and waited for the phenomenon to pass. And then we waited for God, but He did not come.

After the holidays, Oma Ernestine suddenly took a downward turn, her mood becoming even more melancholy than after Opa Hiller had died. I would often find her sitting alone and crying in her black mourning dress, which she wore well after the one-year requirement.

"Please, Wolf, go to *Shabbos* [Sabbath] services with Oma," begged my mother. "It will lift her spirits." I started to go to synagogue with Oma every Saturday morning. But my newfound religious ritual was all too brief. One brisk late fall morning when Oma Ernestine went out to do some shopping, she tripped and fell and could not get up. It was a broken hip. Bedrest was prescribed, and my mother became her own mother's full-time nurse. Oma remained completely bedridden for weeks until she eventually contracted pneumonia and fell into a coma. Days later, on November 29, she died peacefully in her bed, under her unicorn tapestry. She would finally join Opa Hiller and my infant brother Manfred in the Weissensee cemetery, and together they would miss the misery to come.

We all felt Oma Ernestine's loss deeply, and after she left us our lives changed significantly. I am ashamed to say that not all these changes were unwelcome. I suddenly had a bedroom to myself and my mother's physical burden was so lightened that she practically did not know what to do with herself.

Alas, with all her new free time Mutti decided to join Vati and me on our Sunday excursions. As soon as spring reawakened, the three of us headed to Grunewald with a camera, a blanket, and some cookies. Wearing knickers and a cap, my father brought along a walking cane strictly for stylistic effect, while my mother wore a fashionable but impractical suit and high heels. And always, in the crook of her arm, she held her pocketbook tight, as if she were certain it was about to be pried away from her.

I was less than thrilled that my mother had joined our precious Sunday outings. How dare she interfere with my freedom and intrude on my special time with Vati! And how annoyingly nervous she was. Every time the sun shone brightly, she pulled my shirt right over my head and tried to rub Nivea creme all over my pale body. Embarrassed to seen shirtless, I ran away and hid in the woods, while Mutti stood helpless in her high heels, furious, but unable to catch me.

Some days we skipped Grunewald entirely, and simply walked around Berlin. Yet almost as soon as our walk would begin, my mother would begin to complain about her aching feet. Now we had a conundrum. How and where could we stop to rest?

"There's an outdoor garden restaurant over there, Grete. Maybe we can sit down," my father would suggest.

"And spend our hard-earned money on coffee that we could make at home, Arthur? Absolutely not."

The next time we did a city walk, my parents were better prepared.

"Table for three," my father requested, walking right up to the waiter.

"What would you like to order?" the waiter asked my mother, once we were seated.

"Just one piece of cake, and three forks, please," my mother replied.

"And how about coffee?"

"That is all right, we have brought our own coffee to brew. Now if you would not mind, all we need are two cups and hot water. *Danke!* [Thank you!]"

The helpless waiter let us sit at the table for the entire afternoon while we slowly, slowly sipped on our thrifty refreshments and ate our cake one millimeter at a time. We watched the other Berliners, enjoyed the fine weather, and remained blissfully ignorant of how precious these outings would become. How soon we would be forbidden to sit in public! The time was nearing, and we did not see it coming.

It was early 1935, and the world watched helplessly as Hitler brazenly broke the military restrictions of the Treaty of Versailles. It was a steady march of concerning events. In March, he began to rearm Germany. In April he ordered 12 submarines. In May, he banned Jews from the armed forces, a possible indication that he was planning to use those forces. But what Hitler really had in store, and how far he would push the limits of the Treaty, no one knew.

It would not be long before we would find out.

Summer was fast approaching. I had hoped to go back to Friedland for another idyllic summer vacation, but fate had something else in store. Uncle Siegfried and Aunt Irma suddenly joined the ranks of Germans migrating into the city. And that meant my summer plans were wrecked.

"Siegfried," cried my mother, "how could this have happened to you? You, of all people. You have money. You are a veteran with an Iron Cross. Weren't you protected?"

"Oh, Grete. Do not try to make sense of it, because it is beyond reason. It happened so suddenly; I have barely had time to come to terms with it." Uncle Siegfried sat down at our dining room table. He nervously twisted his moustache as he relayed his story.

"Just weeks ago, I had everything. A beautiful house, a fabulous car, all the money I needed. Then one day last week, out of the blue, I get a call summoning me to the police station.

When I arrive, a policeman tells me, in a very business-like manner, that a "receiver" has been appointed over my business, my house, and my car. 'What is a receiver?' I ask. I get no reply. 'What does all this mean? Would someone please tell me what is going on?' It is like I am talking to a wall. No one will answer me. No one even looks at me. It is as though I am not even a human being. Then, some bureaucrat hands me a receipt for all my properties and starts to speak. It's the first time someone has offered me any explanation. 'All your bank accounts are going to be placed in a *Sperrkonto* – a blocked account. Your money is now under the supervision of the Ministry of Finance. You cannot make any withdrawals without permission from the ministry!' he tells me."

"Wait. Do I understand correctly? Are you telling me that all your assets have been seized by the government and there is nothing you can do?"

"That is correct, Grete. My assets are no longer mine. All my wealth has been taken. The house, the car, everything. It is all the property of the Nazis now. Oh, they did leave me one thing: this receipt. All I have is this worthless piece of paper."

That is how my Uncle Siegfried and Aunt Irma wound up moving to Berlin. Robbed of their capital by their own government, they took up residence in a spacious apartment on the Mommsenstrasse in Charlottenburg, just a short walk from 103 Schillerstrasse. To help cover the rent, they took in a boarder – a Chinese engineering student. Things settled into a new normal for the few remaining weeks of the summer of 1935. That is, until the end of August.

The annual Nuremberg festival – the spectacular Nazi rally – was held every year at the end of summer. This year, something was decidedly different. In August of 1935, Hitler announced his plans to eliminate all Jews from Europe at the Nuremberg festival. The rally ended climactically in early September with passage of the Nuremberg Race Laws, where antisemitic ideology was codified into actual law. The Nazis covered every detail. In document after document, they carefully defined who is a Jew, not based on religious practices, but built on a complicated system of "bloodlines." The goal was to help "purify" the German race.

The laws stripped Jews of their German citizenship. They banned sex and marriage between Jews and "real" Germans. The laws disenfranchised Jews and deprived them of most political rights. The Nazis left nothing up to chance, with a list of laws that was extensive, comprehensive, and almost impossible to believe.

Suddenly it seemed as if everything that came before Nuremberg was just a warm-up. Now the real Jewish persecution would begin in earnest.

1936 had started out unnerving. Every Jew had been on edge since the unfathomable Nuremberg Laws of 1935. Furthermore, in March of 1936, Germany had re-occupied the Rhineland, a demilitarized zone along the Rhine River. They had violated the Treaty of Versailles yet again. It was another ominous sign. Might Hitler might be planning an invasion?

But then... there was nothing. We waited, we watched, we listened. Absolutely nothing! No military activity. A distinct lull in anti-Jewish edicts. All was quiet again. Yes, the worst was definitely behind us.

And then, in a 180-degree turn, good news was announced. The Olympics were coming to Berlin! With all the international attention focused on Berlin, the Nazis would have no choice but to tone down their military antics and their antisemitic rhetoric. The Nazis were even fulfilling their promise to improve conditions at home. They had started a bustling infrastructure program, building roads that would eventually become the autobahn. The German people were back to work after years of post-Depression unemployment. Their sense of national pride was restored.

1936 was going to be a good year. Maybe even a great one. You could feel the positivity in the air. It penetrated the population. The enthusiasm of the pre-Olympic nation seeped into our psyches and we dropped our guard completely.

There were some people who remained skeptical. Paul Klein, the department store owner, was one of those people who remained unmoved by the less vituperative rhetoric.

"Arthur, Grete." Paul Klein addressed my parents solemnly at first. "I want you to know that I have made plans to emigrate to Argentina." Then he grew excited. "I would like to propose what I believe will be a fantastic business opportunity for you both. I would like to sell you the clothing store!"

While Paul Klein planned his own exodus, he dangled the alluring prospect of business ownership in front of my parents, and in the high spirits of the year, they were completely seduced.

"The price is right, Grete. It's a bargain!"

"Yes, but is now the right time, Arthur? I realize we will never have another opportunity like this. To top it off, we can afford it. But what if the situation in Germany gets worse?"

"Even the rabbis say this Nazi business is sure to be a passing trend. And look what is going on now, Grete. Antisemitism has quieted down. The mood in Germany is excellent."

"How can we be sure things won't deteriorate, Arthur?"

"You want guarantees? There are none. Sometimes, you simply must take a chance when it comes your way."

It was an opportunity not to be missed. Store owners! It was the highest level of achievement my parents could ever attain – after all, they were not professionals, they had no higher education – not even high school. Store ownership would be the pinnacle of their success.

So yes, this was it. My parents would buy Paul Klein's store. They opted to make Uncle Siegfried an equal partner. Siegfried knew the clothing business well. He would temper my father's propensity to excessive spending, or to forgive a customer's debt with his generous and gullible nature. Siegfried would be a stabilizing force. This made my mother feel confident in the whole venture.

A suitable low price was agreed upon and some convoluted, complicated cash transactions had to be arranged to avoid oversight by the German Finance Ministry. Money was paid "under the table" so that it was not reflected in the bill of sale. To smuggle money out of the country, Mr. Klein converted much of my parents' cash buyout into a rare stamp collection; he would never have been able to leave Germany with cash. Just look at what had happened to Uncle Siegfried's wealth. The Nazis planned to take everything.

Now that the sale was complete, my parents could not even consider leaving Germany. They had made a huge investment, planting their roots ever deeper. We would stay, of course. And Paul Klein would slowly sail off to the safety of South America.

I want to scream to my parents from the future, "Run! Run!" But I cannot. I open my mouth to scream, and no sound comes out. I am in a dream. We do not run.

My parents displayed no doubts about their business decision once it became finalized. On the contrary, they seemed full of renewed optimism. On Wednesdays and Saturdays, my mother went to the store to work as a cashier. On these days she dressed up in her smartest clothes. She had her hair permed and wore it fashionably styled for the customers. I had never seen her pay such attention to her appearance. It was as if she had been reborn.

With our finances no longer an issue, Mutti had to find another outlet for her congenital anxiety. One summer morning, Mutti looked with horror at my scrawny, shirtless, six-year-old body as I was getting ready for a bath. "*Ach, mein Gott*, Wolf! Your shoulder blades! They stick out like birds' wings! Something is terribly wrong. You are malnourished."

Right away, I was the beneficiary of a string of wacky and unproven therapies. Despite taking cod-liver oil and sitting under ultraviolet light every day, I looked even whiter than usual, and all my ribs showed. The obvious next step was evaluation of my feces. Daily examination in our German toilet led to strong speculation that I must have an intestinal parasite.

"Worms! That is the last straw, Wolf. No son of mine will have malnutrition and parasites!"

Immediately, my mother consulted professionals, semi-professionals, and spiritual advisors. The final prescription: a week of treatment in Kolberg, a northern spa resort on the icy Baltic coast.[5]

That summer, while Anita spent another "internship" at Cousin Paula's house learning the finer particulars of household management, and while Vati stayed back to watch the store, I took this brief therapeutic northern interlude with my mother. I was going to a spa by the sea, an extravagance to be sure, permitted only because it was a medical necessity. I envisioned a luxurious resort vacation with a beach, sunny skies, fun and games, other children.

As soon as I arrived, I realized my grave error. There was not a child to be found. It was indeed a *healing* spa. Each morning I was required to drink thick, sour buttermilk. Was this to fatten me up? I conjured up a mysterious kitchen witch who would be checking to see if my finger was fat enough. How grim.

After our morning meal, we trekked to the spa treatment area where a daily regimen of medicinal baths was prepared for me. For several hours each day I was forced to float in a fetid cocktail of healing waters in a large, sawed-off beer barrel tub.

Whenever I was not soaking or drinking buttermilk, I did what I could to create a semblance of a vacation. I went to the beach with Mutti and frolicked alone in the sand, or lay with her in rented wooden beach chairs, trying to find some warmth in the late afternoon sun of the endless northern summer day. If it grew too warm, I ran into the numbingly cold Baltic water up to my ankles; then I ran away from the icy, frothy waves just before my mother could reproach me, and while I could still feel my feet. "You will catch your death of cold!" Mutti screamed hysterically.

The calm of vacation eventually managed to seep into my mother's soul. Each morning, Mutti and I shuffled languidly from breakfast to the spa in our summer sandals – I had never seen her walk so casually, so lacking in purpose. She even held my hand.

On one of our last mornings, my mother and I ambled casually toward the spa, when a guest started running towards us. He was shouting and wildly gesticulating. He looked like a madman. As he got closer, we could hear him more clearly. "The railroad station is over there!" he was yelling, spit exploding from his mouth, his arm pointing in a direction away from the spa.

"What does he mean, Mutti?" I asked.

"I think I understand him exactly, Wolf. He means Jews, get out."

Summer ended triumphantly for Germany. The country had hosted a glorious Olympic Games in a newly built 325-acre Olympic arena. It was the first Olympic games ever to be televised and the arena overflowed with Nazi emblems for all the world to see. Unfortunately for Hitler, the phenomenal African American runner Jesse Owens swept the gold medals, robbing Hitler of the opportunity to display an image of Aryan superiority. The Germans were still able to save face by having the highest number of total medal wins. Yes, it could be said that Germany was victorious on the international arena. And we could not help ourselves. We were Germans too, and we felt like we had won.

The mood in Germany remained jubilant as summer rolled into September. However, my mood quickly tumbled from ecstatic to glum, for the start of school was fast approaching. And glum sunk to gloomy when I found out that as a Jew – under one of the countless new anti-Jewish German edicts – I was not allowed to attend German public school.

"Why can't I go to school with Glatze?" I asked repeatedly, as if persistent whining could somehow reverse my misfortune.

My parents had no answers, for how do you explain the incomprehensible to a child? They were consumed by a much bigger worry: If I could not attend public school, how and where would I get any education? Of course, I would not wriggle out of going to school. Jewish schools for German children rapidly materialized, as if out of thin air. It was simply extraordinary how swiftly and seamlessly a school system could be created for so many Berliner children. A Central Jewish Organization in Germany, funded through a combination of taxes, charitable donations, and ticket sales from artistic events and High Holy Days, coordinated the monumental effort. Schools popped up in synagogues, or at the sites of former orthodox schools. Soon we got word that I was assigned to the school on Klopstockstrasse, just north of the Tiergarten, about a 45-minute walk away.

I put on my new leather *Rücksack* – my backpack – prepared to make the long walk to school on my first day. Just before leaving, my parents presented me with a traditional *Schultüte* – an enormous cardboard cone filled with toys, chocolate, candies, sweets, and various school supplies. The filled cone nearly reached the top of my head. "May your first day of school be a little sweeter," said Vati, as he and Mutti kissed me goodbye. Weighed down by the *Rücksack* hanging off my skinny shoulders, and the human-sized sized cone I cradled in my arms, we all agreed that on my first day, I should take the bus.

I recall stepping off the bus in a foreign neighborhood overcome with nerves. I did not know a soul in the school and had never had a Jewish friend before – in fact, I had never really considered the religion of my friends. The first thing my teacher did was hand us all pencils and ask us to print our names. That's when everyone discovered the calamitous news: I was left-handed! I had always suspected something was terribly wrong with me. Here it was finally: the proof.

Left-handedness was a deviance that had to be corrected immediately. Vati took on the job, as he was naturally the more patient of my two parents. He brought home brown wrapping paper from the store for writing practice. Every day after school I wrote letter after letter with my right hand, dipping my pen point in and out of the inkwell, trying unsuccessfully to achieve perfection. "It's impossible, Vati. I cannot do it. My letters look like the scratch marks of a chicken!"

"Keep going, Wolf. You will get it eventually. Well, I cannot read that letter. Is that an A or an N? Try again."

I tried not to learn anything in school, but the teachers were determined to educate me against my will. I had absolutely no interest in academics. My only interest was in developing a social life. In due time it became evident that I was a decent athlete – a fast runner, and a good wrestler, thanks to Uncle Siegfried. These skills brought me some modest popularity and I gradually began to make some new friends.

In time, I was invited to play at other children's homes and to birthday parties. How elaborate their birthday parties were. Puppet shows! Magic acts! And what toys they had: miniature train sets, castles with moats and drawbridges, and whole armies of lead soldiers exhibited in their stylishly furnished bedrooms. Yes, even their toys seemed to have better living accommodations than me. My prized Army men, sufficient just weeks ago, suddenly seemed austere and inadequate. Even my marvelous homemade kitchen fort lost its luster.

Here I was with these Jewish children who had come from every corner of the city, kicked out of their own public schools just like me. We were living through difficult circumstances that should have created a bond between us. These children should have become my close allies. But they did not.

I did not feel like an equal. I felt like an outsider with my new Jewish friends. Their parents were doctors, lawyers, and engineers. For the first time in my life, I felt socially inferior. Had I inherited these insecurities from my mother? Was it in my DNA? Instinctively I felt more comfortable with the simple working-class kids that lived on my block. Every day that I went to the Jewish school, all I wanted to do was to come home and play on my little quiet block with all my Christian friends.

Whatever my challenges at school, 1936 still reached its conclusion with my parents feeling quite contented. Overall, it had been a banner year for our family. Our best year ever.

We were feeling so good, we decided to celebrate with a New Year's party. That night, the apartment was decked out in multicolored paper streamers and filled with my parents' friends and neighbors. Uncle Siegfried and Aunt Irma came of course.

How silly we all looked in our pointed paper hats! My mother served traditional *Buletten*, Berlin style hamburgers made with ground beef mixed with softened bread rolls, served cold alongside egg and potato salad. She had made Berliner *Pfannkuchen* for dessert – jelly donuts filled with plum jam, a traditional New Year's treat. It was bitterly cold out, and we warmed our insides with glogg, a hot, sweet, spiced red wine. Even I was allowed to drink some.

At the stroke of midnight, we all stepped out onto the frigid balcony with our noisemakers. "*Alles Gute zum neuen Jahr!* [Happy New Year!]" we shouted across the building to our neighbors. We hugged and kissed each other joyfully, while the sky alighted with fireworks and hand-held sparklers. As the sky lit up, flags with swastikas glowed red in the night. They hung from every balcony, as far as the eye could see.

PART II

JEWS FORBIDDEN

4

JUDEN VERBOTEN

As soon as 1937 began, all the optimism we had felt the previous year fizzled like the handheld sparklers of our New Year's Eve party. All our neighbors now greeted us with the *Heil Hitler* salute. Only Dr. Behne, our kind landlord, would say "*Hallo*" or "*Guten Tag*" when he saw us in the hallway. How much this bit of benevolence meant to us! He was making a statement, "I am not a Nazi or a Nazi sympathizer." With this little crumb of kindness, he was treating us as humans, as equals. But even this small act of defiance could get him reported.

A host of new proclamations were issued that were meant to further isolate the Jews of Germany. It seemed as if each passing day brought another restriction, and they kept on coming.

Jews can no longer sit on a park bench.
Jews can no longer go to a movie theater, the opera, the ballet, or a concert.
Jews can no longer go to a beach.
Jews can no longer enter a museum.
Jews can no longer visit a café or eat at a restaurant.

Everywhere I went, a new sign would be posted. The signs seemed to go up magically in the night.

Juden Verboten [Jews Forbidden] or: *Juden sind hier nicht erwünscht* [Jews not desired].

It felt sickening. The wrongness of it. The unfairness. And our own helplessness, too. How could they do it? How could the German people – our friends and neighbors – allow it? Yet they did. Because by then the German people had already become devotees of the government. They were in love with their leaders and fully indoctrinated, and they would do whatever the Reich required of them.

Our only solace was the support and swift response of the Central Jewish Organization in Berlin. With each new injustice, it found an almost immediate solution. They turned one building into a concert hall and another into a theater. The *Jüdischer Kulturbund* was quickly created, a Jewish cultural organization of unemployed musicians and performers that started to schedule regular performances.[1] At every turn, with every loss of freedom, the Jewish community did their best to make our increasingly insular life seem as normal as possible.

As the year progressed, instability was mounting in the rest of Europe and even Asia, with shifting alliances, and bold attacks on defenseless nations. Portentous signs of potential war seemed to be cropping up all over the globe. In Italy, Mussolini attacked and colonized the nation of Abyssinia.[2] Then Germany and Italy allied together to counter an alliance between France and England. Japan mounted a full-scale invasion of China. General Franco began his attempt to overthrow the Spanish throne. Germany sent its support to Franco, while Russia chose to support the Spanish monarchy. It was a dizzying display of a fragile peace dissolving into pieces.

My parents listened to the international news with growing dread. Their memories of the Great War were still fresh, and they could sense the global instability escalating. Hostility seemed to be all around them. It was in their apartment building. It was in their home city of Berlin. And now it was all around the world.

Only within the confines and comfort of our clothing store

could we escape the turmoil of the outside world. In our store, where we were in charge, the political unrest, the antisemitism, and the fear and harassment seemed to melt away.

"Wolf, go get us an *Apfelstrudel.* Hurry," said my father.

I had just arrived at the clothing store after school. I dropped off my *Rücksack* in the back office and was immediately pinned by Uncle Siegfried. We wrestled for a few minutes and ended in a draw, as usual. "Are you two finally finished? Wolf, go to Aschinger's right away," demanded my father as I stood up, repeating his request for dessert. "I am sending you on a sacred strudel mission."

The famous chain restaurant, Aschinger's, was right around the corner, and I regularly picked out a pastry or hot sausage for a few pfennigs whenever I visited my father at the store. Today, as instructed, I ordered a delightful, crisp strudel covered with soft clouds of *Schlag* – dollops of wonderful rich white whipped cream. I carried my treat to the back office, where Vati and I shared the strudel at his desk. When we were done, the store was still dead quiet, and I had my father and uncle to myself a little while longer until the customers started to trickle in.

"What kind of homework do you have there," asked my uncle, eying my pile of books. Siegfried and I had seen each other nearly every day since he had moved to Berlin, and we had become close confidants. He looked at me pityingly with his newly clean-shaven face.

"The usual," I sighed in response. "Can you help me with my art project, Uncle Siegfried? I cannot do art to save my life. I am incapable of drawing a single flower or a tree."

"Have you tried with your right hand?"

I nodded.

"How about your left?" he asked.

I nodded again. "Both my hands can't draw," I moaned.

Uncle Siegfried let out a boisterous laugh and then sat down to help me with my artwork.

As the afternoon grew later, the customers finally started to straggle in after their own workdays had ended. And now it was time for my afternoon entertainment. I closed my books and put my homework away. Then I sat back in my chair, clasped my hands behind my head and waited for the customers to trickle in.

The shoppers were mostly simple German farmers from outer Spreewald, Berlin's backyard of farms, gardens, and forests. After the harvest, the men would make a trip into Berlin to buy what was often their very first suit, usually for Sunday church or perhaps for a wedding. Vati's customers were neither affluent nor sophisticated and Vati "spoke their language," being similar in background and education. This common bond made the customers feel comfortable shopping in a modest store carrying ready-to-wear clothes that occasionally needed just a few simple alterations.

"*Guten Tag. Willkommen.* [Good day. Welcome.] Let us find you a fine suit." Vati fawned over the lone middle-aged man who had just sauntered into the store. After a brief conversation that I could not make out, he pulled a brown tweed suit off the rack. Vati slipped the jacket over the hefty man's broad shoulders. "What a perfect fit," gushed my father. "You cut quite a handsome figure. Let's complete the package, why don't we? Here are the slacks. Please take them to the fitting room and try them on."

The beefy man came out wearing his new tweed suit pants. They seemed to fit fine in the waist and buttocks and just needed to be hemmed. "The alterations – they are all included, *ja*?" the nervous customer asked my father.

"Why, of course!" exclaimed my father. "We just need to get the proper measurements." Vati directed the customer towards the back of the store, where he was directly in my line of sight. Vati gave me a sly wink and then turned back to his customer. "Would you please stand on this ladder, sir? Now go up one more step. Perhaps another." The short man climbed one rung, then the next until he was almost halfway up the ladder. His knee practically reached Vati's waist, and he held tightly to the upper rungs. "Sir, if you don't mind, would you please now lift your right leg. Lift it straight in the air, in a kicking position? Like so." My father demonstrated a goosestep kick with a rigid, straight leg. Holding the ladder, the man kicked his leg out, and my father caught it in the air. He held his leg up at practically a right angle. "Excellent, excellent, sir. Wait! Do not put your leg down. Hold it... hold it... keep holding... Now Mr. Jacob will take your measurements. Siegfried, come," he yelled. "Come to the back. Drop everything you are doing. We have a customer!"

Uncle Siegfried came running toward the back of the store, his tape measure draped around his neck like a long scarf. "What a fine suit," he said to the customer, who beamed back at him with a full-faced smile. With great fanfare, Siegfried slid the tape measure off his neck and through his hands. While my father continued to hold up the gentleman's leg in the air, Siegfried measured the man's inseam, the top of his leg, the bottom of his leg, and around the width of his thigh. All the while he seemed to be marking up his pants everywhere with chalk. Mark after mark, every few inches, as if his leg were a ruler. In between, he kept looking up at me and winking. I suddenly remembered that the man only needed a hem. That's when it dawned on me: Vati and Siegfried were putting on this show solely for my entertainment.

"Please, may I put my leg down for a moment?" said the customer. His leg had been in the air for quite a long time, and he was looking piqued.

"Just a few more seconds," said my father, winking at me again. "We must be very accurate. We almost have it... *Wunderbar*! [Wonderful!]" By now the man was sweating. "Good! Now if you please, just swing your leg straight out to the side. Swing it out. Like so. Perfect."

My father kept a perfectly straight face, while I did everything I could to keep from exploding with laughter. Uncle Siegfried now held the man's leg out to the side while he made chalk marks inside the groin of his pants. He had the man switch legs and hold up his left leg; then he swiveled him around on the ladder like a ballerina *en pointe*, while he placed chalk marks on his legs, by his waistband, and on his butt. Finally, they let the poor man step down. He went into the changing room and came out wearing his street clothes.

My father handed him a receipt for the suit. "It will be ready on Friday," he said.

The weary customer wiped his sweaty brow with his cloth handkerchief. Looking tired, but very satisfied, he exclaimed, "Oh, my, my, gentlemen. I had no idea how hard it was to buy a Sunday suit; this is extremely complicated, all these alterations. *Sehr schwierig.* [Very difficult.] It's so wonderful that it is all included!"

"Yes, everything we do here is custom!" said my father. "Don't you worry, we will have the perfect suit for you!" The man left the store, happy with his purchase and the attention he received. As the front door closed, we all burst out laughing.

We simply had to amuse ourselves inside the store. Because outside the walls of our store nothing was funny anymore.

5

LETTERS AND LINES AND BOARDERS

"Arthur, there is no place for us here in Germany any longer." At some point my mother recognized that we had no future in Berlin. Was it a singular moment; or more of a progressive awakening? I don't really know, but by the time reality finally did set in, the situation for Jews was not just deteriorating; it had turned dire. By the time Mutti finally accepted the truth, it was much too late. The doors of immigration had almost closed shut.

My parents had been living in a fantasy world, their denial bordering on delusion. Here they were, trying to live a middle-class dream, while a nightmare was occurring in front of their eyes. One by one, their rights were disappearing. Friends and family all around them were leaving while they hung on to their grand plan as if their lives depended on it. Did my parents ever admit to themselves: "*We stayed in Germany too long because the clothing store was a real bargain?*" Sometimes, I wonder.

Of course, I'm oversimplifying. I imagine middle-aged people don't easily pick themselves up and leave their whole world behind unless they absolutely must. To avoid making this dreaded decision, my parents hung on to the belief that things would blow over. They were not alone.

When my mother finally acknowledged that it was time to go, at least she did not fall apart. It wouldn't be like Mutti to fall to pieces. Quite the contrary, she now had a new purpose. For all her petty jealousies, anxieties, and insecurities, Mutti was the only one in our family with the discipline, energy, and focus to make something – anything – happen. She was going to have to be the one to save us.

She attacked the problem with the same ferocity she did everything. I watched her diligently refresh her English. Night after night, she furiously read books about foreign countries, straining her imagination to figure out where we might be able to live. But the most critical step she took was to contact an American cousin. To gain legal entry into the US, it was a requirement that a family member – one who was already a US citizen – agree to support our family financially. Mutti now had to solicit a relative to be our sponsor.

She wrote a letter to a first cousin whom she barely knew. His name was Ellis Arndt. Ellis was the son of Abraham Arndt, the only one of Oma Ernestine's six siblings who had emigrated to the US. Mutti had met Cousin Ellis on one single occasion when he visited Germany 10 years earlier. That was the entire extent of their relationship. She knew that Ellis owned an upscale orthotic shoe business in New York called Arch-Aid Shoes. And aid was surely what we needed.

In the best English she could muster, my mother wrote a letter to this veritable stranger, connected to us only by blood.

My dear Cousin Ellis,[1]

I hope you remember our meeting in Berlin nearly a decade ago. There are four of us in my family now. I have a son, Wolf, who is 7 ½, Anita who is now 16, and you may remember my husband Arthur, who now owns a men's clothing store.

You must be aware of the situation here in Germany. It has become quite dire. There is antisemitism everywhere, and Jews are no longer welcome members of society. We thought it would be a passing phase – that is what the politicians and rabbis told us – but every day things are getting worse. Now, the doors of escape are closing almost everywhere, and we are begging, yes begging for your help. I know that we barely know each other. But you are my first cousin, and frankly, we have nowhere else to turn. I am asking you to sponsor our immigration to the United States. It is the largest favor I could ask of anyone, but I believe our very lives depend on it.

Please help our family.

Yours, Grete Jacob Schwersenz

My mother was not exaggerating about the "doors of escape closing." She had investigated all our immigration options and found that opposition to Jewish immigration was international. The Depression and world-wide unemployment had contributed to the resistance, but antisemitism was a pervasive factor. Even Jewish immigration to Palestine had dwindled to a trickle, as the British had restricted entry to placate the Arabs.[2] And strict quotas existed among the other English-speaking British colonies such as Canada and Australia. Some Latin American countries and Cuba were permitting limited immigration; but rumors abounded that people were being swindled into paying large fees for entry visas that turned out to be forged. That was too risky. China was allowing some limited immigration to Shanghai without a visa, where Jews were living in a small ghetto. Hitler was having a good laugh. People were horrified when he said he didn't want the Jews, but no one else wanted them either. The options looked bleak.

Now, having finally acknowledged that we had to leave Germany, we lacked a viable way to get out. We watched Jews steadily departing, but they had started on their visa and immigration applications years ago. They weren't leaving now just because they hoped for employment opportunities elsewhere. They were leaving because the future here was uncertain and perilous. My parents were no longer in denial. They were experiencing real fear.

One day, Aunt Hede and Uncle Arthur Jacobsohn suddenly let us know they had gotten their visas to the United States. We were stunned. They were among the people closest to us, members of our inner circle, any past differences forgotten long ago. How had they managed to get their visas so quickly? Hadn't they just put in their application? My mother could only imagine conspiracies to explain their good fortune.

In a flash, my aunt and uncle and Cousin Ilse were gone, and for weeks we heard nothing. Finally, we received a letter, and we eagerly opened it, hungry for any news. The Jacobsohns had indeed arrived safely in New York, after spending a vast sum of money on first-class cabins for a luxury voyage. They had moved into a neighborhood in uptown Manhattan called Washington Heights. *Everything here is strange*, they wrote to us, *the people loud, the streets dirty*. But they assured us we could survive, even on this odd continent of America.

Their letter was meant to give us hope, to excite and inspire us about our future. But we did not feel reassured. We felt the pain of abandonment and loss, and we feared for ourselves.

We waited and waited, our internal clocks ticking, our anxiety like a dam waiting to burst. We awaited a response from our New York cousin Ellis Arndt, because without him, we could not even consider a visa to the US. Finally, word came from New York: Cousin Ellis, despite his distance in both blood and miles, promised he would not abandon us. Dutifully, he sent to the US consulate in Berlin the cumbersome documentation required to sponsor our immigration. Detailed financial statements, affidavits, tax returns, and reams and reams of paperwork that seemed designed to make the process as difficult as possible.

It took months, but finally all the documents had been submitted. We trekked to the US consulate, located in the center of Berlin. My mother was full of newfound confidence, for Cousin Ellis was a wealthy man, and she believed all our paperwork was in order. Nothing could go wrong. Well, nothing *should* go wrong, at least.

A well-dressed, polite consul greeted us, and we sat down and waited to hear the good news. Donning his pince-nez glasses, the consul pored over the documents. "Uh huh... hmm... okay, I see..." he murmured to himself as he slowly rifled through each page. Finally, he spoke. "*Alles ist in Ordnung* [everything is in order]," he stated. He issued us a case number. It was just a place in a line, but that was still progress. Exhaling with relief, my mother gathered our things. As we stood to take our leave, the consul spoke one last time. "Frau Schwersenz," he called.

"Yes?" replied my mother, looking back over her shoulder.

"Just to be clear, you are going to be on the Polish quota."

My mother paused for a moment; then she looked over her shoulder. "Excuse me? What did you just say?"

"I'll repeat. You are on the Polish quota."

Those six words would change our fate entirely.

"I... don't understand," my mother stammered, the sound of panic filling her voice. She turned to face the consul completely. "There must be a mistake. We are German citizens. We have German passports. We speak German. We do not speak Polish and we have never lived in Poland."

The consul offered no explanation. "Expect a long wait," was all he said.

It was no mix-up. Due to the serendipitous nature of geography and war, my parents' birthplace in Posen, West Prussia – originally part of the German Republic – was now within the annexed borders of Poland. That random line drawn through Prussia – the same one that forced my parents to move when they had first married, the same one that changed Anita's name on her birth certificate to "Annietta" – now categorized my parents as Polish for immigration purposes. Yes, I was born in Berlin, my father fought for Germany in the Great War, and we were all German speakers and German citizens. None of that mattered.

The consequences of our Polish "relabeling" were potentially calamitous. Not only was immigration already tightly restricted, but since 1924 the US had further restricted immigration from "less desirable' countries. Based on racist eugenic theories,[3] Eastern Europeans – Poles included – were not considered high on the desirability scale. As an example, the number of US visas issued each year to German and Austrian citizens combined was 27,000, while the number issued to Polish citizens was 7,000.

We were now part of the Eastern European Jewish quota. There were over three million Jews living in Poland, all trying to get out. Getting a visa would take forever. Years and years if it would happen at all.

In the evening we gathered in our apartment with our remaining friends and relatives and shared the story of our disastrous day at the consulate. Our numbers seemed to be shrinking by the day as members of our circle emigrated. We tried to fill the void with our few acquaintances left behind in Berlin. It didn't even mattered anymore if we liked these people, for we were all in this mess together. Paula Kahnemann, our once despised "snobby" cousin, was now part of our social circle, as was one of Paula's amiable brothers, the young doctor Arthur Arndt, with his wife Hertha and daughter Lotte. How irrelevant and distant the awkwardness between my mother and Paula seemed as we faced the same uncertain future.

These gatherings had become our lifeline. No longer did we speak of trivialities; the conversations now always homed in on issues surrounding the Nazis. We never seemed to tire of it. There was a comforting pattern to the banter. First, the adults would exchange the latest jokes mocking the Nazis. The mood would instantly lighten as Vati or my uncle imitated Hitler or a Gestapo officer.[4] Arms outstretched, they would throw in a little screaming, maybe a goosestep or two. Then, the atmosphere would shift and become more somber. The grown-ups would share the rumors they heard. "Did you hear what is going on in the town of...? They are kicking people into the street, throwing them out of their homes."

They would shake their heads in disbelief as they described the conditions in some city outside of Berlin. Some tongue clucking would follow; then a moment of strained silence as they considered their own good fortune. There would be a pregnant pause. Then an adult would suddenly interrupt the quiet and make a pronouncement: "Well, the Nazis have certainly gone as far as they can go."

Everyone would nod and agree. "Yes, you are right. Absolutely. They will not go any further; it isn't possible. What more can Hitler do?" Obviously, we all lacked imagination.

"Maybe Hitler will be assassinated!" someone would eventually say, throwing some wishful speculation into the banter.

Finally, everyone would speak of their one realistic hope, that the US, Britain, or France would confront Hitler. That meant rescue by way of war. At this point it was the best idea we could conjure up. Hope was all we had left.

A new edict was passed. Jewish storeowners were now required to imprint their names in their store windows. My parents and Uncle Siegfried had no choice but to comply and printed "Schwersenz-Jacob" in white block letters in the window. The effect was immediate: our Christian customers disappeared into thin air.

That put an end to our brief business success. The financial impact was swift and substantial. Siegfried and Irma were no longer able to afford their two-bedroom apartment. It would take time for them to find a smaller flat to rent, but as soon as they did, their boarder, Ho-Pang Yong, would have to move out. By this time, the brilliant civil engineering graduate student had become not only a friend, but a regular fixture in the fabric of our small social life.

Ho was getting his post-doctoral degree at the Technical University in Berlin, his studies subsidized by Chiang Kai-shek's Chinese National Government. He was a lively dinner guest whose fierce Chinese nationalism sometimes made for provocative conversation. Often, he expressed openly anti-Western ideas, but if my parents ever found these sentiments disdainful, they kept these feelings to themselves.

We all enjoyed Ho's company, but I did not realize that my mother had another angle in cultivating this relationship. She was keenly aware of Ho's connections to the Chinese Nationalist leadership and the Chinese embassy in Berlin, and she could not help but be somewhat calculating. *If our emigration to the US somehow does not come to fruition*, she thought, *Ho might be able to help us.* She knew that in a pinch, we might have to emigrate to China. Those needs helped cement a friendship that might have otherwise fizzled.

Finding a smaller apartment for Siegfried and Irma turned out to be a painstakingly slow and difficult process. With an influx of Jews coming into Berlin from all over the country, demand far exceeded inventory. One evening over dinner, my mother tried to shush us all. "I have some news," she announced. She smacked a spoon against the table like a gavel until we came to attention. "Quiet down, everyone. Shh. I have something to tell everyone." She smiled proudly. "I found an apartment for Siegfried and Irma. And the amazing news: it's just two blocks away, on Leibnitzstrasse."

"Oh my! That is incredible! It's just around the corner," chirped Irma.

"How did you do it? Did you have to kill someone?" asked Siegfried. He was laughing, but I wasn't entirely sure he was joking.

"Oh, come now," Mutti scolded, not smiling. "Siegfried, do you remember the Jeruchems?"[5]

"Sure, that elderly couple from Lobsenz who used to be friends with our parents."

"Exactly. I have stayed in touch with them all these years and helped them out, as they were old and had no one. Well, unfortunately, Mrs. Jeruchem just died; she became engulfed in flames as she was trying to light her oven and suffered severe burns. No, Siegfried, I did not have a hand in her demise. Sadly, her husband has just been moved to a home for the aged, and because I have been checking in on them regularly, I learned right away their apartment was going to be vacated. I called the landlord immediately and put your name on the lease."

"That's just awful. The whole story."

"Yes, Siegfried. I know it's terrible that we are benefitting from their misfortune, but right now, you are my priority. I think it's okay to be pleased. And to thank me."

Within weeks, Siegfried and Irma were living just five minutes away. Ho moved out of their apartment as planned, but he did not stop coming over to see us. In fact, he still dined with us night after night. One would have to wonder what interest Ho could have in our family. We were far from fascinating people. We were neither well educated nor well-traveled. What did we have to offer besides a home-cooked meal and pleasant company? He was not coming for the *Sauerbraten* and *Spätzle*, of that I was certain.

As Ho sat evening after evening in our beige-hued living room, speaking longingly of his beloved China, I noticed how his eyes would wander across the room and settle on Anita. They would land on her face, now porcelain-skinned and quite pretty. Then they would move downwards to her elegant pose on the couch, her child-sized hands lying in her lap, her legs crossed femininely at the ankles. Yes, even I could tell that Ho had become quite taken with my sister. Anita, at 17, had finally passed through her gawky, rebellious adolescence to become an attractive, intelligent, and well-spoken woman. A glowing young woman in the throes of love... with someone else.

My sister's love story started nearly a year earlier. Having just come off the optimism and prosperity of 1936, my parents had done something entirely out of character and made Anita a grand Sweet Sixteen party at the beginning of the year. There was live music and dancing, and the most beautiful ice cream cake I had ever seen. It would have been a perfect party, except my father drank a wee bit too much. He began dancing with the mothers of Anita's friends, holding them too close and swinging them around wildly, his thin combover bobbing back and forth with every turn.

When we returned from the party, my mother was incensed. The impropriety! The embarrassment! My parents fought bitterly, killing any chance of happy memories. Now that I think about it, Anita's party was the last time I could recall my parents fighting. Back then, we could indulge ourselves with vanity and petty arguments. It was the last time things were going so well in our lives that we could make ourselves miserable.

Fortunately, despite my parents lapsing into their familiar, bitter marital roles, Anita had walked away from her party thoroughly elated. She had locked eyes with Fips, the 18-year-old accordionist in the band, and he had returned her gaze. Towering over Anita's barely five-foot-tall frame, the tall, Aryan-looking Fips had strapped his accordion to Anita; and with his wing-like arms outstretched over hers, he pulled her arms wide and brought them close again, squeezing the bellows of the accordion, while she tapped the keyboard delicately with her fingers.

At least the piano lessons did not totally go to waste, my mother thought fleetingly, as she watched Anita fingering the accordion's black and white keys.

Over the months that followed, my parents came to be very fond of Fips. And although he was only half-Jewish, they might have encouraged their courtship had these been normal times. Well, these times were anything but normal.

"I won't do it, Mutti."

"You must at least string Ho along, Anita. Just keep him interested. Don't you understand, this might one day mean the survival of the whole family?"

"Mutti, don't make me. Please."

"You must, Anita. You must."

"Ho is twice my age!"

"I'm sorry, but that's not relevant."

"But I'm in love with Fips. I've been seeing him for almost a year."

"And who is Fips? Just a boy in a band. Like it or not, he is not important now. I'm sorry Anita, but you have no choice in the matter."

At my mother's request, Anita flirted with Ho dutifully, her resentment rising like bile with each forced smile.

"You did well tonight with Ho," my mother pronounced several months later. "He seemed encouraged. Keep it up." With that comment, Anita began a diatribe that had been brewing for weeks.

"I have had enough! Ho is always here, having dinner or coffee, or sometimes sitting on the floor, praying. Everywhere I turn, he is here. I cannot get away from him."

"I am just asking you to be courteous, Anita. Be nice. Ho is a fascinating man. He is highly educated and intelligent, with four post-doctorate degrees, and he is completely fluent in German, English, and French. He is far more intellectual and worldly than we are. There is so much we can learn from him."

"And that would be great if he were my professor, Mutti. But be reasonable," cried Anita, exasperated. "Ho is 33 years old. I am almost 17. I know he is intelligent, but do you think I am even slightly interested in him as a suitor? First, he is almost completely bald! Second, night after night we sit here like hostages listening to his never-ending stories about Chinese heritage and culture. Do you think I am one bit interested in learning about Buddhism? I am not even interested in learning about Judaism! And how can you sit there silently, Mutti, while he tells you over and over that Chinese culture is superior to Western culture? Yes, I agree, Ho has a great intellect, but how can you allow him to insult us? Have you completely given up your dignity for the promise of freedom? Well, I am telling you, it is a Faustian bargain. Maybe you can sell *your* soul for freedom, but you're not selling mine!"

Oh, how they argued. Day after day, and night after night. All the while Anita feared that her future had already been determined, and it was by way of China.

Perhaps my mother will be judged a monster, leading Ho on

and using Anita as a romantic lure. Or maybe she will simply be seen as a desperate parent trying to save her family and exploring every angle to get out of Germany. To her, nothing was off the table. We would travel to America, or we would travel to China. Heck, if it got us out of Germany, we would travel to the moon.

6

A KIND OF SICKNESS

"Glatze, Achim!" I sprinted down the steps of my building, calling out to my friends as I headed outside to play. As soon as I approached my buddies, they pivoted away. I tapped Glatze's shoulder, but he kept walking. Not one of my friends would speak to me or even look at my face. As I walked further down the street, the children parted like the Red Sea. They spoke only to each other, and when I came closer, they moved away like I was contaminated. I felt invisible. I stood there, suddenly a pariah. Dumbfounded and devastated, I turned around, and with heavy legs, made my way back up the stairs. What had I done wrong? I must have offended someone, but how?

For days and days, I cried about my abandonment. The sudden isolation was shocking and humiliating, and I could not understand it. "I'm sure it's nothing, Wolf," Mutti tried to tell me, though her words offered little comfort. "Whatever you might have done, kids always get over it. It will pass."

I heard a hint of blame in those words. I had done something wrong to be sure. Now my self-pity was tinged with self-doubt. In a few days, whispers and gossip seeped their way through my building and my parents learned the source of my sudden social dismissal: A Nazi party member in our building had advised all our neighbors to prohibit their children from playing with me. "Wolf," my mother explained, "apparently, this is happening everywhere; it's not you, it's not personal. It is only because you are Jewish."

"Little Wolf," comforted Vati, as he hugged me. "You need to understand that social isolation of Jewish children seems to be part of the Nazi plan. It is going on all around Germany."

But I was an eight-year-old. What did I care about the politics and the rationale and the Nazi plan? It sure felt personal. I had suddenly lost all my playmates and it crushed my soul.

I no longer wanted to go out; I was embarrassed to walk down the street and be thoroughly disregarded. Instead, I took to my bed, lying there in a sorrowful state of mental morbidity, until one day, as if I had willed it upon myself, I became truly ill.

It began with a raging fever and a hacking cough. Within days, a confluence of scarlet spots blossomed on my sensitive skin. The whites of my eyes turned an unseemly shade of crimson, and a crispy greenish crust collected in their corners. I looked like death. My mother became frantic. "How will we ever find a Jewish doctor to summon for a house call? All the decent doctors have already emigrated," she fretted. "And how much will such a house call cost?" she worried aloud.

"Your son has the measles," the shabby doctor declared, verifying my mother's own maternal suspicions. "Cool him down with wet blankets, then warm him up with hot blankets," he advised my parents.

They peeled away their Deutschmarks and handed them over. "That's it? That is your only treatment?"

"Yes, he is young and strong, he will get better in a week. Just follow my instructions exactly."

My mother followed his recommendations to the letter. I was wet and cold, I was dry and hot, alternately shivering and sweating, for days on end. "I don't know Arthur. What kind of treatment is this? Wet blankets? Hot blankets? Where is the sophistication? The specificity? It's been seven days and Wolf is still not better. Now I am certain that man was not a real medical doctor."

"Don't be silly, Grete. Of course, he's a doctor."

"And how do we really know that Arthur? How do we check his credentials? In all likelihood, he is a veterinarian, making cash impersonating a real medical doctor. In fact, I'm convinced of it!"

Yet I lived. Then, just as I was starting to recover, Anita took ill. We naturally assumed she had caught the measles too. Strangely, her symptoms were different than mine. She had fever and was listless, but there was no rash, red eyes or spots in her throat. And she had a complaint I never had, severe chest pain. Could it be pneumonia? Should we call the doctor again? "There is no way we are going to pay for another house call with that charlatan! Let him stick to horses!" my mother declared.

Anita was instead admitted to a small private Jewish health clinic where she underwent a few days of testing and observation. She fared no better there; none of the doctors could pinpoint the diagnosis. She seemed to be a medical mystery.

"One thing we are sure of, is that it's not measles," determined one doctor.

"And it's definitely not pneumonia," said another.

"Or bronchitis," repeated the first.

"So for now, we are calling it pleurisy," the doctors finally concluded in unison.

"And what exactly is pleurisy?" asked my mother.

"It is an inflammation of the lining of the lung."

"Is that your diagnosis?"

"Well, it's more of a description than a diagnosis."

"But what is the treatment?" There was no treatment, my mother soon learned. Nonetheless, a few days later, Anita seemed to have completely recovered.

Life went on as usual. But only a few weeks later, Anita was struck by another attack of fever and chest pain. It seemed identical to the first episode, only it was much more severe. Unable to even get out of bed to go to a clinic or hospital, my parents reluctantly summoned my measles doctor. “Even if he is really a veterinarian,” my mother concluded, “at least he will come to the house.”

The doctor put the bell of his stethoscope on Anita’s chest. “Hmm, aha. I see. Hmm, aha,” he repeated. He said the words meaningfully while his face looked thoroughly perplexed. “A relapse of pleurisy?” he declared, his voice rising into a slight question mark at the end of the statement. It was another useless diagnosis and non-existent treatment which quickly became irrelevant. In just a few days, Anita was miraculously well again.

There had just been two episodes. Still, my mother was beginning to get nervous. It seemed like our health was starting to unravel.

Mutti prayed it was just bad luck. She was due for another check-in at the US consulate. Until now, our visa application seemed to be going nowhere. No progress, just endless waiting. Waiting for the application to be completed, waiting for it to be reviewed, waiting for it to be approved, waiting for our number to be called.

She arrived at the consulate which, as usual, was organized and well-staffed, with numerous well-dressed and pleasant Americans. “Please Frau Schwersenz, take a seat,” said the consul.

Mutti sat down, dutifully. She looked around at the nice, neat surroundings. How tired my mother was of all these pleasantries. How pointless she found all the politeness. Pointless and politeness – anagrams differing by a single useless letter. She wanted a different word – *action*. She wanted someone who understood the word *urgency*. Someone who put their heart and soul into helping with our plight. Someone who realized that we must get out of Germany as soon as possible, before things got any worse, as was sure to happen. But she could find no such individual here. *Don’t they understand what is at stake,* Mutti thought? She became convinced everyone at the consulate had to be antisemitic. It was the only plausible explanation for their indifference.

The minutes passed interminably as my mother sat and the consul rifled through the papers. Then the consul broke the silence. “I am reading here in your medical history that your husband has a groin hernia in his scrotum." He said these words in a dull monotone, without looking up.

"Yes, that is true. He has had it for years, and it does not bother him at all. As you can see, we reported this information at the very start of our application process. Over here." My mother reached over the edge of the desk and pointed to a line on the form.

It was true that my father had a little – well, in truth, not so little – hernia. Sometime during the Great War, my father's intestines had taken a short descent into his bodily trenches. They were now residing quite happily in their basement home in his scrotum. It did not seem to bother him, but he wore a sling-like "truss" just to hold everything in place.

"Why is my husband's hernia an issue?" my mother asked nervously. "No one has brought this up before." Just how on earth could a hernia interfere with immigration, she wondered?

"Well, I am very sorry, but your husband will likely not pass the physical exam," the consul explained to my mother. Now he looked up and sat back in his chair, putting both hands behind his head. "To be honest, Frau Schwersenz, with that hernia, there is no way he will be admitted to the United States."

Mutti stood up quietly and left the consulate. She appeared calm but inside she was panicking. This new problem was quite a blow. Could Vati's hernia potentially delay our visa application? She started her journey home contemplating how to resolve Vati's health issue. *I'll sew up that hernia myself if I have to. With beautiful rows of neat, even, embroidery stitches. Or with a goddam sewing machine if that is what it takes!*

My mother knew a real doctor was required. Somehow she would have to find a surgeon. Yet there would be no time to sew or fix anything because things were about to drastically change.

In March of 1938, the *Anschluss* happened: Germany annexed Austria. They didn't even have to fire a single shot; they just claimed it as part of the Reich. It was the start of Hitler's "expansion," part of his ultimate plan to take over the world.

That moment changed everything. It looked like Hitler could simply expand his territories, along with his antisemitic influences, until all of Europe was one big Nazi Reich. This was a terrifying possibility. The only option was for countries to fight back. Somebody with guts had to try to stop Hitler. That meant war. A war that nobody wanted, quite possibly involving the whole continent, if not the world.

A giant Reich was bad for us, but a Europe at war was terrible too. It would become even more difficult to get out.

And just how were we going to get out, anyway? We were all a mess, physically. Vati's intestines were sitting next to his balls, Anita had a mystery illness, and I had just gotten over the measles. Even if it were possible to emigrate on our pathetic, limited Polish quota in the brief time that was left – before Hitler took over the world or war broke out – we would never pass a physical exam. We would never make it to America.

It didn't look as if we were going anywhere.

7

WALKING ON BROKEN GLASS

Thursday morning, November 10, 1938. Bang, bang, bang! I hear insistent knocking on our door, followed by steady ringing of our doorbell.

Those were the sounds that woke me up from a deep sleep that morning. I quickly stumbled out of bed and rushed toward the front door. What could be happening at this hour? My mother was already at the door, and I stood beside her, still in my flannel pajamas. She braced herself for a moment and then opened the door just a smidgeon. A commanding chorus of "*Heil Hitler*" came through the crack in the door and landed right inside our foyer. Mutti quickly pushed me behind her, and then she pulled the door all the way open.

Standing in the doorway were two authoritative-looking men. They were wearing tan trench coats with black swastika armbands and tall leather boots. Their right arms were rigidly outstretched like weapons, forming the Nazi salute. "*Heil, Hitler!*" they repeated, so loudly they were almost screaming. "We are the Gestapo! We are looking for your husband. Go and get him now!"

My stomach instantly cramped. Where exactly was Vati? Home, probably. With so few customers at the store these days, we almost always had breakfast together. *He must be here somewhere,* I thought.

I wanted to run to find him, but Mutti pulled me tightly next to her, with a grip so firm that I could not break free.

I looked up at my mother's face. She looked petrified, her expression practically frozen with apprehension. She paused for a second. "He is not at home," she said finally, the small, timid words cracking as they left her stiffened lips.

"When he returns, he must report DIRECTLY to the police station!" one of the Gestapo agents shouted. They clicked their heels together, turned, and abruptly left.

Mutti closed the door behind them and loosened her grip on me. She turned around. I followed her as she walked the length of the hall unsteadily toward the living room. She stood there, ghostly pale, covering her mouth and chin with her whole left hand, her thumb resting on her left cheek, one finger lying on the tip of her nose, tapping it every so often. Then she shook her head from side to side. She sat down slowly, holding the arm of the couch tightly with her right hand as if she could no longer support herself.

"Where is Vati?" I finally asked. "Is he home, Mutti? Were you lying to them?"

"Go put your clothes on, Wolf."

I quickly threw on some street clothes and before returning to the living room, took a detour to look for my father. I peeked into the bathroom. No Vati. I slipped into my parents' bedroom, but I could find no sign of my father. He was nowhere to be found. When I returned to the living room, my mother was still sitting as stiff as a statue on the couch, seemingly lost in thought.

Just then the phone rang. We both startled; Mutti jumped up and ran over to the mantle, where our phone sat like a monstrous black bust amongst the elegant porcelain figurines. The little figurines trembled nervously when the phone rang urgently for a second time. Mutti hurriedly picked up the receiver. "Yes? Who is this?"

All I could hear was a blur of excited rambling, and then my mother saying, "Slow down, Siegfried. I can barely understand you. What is the matter?" I walked over to the mantle, and my mother held the receiver out so that we both could hear.

"Where is Arthur?" Uncle Siegfried was speaking on the other end of the line. Barely pausing for air, he continued. "You must hide him, now. Or find him, wherever he is, and tell him not to come home." My stomach turned. "The Gestapo are everywhere," he continued. "They are going to all the Jewish homes and rounding up all the Jewish men. I was arrested this very morning. That's right; I was arrested. The Gestapo came at five o'clock this morning and pulled me right from my apartment."

My mother's eyes grew wide as Siegfried kept speaking, the words racing out of him like a bumble bee in flight. "They pulled me out onto the street and threw me in with a large group of Jewish men. We were in the cold for hours, standing at attention. No one spoke. No one knew what was happening. We thought we might be shot right there on the spot. Some people thought we were going to be sent to prison or to a work camp. There was panic on everyone's faces. You could practically smell everyone's fear.

"All around us we saw our city on fire. Mobs of Germans were roaming the streets. They were smashing stores. They were beating up old Jewish men right on the sidewalk in front of us. They spit on them and hurled mud at them. You could hear glass breaking everywhere around us. The police stood by and did absolutely nothing. It was a madhouse, Grete! It was as if hell itself had broken loose.

"Then our group was put into a line. We finally heard our fate: we were being sent to the Oranienburg concentration camp just north of Berlin. We were ready to start marching. I could see perhaps thousands of men from the city marching already, and our group was supposed to join them. At the last minute, I called over to one of the guards. I began desperately pleading with him; I told him that I was a wounded veteran of the Great War and I had fought valiantly for Germany. The guard pulled me out of the group. 'Today is your lucky day,' he said to me. 'Your Iron Cross has saved you.' And then he released me. I limped away, knowing that all the other men were being taken to the concentration camp. Every one of them. I felt such a mixture of relief and guilt. But I did not look back. I just kept walking until I made my way home. I have only just gotten back. I called as soon as I walked in the door."

"*Mein Gott*! Oh, my God. Oh, my God..." my mother kept repeating, over and over.

"But Grete, where is Arthur now? You must start thinking clearly. Where did he go this morning?" Siegfried sounded urgent.

I looked at my mother, the same pressing question on my own mind. "He went out to take care of the insurance documents for the sale of the store," Mutti replied. "Remember, Siegfried? Today he had to submit the paperwork to the Ministry of Finance to approve the sale of the store to our buyer, Herr Herzog."

"Of course. In all the commotion I had forgotten. You say Arthur is just doing some paperwork this morning? Then the store will be sold? Well, you can still do something. Right away! Arthur's life is more important than the store. Do not hesitate. Men all over Berlin are being rounded up and sent to concentration camps. Figure something out! Go out and find Arthur now. If you do not find him and hide him, I'm afraid he will be next!"

Mutti hung up the phone. By now, the buzz of commotion had crept in from the streets below. The smell of smoke from the fires outside had also begun to seep into the apartment. A sense of worry and dread overcame both of us.

Everything started to make sense. Now we understood why the Gestapo had been to our door: they had already come to take Vati away. Siegfried had painted a good picture of the events that had happened over the course of the previous night. The violence, the knocking on doors, the roundups, the fires, the massive destruction of property. The murders. And it still wasn't over.

Neither Mutti nor I had seen Vati since we had woken up this morning. Where was he now, we wondered? Would he even return? Perhaps he had been rounded up already and sent to a concentration camp. Or maybe beaten and sent to a hospital. Crazy to think but yes, that might be better, safer. How would we even know? If he were alive somewhere, maybe he should not come home. It might be better for him to run somewhere and hide, to not come back at all. He could save himself, although we might never see him again. Mutti and I went over each of these scenarios. We talked until our throats were dry and we had made ourselves sick with worry. And then the front door opened, and Vati walked right through it.

"Vati, Vati!" I ran to my father and hugged him tightly.

"I'm fine, little Wolf. Don't worry, I'm okay."

"What is happening out there, Arthur?"

"Everything is terrible outside, Grete. It looks like a war has passed through. Lootings and beatings are happening everywhere. They have set fire to all the synagogues. Destroyed all the Jewish-owned shops. But they are rounding up the men – this is what is really scaring me."

"We must think fast, Arthur, what is our next move?"

I was all ready to hear my parents' contingency plan, but they did not have one. No escape route, no underground bunker, no place to run and hide. Nothing. They had never considered this possibility. They talked, paced, sat, got up again, paced some more. Their minds were a muddle, they were panicked and unfocused. Any strategy would have calmed me. It was the absence of a plan that was terrifying.

Finally, under pressure of time, my parents devised a flimsy scheme. It was neither clever nor original. It was, frankly, rather pathetic, and simply desperate. They would head to the private Jewish clinic where Anita had just recently been an inpatient for a few days. "We'll beg them to admit Vati. We'll make up some medical excuse. And we've met the doctors there just recently," my mother finally stated with conviction. "We already have a relationship. They will have no choice. They will have to admit him."

What kind of special relationship did my mother imagine she had with the doctors? Even I thought the plan sounded weak. But with limited options and no safe havens, it was the best they could devise. My mother then turned to me. "If the Gestapo returns, tell them Vati had an accident on the way to the insurance company. Tell them he has been hospitalized."

"You mean, lie?"

"Yes, that's exactly what I mean."

"Why are you telling all of this to me? I'm only an eight-year-old!"

"Wolf, look at your sister. She's of no help to you now." I turned and looked at Anita. Thoroughly incapacitated, she was lying listlessly in a cot in the living room, barely able to lift her head from the pillow, in the middle of yet another health crisis. The episodes were coming once a month now and they were ferocious.

My parents stood by the door. They had their coats on and were ready to leave. "Wolf, I am putting you in charge!" exclaimed my father with finality. With a forced smile he saluted me as if I were a soldier. Then he turned on his heels and both my parents walked out the front door.

I sat in the living room as the grandfather clock ticked relentlessly. How much time had passed? A half hour, an hour? Time had lost meaning to me. Anita was there in body only, and I felt utterly alone. I sat on the couch, praying that the doorbell would not ring, but then it buzzed like an unwelcome alarm clock. Palms sweating, hands trembling, I opened the door. There was just one Gestapo agent this time. The lone officer looked just as fierce and intimidating in his crisp tan trench coat as the two Gestapo agents did earlier that morning. *"Heil Hitler!"* he thundered; his arm raised. "Where is your father?"

"M-my f-father has been in an accident this morning and he is at the h-hospital," I stuttered. It did not sound believable, even to me. A prepared answer... a preposterous story. A nervous delivery from a bad actor who did not know his lines.

The Gestapo agent remained expressionless and he did not leave. "I must search the apartment," he said as he pushed past me into the foyer.

No one had prepared me for a search. It was not part of my rehearsal, and I had no idea what I was supposed to do. The Gestapo agent walked confidently through the apartment, his trench coat dusting the surfaces of the furniture as he swept by.

Methodically, he entered each room as I followed nervously behind him. He began in the bedrooms, probing every corner and rifling through the closets. He pulled out all the linens and my mother's fine embroidery; he knocked down hats and boxes indiscriminately with his stick. He looked under every bed. Then he walked into the living room. With each leather-booted footstep, the little porcelain figurines quivered nervously on the mantle. Only Anita remained motionless. She lay like the dead on the cot, not moving a muscle. The officer paused and glanced at her briefly, but then seemed uninterested and turned instead to the furnishings. With his gloved hands, he lifted each of the Persian rugs and tapped firmly on the floors with his stick – a stick I rapidly realized was not meant for walking. I knew he was looking for an adult – either my father or someone else – hiding somewhere, anywhere, even under the floorboards. His search was exhaustive, and after a while, I almost imagined that he would find my father hiding somewhere. "*Aha!*" he would cry out, and then he would drag Vati out of the apartment. I could not help myself; my whole body and soul felt guilty, because I was keeping a secret and I had lied, and I was sure the Nazi officer could see the mendacity written all over my face.

He found no one hiding in the apartment, of course. The Gestapo agent was finally satisfied and turned to me to take his leave. Very briefly, his tone softened. "I'm sorry I had to search your home, son," he offered, politely. "Before I leave, I have one other message for you." He instantly became stern again, his voice and face tightening. "Tell your mother as soon as she returns that she must report to the police station!"

I shut the door behind him and waited until the sound of my pounding heartbeat and the weight of my guilty conscience gradually faded. And then I just sat there, not moving and uncertain what to do, in state of psychological paralysis. Was it morning or afternoon? Had I eaten? It felt as though hours and hours had gone by. I held on to the thought that my mother would soon return having left my father safely tucked away at the clinic. All would be well again.

Just then, both my parents walked in the door. How happy I was to see them both! Then it hit me; Vati was not supposed to come home. "Vati, why are you here? I thought you were supposed to stay at the clinic."

"No, don't worry, *mein liebes Kind*. I was just too healthy, so they would not accept me at the clinic. Do not concern yourself, my little Wolf, we will think of something else."

I proceeded to tell them how the Gestapo agent had come and thoroughly searched the apartment. As I recounted the story, I saw their complexions turn as white as hospital linens. If they had somehow convinced themselves that events of the last 24 hours might be calming down, and that perhaps my father could just stay home, my story instantly disabused them of that belief. "Well, that's that; we cannot stay in the apartment," announced my mother firmly.

They still had no idea what to do next. They murmured and talked in circles and seemed paralyzed with fear. And they could think of nothing; they could not conjure up a more innovative escape plan; the best they had was the same concept, only this time they had a new location. "We will go to the main Berlin Jewish *Krankenhaus* [hospital]," my mother finally stated decisively. "It is huge. We will have no trouble getting your father admitted there." And once again, my parents left me alone with the shadow of my sister, heading this time to the public Jewish hospital in Berlin Mitte.

On November 10, 1938, the Berlin Jewish Krankenhaus looked more like a war zone than a hospital. The emergency room was teeming with patients, and more were filing in by the minute. In the previous 24 hours, injuries, beatings, and burns had led to hundreds of surgical emergencies. In addition to the wounded, throngs of Jewish men in the same predicament as my father were trying to save themselves with fictitious claims of illness. Men and women mixed in with the truly maimed were pleading and crying, begging for admission and safe haven. The woefully inadequate staff was desperately trying to triage the patients and create some sense of order, but they could not make a dent. There was misery everywhere and the staff was stretched to its limit.

"Please help us," my parents implored as the staff passed them, but their pleas were drowned out by the din of everyone else's suffering. My tiny father could not get anyone to notice him, and it became all too apparent that the hospital was going to bypass him just like at the clinic. Now that my parents were witnessing the hospital nightmare with their own eyes, it made perfect sense that only true emergency cases would be admitted.

"Grete," my father said. "I simply can't be turned away again. I'm going to become an emergency case even if it kills me." And without missing a beat, he hurled himself onto the middle of the floor of the reception area. *"Ach, Aaach,"* he wailed at the top of his lungs.

At first, the nurses stepped right over him. Vati kept on wailing. A gentleman in the waiting room called over to a passing nurse. "Don't you think you should tend to that man?" He pointed to my father. "It looks like he is in excruciating pain." The nurse continued walking.

My father continued to lie sprawled out in the middle of the floor. Holding his groin firmly, he alternated between quiet moans and bursts of intermittent screaming. It took nearly an hour until a nurse finally walked over to him. She pulled down my father's pants right there in the reception area and eyed his groin. Then she jumped back, and with a horrified look on her face, exclaimed, "Oh my, just look at the size of that thing!"

Vati's enlarged scrotum was out of its truss and his hernia looked impressively swollen. "Can you stand up?" the nurse asked.

Vati writhed again in mock anguish. "I can't get off the floor," he whimpered weakly. "It's my hernia. It's stuck. It must be strangulated."

Hours later, the door to our apartment opened and my mother walked in. This time, she was alone. Plunking herself down into a chair, she looked completely depleted. Slowly, she told me the tale of the hospital, and Vati's award-winning act of a lifetime. "For once, his antics paid off," she sighed, shaking her head from side to side, as if she couldn't believe it herself.

Suddenly I remembered; I had one more piece of terrible news to deliver. "Mutti, I'm sorry, but the man in the tan trench coat gave me a message. He said that since Vati isn't here, you have to report to the police station instead."

"*Ach, mein Gott!*" she cried, sitting up. "Are they now going to arrest me instead of Vati? Will it never end?"

Mutti pulled herself wearily out of her chair, knowing she must comply with the order. She brushed off her coat and smoothed her hair. She kissed me goodbye as if it were going to be forever and told Anita to take good care of me. With leaden feet, she went back downstairs to the disordered streets below, checked in at the police office and waited to be taken away.

"Frau Schwersenz!" said the officer. "We have been informed that you have a short-wave radio. All Jews' radios are being confiscated. You must turn yours in immediately."

She turned the radio in. The day was finally over.

Vati remained in the hospital for a week recovering from his hernia surgery, while Berlin recovered from its own self-inflicted wounds and savagery. It was only later that the events of the prior 24 hours, from November 9-10, 1938, got their name. *Kristallnacht*, the night of broken glass.[1]

What started Kristallnacht? A few days earlier, a Nazi diplomat had been killed by a Jewish teen. Kristallnacht was payback. But the exact cause was almost irrelevant; the antisemitism that was being stoked over the prior months was a powder keg that could have erupted at any time, for any excuse. During that endless night, Nazi mobs torched and vandalized thousands of Jewish homes, schools, businesses, hospitals, and cemeteries. The police were instructed not to intervene. SA officers (Stormtroopers) and Hitler youth were dressed as civilians. This made the uprising appear to be an expression of "outraged public reaction," rather than a government sponsored act of terror.

When the final tally was taken, 191 synagogues across Germany were burnt down. Hundreds of Jews were killed, and 30,000 others were rounded up and sent to concentration camps. As an ultimate act of sick irony, the Nazis held the German Jewish community responsible for "property damage due to the rioting." The price tag was one billion Deutschmarks.

That horrific night both Uncle Siegfried and my father had come within a hairs' breadth of being taken. My father thought only serendipity had saved him. Siegfried was certain it was an act of providence.

Even our clothing store survived. Standing distinctly intact on its corner, surrounded by mountains of glass, nearly every store around the clothing shop had been vandalized. This was neither an act of luck nor divinity. Our store had been heavily safeguarded since it was in the process of being sold to a German. The sale would go through as planned. However, since the paperwork had not yet been finalized, Mr. Herzog saw an opportunity to renegotiate the terms of the sale and purchase the store at a lower price.

"Ach, what difference does it make," my mother muttered.

Had I heard her correctly? Did my mother say she did not care about the money?

"It doesn't matter anyway," she continued, letting out an exasperated sigh. "All the money will be deposited into an account controlled by the Ministry of Finance. Any profits we might have made are going into the hands of the German government."

1938 was clearly a turning point, a harbinger of worse things to come. Just a few weeks after Kristallnacht, my mother's haughty cousin Paula Kahnemann spat at an SS officer when he cursed at her and called her some Jewish epithets. She was too proud; this was Paula, after all – Paula whom we had disparagingly labelled a "snob," but who in fact was a woman of fierce dignity and determination. The next day she returned to her apartment to find her door taped shut and the SS looking for her. Fearing for her life, she and her family used their means to smuggle their way to Yugoslavia[2], eventually finding passage out of Europe on quite a nice passenger ship headed for Cuba. Unfortunately, they gravely miscalculated. The ship would never make it to Cuba, or anywhere safe for that matter. They had boarded the ill-fated ship the *St. Louis*.[3]

Now Paula was gone. Even her nice younger brother Arthur had left with his family. When the New Year rolled around again, our circle was reduced to just Uncle Siegfried and Aunt Irma, my mother's elegant cousin Ella Hammer, a second cousin, Erma Ruschin and her husband, and our friend Ho-Pang Yong. We could not imagine what was in store for our little band of left behinds.

I thought about death now all the time.

8

MINUS ONE

Time was moving relentlessly forward. It would not stop and wait for our visas. By the time 1939 rolled in, we had no store and no money. All we had left was hope. Hope that things in Germany would not deteriorate further. Hope that there would be enough food on the table. And there was also work. Work kept our minds occupied and pushed back the fear, the stress, and the constant worry. There seemed to be endless planning and organizing and scheming. There were trips to the consulate, trips to the Jewish Organization. And there were decisions to be made, endless decisions and decisions and decisions.

I was still going to school every day. This should have created a sense of stability, but instead, it was a revolving door of uncertainty. There was a constant flow of people coming and going. Children and teachers departed as they got their visas to emigrate out of the country. New students flowed in as their own schools or synagogues were vandalized or destroyed. People coming in, people going out. Appearances and disappearances. Your friends could be gone tomorrow.

The Jewish Organization tried its best to create some sense of normalcy for us children amid the chaos. They established an afterschool daycare program which I attended each day with my classmates. Together, six of us trudged across the Tiergarten. We passed the Kaiser Wilhelm Church and kept on walking into the main shopping district, turning onto Tauentzienstrasse. A few blocks further on, we entered an apartment on the ground floor of a nondescript building. In this little haven, I felt relatively safe and happy. Supervised by the kindest of volunteers, I ate a simple warm meal, played ping pong, did my homework, and tried to temporarily forget about the constant apprehension that awaited me at home.

On the occasions that I was not in school, I traipsed to the US consulate with Mutti, where I sat impatiently, being a novice at the bureaucratic process.

"What is taking so long?" I muttered, as I waited for us to be called in for our review.

"Be patient, Wolf. You must get used to waiting. Bureaucracy is slow. I expect this to be a routine appointment to review our documents. Vati's hernia is fixed and there is nothing left to be done now except wait."

Eventually we were called in to sit down for our interview. "Hmm... uh... I see," the consul said, as he rifled through the endless stack of papers. "Uh huh," he repeated a few times. And then he suddenly looked concerned. His forehead furrowed into three depressed horizontal lines. He cleared his throat. "I'm sorry to tell you this, Frau Schwersenz, but after careful review of your paperwork, it appears that your cousin in America, Ellis Arndt, does not have sufficient funds to support four people. Therefore, your application will only be valid for three visas to the United States." He took out his stamp and slammed it down on the papers three times. *Bang, bang, bang!* One stamp for each member of our family... minus one.

"Three visas, not four," Mutti said as we walked home. She seemed dazed. "Three, not four," she kept repeating. *Three. Not four.*

We would not be leaving Germany together.

"I know what to do. I will try to cross into to Switzerland," my father volunteered. "I will bribe a guard and smuggle across the border."

"And if you don't make it?" my mother asked. "Then what?"

"Then I will be shot, most likely."

"It's out of the question. We will find another way."

All my parents' certainties had slowly been eroded over the years, but they had held on to one bit of faith – that we would remain together as a family unit. Now that last shred of confidence had been trampled.

"We are all going to get out of Germany, somehow, even if it isn't going to be together." My mother had decided. So that's what was going to happen.

The British had devised a plan that might offer a way out for one of us. Recently, they had been placing ads in German magazines for domestic workers. In some cases, the ad was merely a ruse – the English were graciously helping Jews escape on a work visa. But for the 20,000 Jewish women who ultimately escaped Nazi occupied territories in this way, it was more like a quid pro quo: we will get you out of your predicament in exchange for unpaid, backbreaking domestic service. Or, put another way, *we will save you, so long as we get a free maid as part of the bargain.*

That is how Anita was the one who ended up foregoing a US visa. She would head to England and be sacrificed – or saved – depending on what happened to the rest of us.

Anita could not seem to escape her destiny to become a domestic. She hastily submitted her application.

We were officially poor again. Our apartment was devoid of furnishings. We had no assets, and we were out of cash. Every day, our situation kept deteriorating. It was astonishing, really, how much deprivation we could get used to. We did not know how much more misery would be imposed on us, but there didn't to be a bottom. "Things can't get any worse" was a phrase we stopped saying long ago, and anger seemed like a waste of energy. The Germans were determined to whittle away at our resources, our morale, and our humanity.

Another edict arrived. "What is it this time; do we have to turn over a kidney?" said Mutti.

"All Jews must turn over any valuables to the local police," Vati read. "I think they mean everything. Any gold or diamonds... it's all going to be property of the Nazis. And I think we have to comply. They can search our apartment at any time."

In truth, we had hardly anything of monetary value left. The prior year, we had moved out all our home furnishings. Our best linens, my mother's prized Persian rugs, our furniture, the piano, and even our cozy down blankets, were packed, loaded onto "lifts," and shipped to Rotterdam for safe storage. It was an incredibly tiresome and expensive project meant to safeguard against the Nazis taking our property. Everything had been insured, and we fantasized that we would be reunited with our belongings after making our way to America.

Every material thing that we ever had was gone. The few remaining valuables left were just some small baubles, treasured mainly for their sentimental value. Giving them away to the Nazis would be painful. It sure felt like we were donating a vital organ.

One evening, as we sat with our cherished, ever-shrinking social circle, my mother's cousin, Ella Hammer gathered us around conspiratorially. She lowered her voice and said, "Listen up, everyone. You must swear to secrecy. Do I have your word?"

"Yes, Ella. Enough cloak and dagger talk. Go on already."

"Good, because this is very important. I have become friendly with a Christian woman who works for the Dutch Red Cross. She travels regularly to and from Holland and she has made me an offer. She has agreed to smuggle our valuables out of the country."

"Is it worth the risk, Ella? We do not have much," my mother admitted. "Just a gold watch chain of my father's, some gold wedding bands, a diamond brooch, and a diamond ring."

"Do you really want to turn those over to the Nazis, Grete? You will never see them again!"

"I realize that. But what reason do you have to trust this Red Cross woman? What is she asking for in return?" asked my mother, spouting her usual cynicism.

"Nothing at all, Grete," Ella replied. "She is part of a network of brave Dutch citizens looking to aid the Jews. I know, it seems impossible to imagine in these times. What person out there would want to help the Jews? Who would put themselves in danger? Believe it or not, there are people out there who are trying to help us."

My mother still could not fathom this dangerous act of selfless charity; however, no other options seemed more appealing. Reluctantly, we handed over our trinkets of gold and our few carats of diamonds to Ella, who passed them on to a Red Cross worker we had never seen, who then delivered them to yet another stranger in Holland whom no one had ever met. What would happen to the jewelry after that, we had no idea. We were given a code name of a person who would presumably contact us in the future. It all seemed quite cagey. Yet somehow, giving our jewelry to a nameless Red Cross worker and a chain of anonymous underground aides, felt more satisfying than handing it over to the Nazi authorities. As we entrusted our items to Cousin Ella, we had not a shred of hope that we would ever see our jewelry again.

That summer, there was a noticeable shift in the Nazi propaganda. The Germans had acquired a new enemy besides us Jews: this time it was Polish people. By August, the press started reporting daily "atrocities" committed by the Poles against the Germans. We guessed it was a fabrication, and we could see the old Nazi playbook in use again: create outrage to rile up public anger against a target. That will then justify the necessary "intervention" to protect the Germans. By the end of summer, the Nazis made their predictable announcement: "We must protect the Germans living in the Polish corridor!" The German propaganda machine had created adequate public support to justify the invasion of Poland.

Germany attacked Poland on September 1, 1939. That day was

the official start of World War II, and we were smack in the middle of it.

Vati and Anita sat quietly in their train car. Both felt so much sadness, so much apprehension at their impending separation. They had so much to say that they barely spoke at all. Vati tapped his pants gently. Yes, he could feel it, the 300 Deutschmarks – or about 75 dollars – that Mutti had deftly sewn into the lining of his slacks, in case of an unforeseen emergency. It gave him a bit of security to know it was there. They both had all their papers. There was no reason the trip should not go smoothly.

It would take about nine hours to complete the 600-kilometer (380-mile) train ride to Rotterdam in the Netherlands. Vati was planning to accompany Anita for the whole train ride. Once in Rotterdam, they would part ways. Anita would take a ferry from Hook of Holland to England by herself – that might take another 12 hours – and Vati would take the train straight back to Berlin.

Anita's ferry would likely land in Harwich, England,[1] and from there she would take another train into London. Anita contemplated her long journey, and her upcoming position in England as a domestic. Was there a legitimate job waiting for her in London? Time would tell. She had to get there safely first.

A couple of hours into their journey, the door to their car opened, and a group of five young SS officers sauntered into their compartment. Anita looked up at them. She could not help but notice how handsome and blond, young, and fresh-faced they were. Fips could easily fit right in, she realized with a twinge of sadness, knowing she would probably never see Fips again. She turned back to the window to avoid eye contact. She must have turned too late, for one of the young men had spotted her. "Why, aren't you a pretty little Jewess!" he called out, in some perverse version of antisemitic flirting. "And who is the little Jew traveling with you?" he added, laughing and pointing to my father, who was unsuccessfully trying to render himself invisible by shrinking further into his seat. "Are you and the little Jew trying to run away from Germany?"

My sister's normally fair complexion turned red. Some mixture of rage and shame rose to the surface, but she suppressed it and tried to answer politely. *Pride has no place here,* she reminded herself. *Remain calm and do nothing to incite any anger.* After all, the officer was merely being offensive. Quite pleasantly she replied to the young man, "No, we are just traveling." Her voice shook ever so slightly.

It was all over in a matter of a few minutes. The young men eventually moved on, the compartment door closed, and Vati and Anita exhaled with relief. *That's it. Incident over.* They gave each other a nervous smile of relief.

Hours passed. Daylight faltered and Anita and Vati fell into a shallow sleep. The darkness deepened as they continued to rattle north. *Thwack!* The door to their car banged open, jolting them awake. It was dark and their eyes had yet to adjust to the dim light. Noisy young men had just entered their car. How many men were among them this time? It was hard to tell. More than before, it seemed. They slurred their words and lost their balance. *They sound intoxicated,* thought Vati. *This is not good.*

Anita's eyes adjusted, and now she could see that it was the same posse of young officers as earlier, along with a few additional men. In the dark of night, the young, slightly drunk men seemed bolder and more menacing. They were speaking loudly, and this time, they had not returned to flirt. "You, there! Dirty Jew! *Untermensch.*[2] Sleepy eyes!" They spat these common anti-Jewish epithets at my father. How common their slurs were! The men seemed quite self-satisfied with their base and unoriginal insults. They laughed and guffawed in the aisle, while Anita and my father sat motionless, hoping that they were only facing harmless verbal nonsense.

The train slowed as it pulled into the next station and then came to a halt. In a split second, the men grabbed my father by his underarms and legs and lifted him right out of his seat. Then, right before Anita's eyes, they carried him off the train.

Anita barely had time to register what had happened. It was as if she had blinked and then, in a flash, Vati was just gone. She let out a scream. "Vati!" she shouted out the window as the train began rolling out of the station. Anita pounded on the train window. She called and cried out, but there was no one on the platform who could hear her. In her car, the passengers buried their heads in their books and newspapers. There would be no help for Anita tonight. The train began picking up speed and continued its journey to Holland. Minus one passenger, that is.

My father opened his eyes and found himself lying on an empty train platform. Surrounding him were. the Nazis from the train – drunk, young, merry, and menacing. It was the middle of the night and the station was eerily silent except for the sounds of the young men. No one else was there, and no one else seemed to be coming. A tornado of thoughts began circulating in his mind. *What will become of Anita,* he worried. He had just left behind his young daughter on a train, alone and unprotected. *How will I know if she arrives safely?* But perhaps his worst thought was: *How will I explain this to Grete when I get home?* He looked around at the intoxicated Nazi neophytes. *I won't have to explain it,* he then realized, despairingly, *because there is no possibility that I am ever going to see home again.*

The elated young officers were hooting and hollering, their voices echoing in the empty station. How excited they seemed about their new acquisition at first. But having just gotten their brand-new toy – Vati – they seemed uncertain how to enjoy their prize. "What should we do with the Jew?" one of the young men said.

"I have a good game," said another. "Let's call it 'Run, Jew, Run.' It should be entertaining." He turned to my father. "Get up, Jew. Run across the tracks."

My father wisely did not utter a word of resistance. Picking himself up off the ground, he briskly walked back and forth across the train tracks. But no sooner did he return to the platform, than one of the officers kicked him and he fell to the ground. My father immediately stood back up, but another officer kicked him until he fell again. "Get up, you dirty Jew. *Mach schnell* – go faster this time – or we will beat you!" Vati got up and followed his orders. This time he ran across the tracks. He ran back. When he returned, one of the men kicked him again and he went down. "Faster, Jew!" he shouted, and then laughed.

Up Vati rose again. Back and forth he ran over the tracks. Faster, this time. Getting kicked. Falling down. Back up again. Running across the tracks. Up, then kicked, then down, then up again, then running. Back, forth, up, down. Again. Again. Running for his life. Again, and again and again. The young officers were all laughing now.

Eventually, they grew bored with their game. One of them dragged my father into a small shack. "Take off your clothes," he ordered.

Vati stripped to his underwear. Shivering from both fear and cold, he sat in the dim light in the shack. Vati could finally really see his captors. How innocent they looked with their smooth, hairless faces, their boldness a facade. Boys, barely older than Anita. As individuals, perhaps they had some humanity left. As a group, not very likely.

Vati sat in his boxers, while one of the young officers – the obvious ringleader – sifted through his clothes. "I knew it! This filthy Jew was going to escape Germany," the officer began to shout. He had found the 300 Deutschmarks Mutti had painstakingly sewn into Vati's trousers.

"I don't know, maybe not," suggested another boy in the group. He seemed a bit kinder, but maybe he was just weak. "He may have been just trying to smuggle the money out."

"Well, I really don't care," yelled the ringleader, his fair face flushed with outsized anger. "We need to decide now. What should we do, brothers? Shoot him, arrest him, or let him go?"

A debate ensued among the young men. They stepped outside the shack, out of Vati's earshot. Another hour passed, maybe more, as Vati sat shivering in his undergarments, alone in the shack, waiting. How would his fate be decided? What on earth were they doing – rock, paper, scissors? Had they ever even killed anyone?

It seemed like hours had passed when the men finally returned to the shack. "Get up," shouted one of them, a man-boy who still had pimples on his face. He threw my father his clothes. "Start moving."

Vati stepped out of the shack onto the abandoned platform and began walking. He walked slowly and steadily away from the men, as tall and proudly as he could. All the while he wondered if he would ever hear the splitting sound of the shot that was going to end his life.

The next day, the front door opened, and a man walked into our apartment who I barely recognized. It was Vati all right, but he seemed to have shrunk; his clothes hung limply from his bent body. Looking pale and exhausted, he told us the lengthy tale of his harrowing journey.

"... and then they just put me back on a train headed to Berlin," he finished.

"But what became of Anita?" shrieked Mutti.

"Grete, did you hear me? I just narrowly escaped death!" my father exclaimed. "For the second time!"

"I don't care about that," wailed my mother insistently. "I just want to know what happened to Anita. That is all. Did she make it to Rotterdam? To England? Can't you tell me that much."

"I have absolutely no idea, Grete. How could I possibly know? I was in my underwear. At gunpoint! How would I know where Anita is?"

I could sense an argument developing as Vati searched for comfort and Mutti searched for answers, prepared to blame somebody for something to assuage her anxiety. But just then, Mutti turned to me and saw the anguished look on my face. Just yesterday, I had said goodbye to a sister who had been like a mother to me, and I was lonelier than I had ever been. And I worried about my father too. With Vati exhausted and shaken, and Anita gone, who would comfort me? Something changed in my mother at that moment and the yelling stopped.

That night, Mutti made us a simple supper of cold open tomato sandwiches. She mustered up a facade of composure and spoke reassuringly. "Be calm everyone," she said. "Wolf, in the morning we will figure out how to get word from your sister. Tonight, we will go to bed early. There is nothing more that is going to happen tonight from all our worrying."

It would be weeks before we heard that Anita made it to England. She had arrived unharmed but homeless in a country that would soon be Hitler's primary aerial target in the war.

PART III

WAR

9

VICTOR, VICTORIOUS

The invasion of Poland was as vicious as it was victorious. The Germans defeated the Poles in just three weeks.

Bismarckstrasse was just one block from our apartment, and from our balcony I was able to watch the victory parade as it passed impressively along the majestic eight-lane boulevard.

Starting at the Reich Chancellery, Army units 20 across and 50 deep goose-stepped in perfect unison. Motorcycles with their attached side cars followed. Artillery pieces came next, followed by a row of tanks, and after them, a phalanx of goose-stepping SS units. Each unit had its own band and its own military flags, and the crowd screamed uncontrollably each time a unit passed. Fighter planes flew overhead in perfect formation, adding to the spectacle.

The crowds were at least 10 people deep. Everybody was carrying flags and exploding with fervor so wild that they had to be held back by military police and soldiers.

The parade went on for hours and came to a climactic end, when a group of Mercedes-Benz convertibles suddenly appeared, carrying Generals, Nazi ministers and finally, the Führer himself. As each officer gave his formal *Heil Hitler* salute, the mob became delirious. The excitement was contagious. Everybody felt it. I did too.

The excitement of victory would only be transient, of course. By the time the war was in full swing, there was plenty of suffering to go around, even for the victorious nation of Germany.

At first, Hitler plundered the food and natural resources of the countries he invaded. It was a Roman-style war strategy that was ultimately doomed. Inevitably, food supplies became scarce, and rationing began.

Like every family, we received a ration book containing coupons for basic food necessities. Each German adult was allotted 1,600 calories per day. Our ration coupons had the letter "J" – for Jew – imprinted on them. We soon learned that the "J" restricted our shopping times to the hours of 6 to 7 p.m. By the time we were able to patronize the stores, all items – even those not rationed – were simply gone from the shelves.

Despite the food shortages, I kept on growing. The bottoms of my pants steadily crept above my ankles, and my waistband loosened as I got skinnier and skinner. When a new edict was passed banning Jews from buying any new clothing, my mother used her creative sewing skills to lengthen and take in my trousers. The Central Jewish Organization also stepped in, rapidly coordinating a used clothing exchange that allowed us to swap sizes. Despite these interventions, in no time we Jews all looked undernourished and shabby.

The war instigated a huge shortage of labor, since all men of working age had been drafted, and defense industries were operating at peak capacity. To fill these heightened labor demands, the government instituted forced labor for all able-bodied citizens. My father was assigned to lay railroad tracks for an airplane factory just on the outskirts of the city. The job required hoisting an entire train rail on his shoulders. Although he did this in a group with four other people, it was a hard job for such a slight man, taking a toll on his feet and on his back, not to mention his psyche.

Uncle Siegfried's status as a wounded veteran spared him forced labor, but his wife Irma had to work in his stead. She began making parachutes at a nylon factory, where pay was nominal, the work laborious, and the smell of the synthetic nylon, by her account, was putrid. Her days of having never worked were over.

While the slow and steady erosion of "normal" had started long ago, it seemed as though the war accelerated the decline. What *had* normal been like? We could barely even remember. Playing on the street... Sitting in cafés or on park benches... Furniture in our apartment... Adequate food and clothing... Those things were all a distant memory.

Only socializing with our little circle of friends and family had a cadence of predictability to it. But even that little routine eventually succumbed to the pressures of war.

"I'm afraid that I must be departing Berlin," Ho informed us one day. He expressed his sincere sadness and then explained his predicament. "The Chinese government is recalling me from Germany. Hitler is allying with Japan, our sworn enemy. All diplomatic relations between China and Germany have broken off and I cannot be a guest in this country any longer."

Yet another friend was going. While we shared our heartfelt disappointment, Ho quickly interrupted. "Please, I must continue. The good news is that I am being sent to England to continue my research. I hope to connect with Anita when I arrive in London. You must know by now that I am very much in love with Anita and I want to take this opportunity to make you an offer. I implore you to think about this carefully. I can get all of you visas for China, where you can join my family in the Xinjiang province in northern China. My family is quite affluent and would make you most welcome. However, this offer is conditional. Anita must agree to marry me for the offer to stand. Please, talk this over amongst yourselves. Then write to Anita. Discuss it with her. If Anita marries me, you all come to China. That is my offer. Remember, you may not have other options."

You may not have other options. This sentence loomed over us. Was that a warning or a threat? An invitation or a premonition? We were not completely sure, but we took his words to heart.

China. My mother had kept the option open only as a last

resort, but she was quite afraid of emigrating there. Her second cousins, the Ruschins, had recently fled to Shanghai but we had heard nothing from them since they emigrated.[1] My mother's knowledge of China was therefore limited to whatever Ho had told us and what she had read in the popular Pearl Buck novel, *The Good Earth*. All she could remember from the book was famine, foot binding, and locusts. She had no realistic vision of modern life there. She was uncertain if Ho could be held to his word. However, between Ho and my parents, there seemed to be a tacit understanding of mutual self-interest. Ho was using our situation to "nab" Anita and he knew we were using him to procure our freedom.

No, not China. My mother still fervently hoped to get us safely to America. With Ellis as our sponsor, it still seemed possible. The finances seemed to be worked out; all we needed were three visas now. The medical issues were resolved. Really, what could be the problem? *Thank you, Ho, but we do not need China right now.*

Ho went off to England, and we passed on his offer, with our sights set on America.

Another trip to the US consulate was coming up, and with the health and financial concerns all resolved, it should go quite smoothly. A nice long wait, polite gestures, a seat at the desk with the consul while we watched him rifle through the documents. That's what we expected, and we approached the visit with guarded optimism.

But something seemed to be taking an awfully long time. The consul looked through the folder. And then he looked through it again, and again, and again. He spun his chair around to a file cabinet and, pulling out a file drawer, picked up another folder and looked inside. He scratched his head and turned back to us. Our hearts were racing; we were barely breathing. Finally, the consul spoke. "I'm terribly sorry, Frau Schwersenz. I am trying very hard to locate the documents for Ellis Arndt's sponsorship application, but I simply do not see them anywhere. It is as if your whole application has disappeared into thin air!"

"That's impossible. Look again," pleaded my mother, her voice straining. "They were all there on the last visit. Please, look again. They must be there."

"I am sorry, I have looked and looked, but the papers are not here. They must be either lost or somehow misplaced. There is nothing more that we can do. I am sorry but there is only one option. The fastest thing you can do is to get duplicates of your entire application and all supporting documents and affidavits from your sponsor. Only then can we proceed."

Mr. Consul, don't you understand? We are now at war! This delay, this misfiling, might now cost us our lives. My mother may have thought those words, but she did not say them aloud. Yet how was it even possible that we could be besieged by such bad luck and gross incompetence? Never, not in a million years, would she have believed that these recurrent problems in our application – from Ellis's financial concerns to my father's health "problems," and now the "missing" documentation – were part of a deliberate program to delay and deny our entry into the US for as long as possible.[2] Years later it would come to light that the US consuls were specifically told by the State department to "postpone and postpone and postpone" all visa applications.

My mother smiled, politely thanked the consul, grabbed my hand firmly and walked out. In her mind she was already planning, calculating, getting into action mode. She would have to contact Ellis again. The poor man would have to begin making duplicates of our entire application. Every single signed affidavit, every notarized page. It would take weeks, maybe months.

1939 ended somberly. We rang in the New Year with only Aunt Frieda and Uncle Alfred, Uncle Siegfried and Aunt Irma, and Ella Hammer. What was once a healthy circle of friends and family seemed to have contracted into a tiny speck made up of a few straggling leftovers. Our group barely took up any space in the living room. No one could muster up the spirit of the New Year. Uncle Siegfried tried to lighten the somber mood. Standing up, he held a glass and clicked it with a spoon until he had our attention. "I have some news," he announced. "Irma and I have finally put in our application for emigration to the United States!"

I had no idea that my uncle had waited so long, all this time believing his Iron Cross would protect him. Nothing would protect him now. We all knew it was far too late.

Berlin was suddenly abuzz. All around, there were preparations for war. The whole city seemed transformed.

German men all strutted about in their Army uniforms. Inside the Tiergarten, trenches had been dug right next to the path where I normally walked from school to daycare. The lovely Lake Lietzensee, situated in a nearby city park, was now covered with artificial grass and fake cardboard houses. The goal was to disorient the British pilots peering down from the night sky so they would no longer see the *Funkturm* radio tower in the lake's reflection. But the effect was to disorient me; I could no longer recognize my city.

Heading from school one afternoon, I walked with my half dozen Jewish friends through the Tiergarten and ran into a group of non-Jewish German children walking in the opposite direction. We stared at each other with nervous hostility, and then we opened fire. Throwing our small bodies into the trenches for cover, we began our attack, launching stones at our enemies with ferocity. They responded in kind, throwing stones back at us. Our battle lasted for an hour, maybe more, until both sides broke off from sheer exhaustion. For a while, adult onlookers stood by and watched but they did not intervene. It was as though they sensed this mini war was not just child's play. We felt we were fighting our real enemy; and for the first time since this whole mess began, we had an outlet for all our rage and resentment. Our battle had no clearcut winner, but at least here, in our Tiergarten trenches, we did not feel completely powerless.

That first winter of wartime seemed endless. I was always cold and hungry. While everyone in Germany lacked food and heat, it certainly seemed that our Jewish rations were scantier. Not uncommonly, an antisemitic grocer would intentionally cheat us on our portion of cheese or meat after seeing the "J" on our rations card. Often, we would return home from the shops in the evening, exhausted and nearly empty handed. My mother would feel hopeless as she stared at our measly allotments, knowing no one would come to our aid.

Mutti continually worried about the next stage of deprivation. "What if we lose the apartment?" she asked my father one evening. "I have heard rumors that landlords are being pressured to evict Jews. No warning at all. The one thing we must have is shelter from the cold. It is imperative!"

"It's out of our hands," sighed my father, the fatalist. He had no solution to offer. "No one can predict what will happen next. All we can do is hope for the best."

One evening, after another failed shopping expedition, my mother and I trudged home, frustrated by our pitiful grocery pickings. At the top of the stairs, we saw our landlord, Dr. Behne, waiting for us in front of our apartment door. He was carrying an official-looking briefcase and he seemed to have been standing there for quite a while. My mother paused on the steps, her hesitation meaning: *Please don't let it be so.* As if not going up the stairs could stop the inevitable. We finally continued a slow ascent to our landing. "Good evening, Frau Schwersenz." Dr. Behne lifted his briefcase in the air. "I have something I need to give you." He leaned the briefcase on the railing and opened it. Then he pulled out a package of white paper. So this was it. Eviction papers. "This is for your family," he said softly, his voice sad and gentle, his eyes downcast.

My mother slowly unwrapped the paper package. In the center of the paper wrapping lay a small, ordinary little whitefish, its one eye staring at us immutably. My mother's own eyes, rarely wet with emotion, welled up with tears of gratitude. She leaned against the railing as if she suddenly could not support herself. "Dr. Behne. In all this time, this is the only act of kindness we have ever received. Thank you."

Carrying our meager groceries, we stepped inside the apartment. No eviction papers. It was still ours for now. But how unrecognizable it had become! The floors were bare and uncarpeted, the not-quite-grand furniture and rugs in storage somewhere in Rotterdam. Every ornament, each bit of silver, every picture, even Oma Ernestine's ugly tapestry, was gone. All that remained were the beds and a kitchen table and chairs. The apartment looked drab and dark. It was the color of despair and it echoed with the emptiness of a way of life that was over.

With our coal rations cut, our heating stoves sat cold and idle in the corners of their respective rooms. Perhaps that winter was particularly bitter or maybe it was quite average, but without adequate heat or clothing, or food in our bellies, we were cold all the time.

Eventually, we stopped pretending to live like normal people; we even stopped caring what we looked like. The three of us dragged our beds from the bedrooms to the living room so we could all sleep together in one room. The living room, barren but for the three beds lined up in a row, resembled a hospital ward. Intermittently we turned on the gray-tiled heating stove, meticulously rationing our remaining fuel. Still perpetually cold, we donned layers upon layers of old sweaters until we looked like the homeless. All we were doing now was trying to survive.

We were not alone in our icy isolation. My school could not get adequate fuel and announced it would close its doors for the six coldest weeks of winter.

It did not reopen.

The crocuses arrived, exploding with color, and marking another spring, all the while blissfully ignorant that Germany and the rest of Europe had become further entrenched in war. Throughout the winter, Cousin Ellis had been trying to replace the missing documents, but our file was not complete yet, and it looked like the clock was just about to run out. We could no longer simply wait for our visas to the United States to materialize while the war was progressing through Europe. We had to find an alternate plan. It looked like our road to freedom was going to be through

China after all. That meant Anita was going to have to rescue all of us.

Getting ourselves out of Germany and into China would be no easy task. We were technically stateless, having "lost" our German citizenship. We needed to acquire a laundry list of paperwork. Temporary German passports from the German police. Permission to exit Germany. Transit permissions to pass through other countries, often lasting just a few weeks. Visas to get into China. Everything had to be obtained in the correct order, and everything had its own expiration date. If one pass expired too soon, the rest of the travel plan would unravel. It was a bureaucratic nightmare.

And the travel plans themselves had to be arranged. Every Jew trying to leave Germany had to arrange the booking of all transit tickets through the Central Jewish Organization in Berlin. We headed there next, praying for a passage to China.

The Central Jewish Organization[3] was an all-volunteer grass roots organization that had been such an impactful part of every Jew's existence in Berlin. It had arranged schooling, clothing, cultural events, and now our travel. Until now, it had been just a concept. I had never seen it, and I imagined something like the US consulate, or perhaps a ticketing office, like the one at the Bahnhof Zoo Station. However, I had no context for what we encountered.

Perhaps the site of a disaster would be closest. We entered a desperate scene of biblical proportions and waded through a sea of ragged-looking people filling the halls and the main room. Hundreds of people just like us were desperate to get out of Germany. Everyone was simultaneously pleading with a skeleton staff of harried agency workers. "Help us, help us. You must help us find an escape plan," they begged. The overwhelmed personnel were powerless to aid the mountains of frantic people. Around us, papers seemed to be flying in the air. Jews were shouting and crying; they seemed to have given up politeness long ago. They were arguing and gesticulating, or they held their arms out as if in supplication; whatever it would take. They were fighting for their lives.

We walked into bedlam, chaos, and disorganization. And

somehow, we walked out with a booking. It was our first bit of good luck. We would be on an Italian ship. It was leaving from Genoa, Italy on June 10, 1940 and was headed for China.[4] Yes, this was real. We had an escape plan. We would finally be leaving Germany!

Or maybe not. The war was progressing at breakneck speed. Like an avalanche rushing down a mountain, Germany was burying countries in its path, and there seemed to be no stopping it. In April, German troops invaded Denmark, meeting practically no resistance from the Danes. Then, Germany attacked Norway. The Kingdom fought bravely, but it was no match for the German Army and was immediately occupied. In May, German troops invaded Belgium, Luxembourg, and the Netherlands, and on June 5, they invaded France. The French initially retreated, woefully unprepared for Germany's new form of "mechanized infantry." Soon after, it surrendered, leaving an occupied portion of France and a puppet "independent" government in Vichy France.

The European countries were toppling like dominoes. Germany seemed to be reaching its goal of taking over all of Europe, if not the world. Suddenly, Italy decided it would join the war. It did not want to miss out! On June 10, it declared war on France and Britain. *Not Italy! Our ship leaves from Genoa!* When Italy entered the war, the door to our passage to China by way of Genoa slammed shut. Once again, we were trapped.

Trapped in Germany, but still alive. That was some consolation, I suppose. "Look, Grete, at least we have a roof over our heads, and we are living in Berlin, and that is better than Jews are faring elsewhere," Vati declared, reassuringly. We had to feed ourselves these little crumbs to maintain some semblance of optimism. He was right, though. Berlin was safer than elsewhere. We heard rumors that Jews from smaller German cities – Frankfurt, Munich, Leipzig – were being "resettled" in the east.

"Just 24 hours' notice, and you're told to pack a single suitcase, then you're transported to a ghetto in Riga in Latvia, or Lodz in Poland." These stories were circulating like wildfire. It sounded like a nightmare! But us Berlin Jews presented a particular obstacle to resettlement. There were just too many of us. The Germans could not transport the huge Jewish population out of Berlin in the middle of a war. Our numbers neared 100,000 and the logistics were confounding. Until the Nazis could develop a clever way to expel the bulk of us from the city, Berlin was still the safest place to be.

There was nothing to do but wait. Wait for a miracle to materialize.

One warm day in late June, my father approached Uncle Siegfried, looking very agitated. "What is troubling you, Arthur?" asked Siegfried, putting his bear-like arm around my father's compact shoulder. "Sit down, my friend."

Like a man at confessional, Vati sat across from Siegfried and proceeded to confide in him. "Siegfried, I must speak with you confidentially. I really don't know what to do and need your advice. Do you remember when we were supposed to turn over all our valuables to the police..."

"Yes..."

"And instead, we gave our things to the Red Cross worker from Holland..."

"Go on, Arthur."

"Well, I... I kept some."

Siegfried raised one eyebrow in surprise and alarm. "Kept some... what?" he asked.

"Some jewelry. They were just a few trinkets, Siegfried. Nothing much. I do not even know why I did it. I just was not ready to give up everything. Now I am having second thoughts and, frankly, I am really frightened. We could be searched at any time, and I have no idea what to do. I need your help. And please, Siegfried, I am begging you. Don't tell Grete."

"Are you insane?" Mutti's face was contorted with rage. She held her forehead with the palm of her hand as she continued to scream. “You could go to a prison camp. Your stupidity could get us all deported. We will all be shot!”

It had taken Siegfried under an hour to tell his sister. Secrets were secrets, and loyalty was loyalty, but blood was a bond you did not break.

My father needed a practical solution to this problem, and my mother’s moral attack was of no help. And yet she was not exaggerating with her admonitions. The six concentration camps of the “Greater German Reich” – Oranienburg, Sachsenhausen, Buchenwald, Dachau, Flossenburg, and Mauthausen – were up and running, and we could be sent there for even the most minor transgression. These were forced-labor camps, and not the extermination camps of horror – like Auschwitz – that would later be created in Eastern Europe. But starvation, slavery, inhumane conditions, and death still reigned in these places of internment. “You must get rid of it immediately,” Mutti ordered my father. “All of it.”

“But...”

“Not another word!”

Late in the night, when the early-summer sky finally darkened, Vati and Siegfried surreptitiously slipped out of the apartment, bringing with them the few remaining items of gold and silver jewelry. They walked quickly and quietly, avoiding police, SS, Gestapo, Stormtroopers. Avoiding even our own Nazi neighbors who would likely turn them in. They crept into the Tiergarten and tiptoed to the bank of the Spree River which ran through the park, snaking a path northbound.

Vati’s heart was beating fast. He could not risk getting caught. Still, he took a moment to look at each piece. A few simple rings. A gold chain. Hardly anything. The cold metal had warmed in his sweaty hands. Now it was slick and slippery. He held it a moment longer. Why was it so hard to part with it? He almost didn’t understand it himself. Still, they were the last things of value that he owned. He pulled his slim but muscular arm behind his head, closed his eyes, and threw the little handful of jewelry as far as he could into the cold flowing river.

10

SCHOOL'S OUT

Instead of school, we were given worksheets, and the days felt idle and isolated. Longing for companionship and routine, I still went to the daycare center several afternoons a week, where I noticed another boy. Taller than me and probably older, he was just as pale and lanky, with an impish grin that bespoke of trouble. Both of us walked the same 40-minute route home until we reached Bismarckstrasse. Then the boy took a turn and headed northbound.

Heinz Spiegel was two years older than me, but light years ahead in knowledge and experience. He was the first Jewish boy I had ever really befriended. That summer, in the middle of craziness and confusion, loneliness and uncertainty, Heinz and I became closer than friends. We became brothers.

Heinz quickly became my mentor. He saw huge holes in my education, and he knew he must immediately get to work filling in the gaps. "What do you know about sex, Wolf?" he asked.

I knew nothing. "Do you even know how babies are conceived?"

I did not. "You don't know how to smoke? But you're already 10! Un-be-liev-able! What has anyone been teaching you all these years?"

On a quiet weekday, my real schooling began. Heinz presented me with two unfiltered cigarettes he had somehow procured. It was risky to be caught smoking at such a young age, but our manhood depended on it. To evade detection, we slipped into the stairwell of a plain apartment building and sat in a corner, hiding in the dim light. We lit our cigarettes and held them with simulated nonchalance, curling our forefinger over the top and our thumb on the bottom, as proper Europeans. I started to inhale, surrendering to the usual fits of coughing, nausea, and dizziness of a virgin smoker.

On the floor above us, we heard the unexpected creak of a door opening. We froze. "Who is there?" came the husky voice of a male adult. The owner of the voice leaned over the banister. The worst of all possible people to catch us! A middle-aged, corpulent man in a half-open Army uniform! He started to race down the stairs. We quickly tossed our cigarettes out the stairwell window, and then we started to run.

The chase was on. Red-faced and yelling, the officer sprinted after us down the stairs. "What are you two doing? You delinquents! Why aren't you in school! You cannot smoke! I will find your parents!" He chased us out onto the street screaming and gesticulating, but after half a block we turned and saw he had given up soon after we left the building.

"Why do you think he stopped... following us, Heinz?" I stammered between fits of wheezing.

"We were just lucky. He was probably too fat to keep running," answered Heinz. "But I don't think he could tell we were Jews, or we would have gotten the beating of our lives."

He was right. With our prepubescent, cherubic faces, our noses that had not yet taken their downward trajectory, and the fair skin and blue eyes of Germans, we might not have been immediately detected as Jews. With our lungs still hacking, we ran away, aptly chastened.

I followed Heinz everywhere with blind devotion. Heinz dared me to do things I would never have mustered up the nerve to do on my own. "Go into that pharmacy and tell the clerk that you want to buy prophylactics." I had no idea what prophylactics were, but I asked for them at the counter anyway. The pharmacy clerk became apoplectic and came running out from behind the counter ready to box my ears. I skirted out of the pharmacy fast as a jackrabbit, unsure of what I had done. Minutes later, I found Heinz in stitches, and in between fits of hysteria he eventually explained what I had asked for.

I did not care that the joke was at my expense, I was just happy to laugh at anything to take a break from the bleakness. That became our trademark; we would walk into all the shops together, and I would walk right up to the pharmacist. "Excuse me, where do you have the condoms?" I would ask, just to see the robust range of reactions. Always, the store clerk or owner would run me out of the store, full of shock and outrage. I ran like the wind. I felt like Jesse Owens. I could outrun them all.

Our wanderings often took us to Grunewald, the forest preserve where, in happier days, I had hiked and biked with my father. Midweek, we could stroll Grunewald's quiet, empty paths without fear of being accosted by German children. On one such afternoon we were enjoying our blissful solitude while walking randomly through the desolate dirt paths. We talked about the war, we giggled about girls, we complained about our parents. Then we took a break to bask in the late-September sun, happy to be free of school and responsibilities.

After our short rest, we began walking again through the woods, slowly making our way back toward the train. We walked side by side in silence, having temporarily run out of topics of conversation, when the gentle harmonies of distant singing suddenly broke through our quiet contemplations. It sounded like a church group. Was it a boys' choir? We could not help but approach the sweet serenade.

The voices became louder as we came to a clearing. No sooner had we approached the source of the voices, than we realized our grave error. In the clearing were over a dozen Hitler youth, singing in perfect harmony. There was no mistaking them in their classic brown uniforms. Then we saw that they were armed, each of them carrying a dart gun for hunting small animals and birds. We looked around us, but here was nowhere to hide. We were completely exposed, and they had definitely seen us. All we could do was tiptoe past them quietly and pray that we would not be accosted.

We had walked about 50 yards without incident, when Heinz and I finally exhaled. We did not dare speak, but we each thought, *they must be so occupied with their singing that they cannot be bothered with assaulting us.*

Mid-thought, something whirred past my head. A moment later, a volley of shots rang out. Suddenly, there were darts flying everywhere. We were under attack! We bolted into a run. The darts whizzed past our ears, sailing in all directions. We made zigzags through the woods, out into the open paths and back into the woods again. We ducked and jumped, desperately trying to avoid the crossfire. Without stopping, we made it out of the park and kept running until we reached the train station. We made a mad dash up the stairs, taking three steps at a time up to the platform. The elevated train pulled in just in time; it opened its doors like loving arms and we threw ourselves in. Then we collapsed in our seats, still panting and red-faced. We checked ourselves for injuries and took the train home, secretly smiling to ourselves, reveling in the joy of our survival, while we sat, sweating, in total blissful silence.

At the end of the summer of 1940, Heinz and I received notice that we would be transferred to a new school, situated in a reformed synagogue on Joachimthaler Strasse near the fashionable avenue Kurfürstendamm. The synagogue was one of just a few that survived the Kristallnacht burnings. Flanked by German businesses on both sides, it was lucky to be spared destruction that fateful night.

An orientation and brief assembly were held in a large auditorium. "I am sorry to say, there will be no classes again this fall," a teacher announced. "Instead, we will be giving you homework assignments which we will collect twice a month." A collective groan rang out through the auditorium. The news was terrible. We were all desperate to go to school! How we yearned for the interaction with other children. We were sick of homework packets and more busy work. We all wanted to learn. Even I did. And what we wanted most of all was routine.

After the assembly, most of the children went home, but I lingered back with Heinz and a few of the boys and girls. The lights were turned off and the synagogue was plunged into total darkness. The girls decided to play an impromptu game of hide and seek. Suddenly, they had all disappeared. We began calling for them. “Yoo-hoo. Where are you hiding?”

Giggles and snorts. The scuffles of little footsteps. The swoosh of fabric. “We are over here. No we aren’t. Come and find us!” they demanded.

I did not know what to make of these strange creatures who were teasing us with their paradoxical summons. They were everywhere and nowhere. They called out to us but ran away. I felt my heart beating. No, I could hear it beating. The blood was whooshing in my ears like a murmur. *Zhoom. Zhoom. Zhoom.* I felt lightheaded. The girls were hiding in closets. They were behind pews. They were throughout the building. We could not see them, but we could feel their mysterious presence. It was intoxicating. We found them one by one and pulled them onto our laps. In the darkness, their soft skin and sweet breath seemed intensified. The girl in my lap clasped her small hands around my neck and brushed my cheek with her velvety lips. I knew nothing of girls, nothing of sex, but in the darkness of that abandoned synagogue, in the epicenter of Nazi Germany, I felt the first twinges of desire.

We finally dispersed and walked lazily home from the school that would not be school. Heinz and I headed towards Bismarckstrasse, where we usually parted ways, but Heinz could not cross because another victory parade had just started to come through.

It was another German war success! The triumphs were piling on, one after another. We squeezed between the mobs of people rapt in exuberant delirium. Winding our way through the sidewalks, sliding between pressed bodies, we watched the excitement spread like an infection. People of all ages were screaming. They were in a state of total exhilaration. They yelled in unison. It was as though they were hypnotized.

On the sidewalk, the atmosphere was like a carnival. Pop-up street theaters had appeared out of nowhere near the subway stations. Costumed actors walked back and forth on the streets. They were dressed up as unflattering caricatures of Prime Ministers Churchill and Chamberlain; Foreign Minister Anthony Eden with his distinctive guardsman's moustache; President Roosevelt in his characteristic pince-nez glasses; Jewish money lenders with exaggerated, long, crooked noses.

All of Germany's adversaries were there in larger-than-life costumes. The ugly enemies had all turned out for the peoples' entertainment.

That very night, on August 25, 1940, and into the early morning of the next day, the screaming siren of our first air raid woke me from a fitful slumber. I had never heard such a noise before. The sound rose and then lingered in deafening volume, then suddenly dropped as if it had run out of air. Then it climbed back up again, as if it had caught another wind, building to a feverish intensity. Over and over, it played its atonal tune. It was jarring and blood curdling. British RAF planes had set off the sirens in response to a German bomb dropped on England the day before – quite possibly in error. Britain was sending an announcement to Germany that it would defend Europe against German aggression at all costs. Germany was stunned. They never thought it could happen, that they – correction, that we – could be the targets. Despite a massive show of air power, minimal damage was done. The raid was primarily for show, and the only casualty was an innocent elephant in the Tiergarten zoo.

War was everywhere now, even in the air. It had seeped into the consciousness of every German, including me, and I became obsessed with it. I had one desperate hope: for the Allies to change the course of the war. Germany simply could not continue its campaign of victories. Every battle won by Hitler seemed to count against our very survival.

Vati somehow obtained an oversized map of Europe and brought it home. We hung it on the wall, turning our living room into an ersatz war room. I mapped out the entire front, putting colored pins into each of the captured towns. Mutti was afraid that someone might discover the map and misconstrue it as anti-German, so we hid it under a blanket just in case anyone entered the apartment.

The map with its little colored pins was our only decoration.

11

FLAT EARTH

The cold steadily crept back in as the fall of 1940 approached. The Nazis had successfully conquered most of Western Europe and now they set their sights on England. Protected by a powerful navy, surrounded by an ocean, with far-flung colonies and commonwealths that would surely come to its aid, Britain was not likely to succumb as easily as the continent. Germany's best strategy was constant air attack, a blitzkrieg. They were sure that an endless attack would break the will and the spirit of the people. They could not have been more wrong.

The British responded to "the blitz" with their own dizzying display of aerial annihilation throughout September. Some basic bombing etiquette that hitherto had confined bombing to military targets was lifted, and all of Berlin – along with its citizens – was fair game. *We* were the targets now, every one of us. The British were intent on as much destruction as possible. To flatten us, if necessary.

The air raid started with the deafening sound of the siren, and we ran hastily to our basement, grabbing some meager rations to take with us. We sat for hours, confined to our makeshift underground shelter while we listened to the screams and explosions of bombs and anti-aircraft fire.

After the raid was over, we lumbered upstairs. It was the wee hours of the morning, and I crawled wearily into my bed and fell dead asleep. Just an hour later, there was another siren. Another air raid! We headed back to the basement for the rest of the night, listening to the bombings continue until the sky just started to lighten. By then it was 5 a.m.; the sleepless night was over. "If the bombs don't kill us, the exhaustion just might," my father mused, but he had to keep this little joke just between us. Because we sat in that basement by ourselves, separate. Our chairs had been pushed off to the corner by our German neighbors so we would not contaminate them with our Jewishness.

For weeks at a time, it seemed as if the air raids were nightly. They started at 11 p.m. like clockwork. Every night that we sat in the basement, I was in a state of worried confusion, my thoughts a chaotic tangle. I was afraid that a bomb might fall on me, while I simultaneously hoped that a bomb would fall on the Germans. Then I would remember *we* were the Germans too.

Suddenly I had an identity crisis. With our German citizenship revoked, the Polish quota we were filling for our US visa, our own country trying to evict us, and being identified as Jews rather than Germans, I did not know who or what I was anymore, and I started to lose track of which side I was on.

While I would eventually grow accustomed to the wailing of the bombs, I never adapted to the sneering glances and condescending attitudes of our neighbors. Those looks pierced my soul. We sat apart as though we had leprosy. And while our neighbors could take comfort in the solidarity of their shared air-raid experience, we could have no camaraderie with our cellar-mates.

Sometimes, overcome by boredom, I ran to the entrance just above the shelter. I could just catch a glimpse of the outside. The sky was eerily illuminated. There were searchlights sweeping the sky, maybe six or eight of them. I followed the beams crossing each other like giant X's in the night sky until they lit up the British planes flying in perfect formation to reach their intended targets.

We left the basement shelter happy that our building was still standing, but not feeling entirely free from danger. Mutti cautiously reentered our apartment, while Vati checked every inch of the floor and in every corner to make sure there were no lightweight incendiary devices dropped by the Britons that could burst into flames. Outside, in the light of the morning, I saw German children scurrying around the streets. They were looking for reusable shell fragments they could proudly present to the Nazis. I walked through the streets alone, and I looked for shrapnel too, as a souvenir.

It was always eerily silent the morning after an air raid. Rubble covered the ground, muffling the street noise as if a fresh coating of snow had fallen overnight.

After a particularly heavy night of bombing, I started my usual walk to daycare one morning, stepping tentatively through piles of debris. The rubble thickened and the destruction worsened as I got closer to Kurfürstendamm and then turned onto the nearby busy shopping street, Tauentzienstrasse. I seemed to be nearing the epicenter of the previous night's bombings. It was unnervingly close to the daycare center, and the magnitude of the destruction was just starting to come into focus. Mountains of broken brick and debris littered the streets. Every building had been struck and damaged, and some structures were gutted open like a fish. I felt disoriented; my familiar neighborhood was not recognizable anymore. My shoes slipped and crunched on the broken glass, unable to find any foothold on firm pavement underneath.

A loud crash exploded next to me as a huge pane of glass suddenly fell from the window of a blown-out building, shattering to pieces. It had come clear out of the sky, and I was shaken; I had missed being impaled by a matter of inches.

My heart was pounding heavily as I continued crunching onward. Danger seemed to be everywhere. It was in our apartment ready to burst into flames, it was in the basement in the menacing looks of our neighbors, it could simply fall out of the sky at any moment.

I walked and walked, thinking of only one thing. I had to get to the daycare center, for it was my only place of refuge. I waded and climbed through block upon block of glass and rubble until I finally reached the center. Then I shut the door behind me, closed my eyes to the chaos outside, and threw myself into the tender, comforting arms of one of the volunteers. I had made it.

Just a few minutes after I walked in, the doorbell rang. One of the volunteers opened the door, and a ball of fire flew through the entrance and struck her. It was a straw doormat that had been set ablaze. We could hear the uproarious laughter of the perpetrators – two Nazi youths – as they fled the scene outside the center. The fire was extinguished, and no one was hurt, but that was the end of my sanctuary. The daycare center closed permanently.

Heinz and I only had each other now, and from then on, we roamed Berlin like street ruffians. The streets were endlessly busy with maintenance. Prisoners of war – first Poles, and later Russians – worked steadily at gunpoint fixing bomb craters and removing rubble. How gaunt, disheveled, and depressed the men looked! Most people passed them by as if they were invisible. It was not long before we did the same.

"I need you for a mission, Wolf."

Mutti had cornered me just before I was about to start my daily wandering with Heinz. "We must scour the streets and stores to find some food to celebrate Vati's birthday. I will need your help for this."

She took me completely by surprise. A celebration in the middle of all of this? It was a crazy idea. There was no way she could pull it off, with resources so scarce and food in such short supply. Our larder was always empty, and we were hungry all the time. My parents had even begun giving me some of their own rations; they feared I had become too skinny.

Nonetheless, I put off my daily drifting and dutifully accompanied my mother through the rubble to all the grocers and the remaining shops that were still standing. Barren display cases greeted us in store after store. Empty shelves lay dusty and bare. We searched for hours, managing only to scrape together a single orange and a few potatoes. Wearily, we brought home this sad sack of staples and placed it on the table. "I am sorry. This is all we could find." I showed my father our paltry prizes.

"Nonsense, Wolf, it's a bounty!"

Vati immediately set to work. Like a silent movie star, he began a boisterous display of culinary competence. First, he boiled the potatoes. Then he delicately carved them one by one into fine slivers. Stretching out the action in dramatic detail, he placed the slices of potatoes ceremoniously in a serving bowl. He next peeled the orange, slowly – very slowly – in one continuous serpentine coil. He thinly sliced the orange's flesh into segmented circles and added them to the bowl with the potatoes. Then, with a dramatic flick of his wrist, he dropped in a single spoon of mustard. Finally, he took out two large serving spoons from the kitchen drawer. With extraordinary flourish, he vigorously tossed his creation until a potato, orange and mustard mélange flew out of the bowl and into the air and landed back down in a golden spectacle.

Vati doled out a serving for each of us. He took the first mouthful while we held our breath and waited. He closed his eyes and was silent for a moment as if in prayer. Then he spoke, his eyes still closed. "Mmm, yum… *Ach mein Gott*, this is so delicious!" Vati exclaimed with wild exaggeration. His eyes popped open. "What an amazing salad! This might be the best meal I have *ever* had!"

With that, we all dug in. I ate my few pieces of potato and orange. For a moment, my tongue was fooled by the power of suggestion. *What a delicacy it was indeed!* I tried closing my eyes too. The spicy, salty tartness of the mustard! The bright, sour sweetness of the citrus! The smooth neutrality of the potato! My goodness. YES!! It had all the elements. A perfect balance. Delicious! We all shared and delighted in the feast, dragging out each mouthful, making the meal seem momentous.

It was ridiculous, and wonderful, and funny and sad, and I can still taste it in my mouth.

New Year's Eve of 1941 was a quiet and somber affair. With so few people left in our circle, we had nothing to do other than have a simple dinner at Irma and Siegfried's apartment. There was no celebration, no glogg, no fireworks.

Siegfried shared his own immigration update. "Good news! Irma and I were able to get an affidavit for immigration to the US. Our case will be ready for review in 1944," he told us, excitedly. It was so preposterous, we might have laughed aloud under different circumstances. Too heartbroken and exhausted, we neither laughed nor cried. By then, we had stopped sharing jokes, rumors, and worries; we were even past the point of talking. All we could do was try to inhale the scent of each other and feel the warmth of the loving bodies near us. All we had left now was our time together; but how much time we did not really know.

We left their apartment well before midnight to avoid being caught in an air raid. A full moon lit the snow on the ground, marking our way home. A drunken man weaved his way up the street and approached us. He might have been wanting to talk, or to beg, or just say Happy New Year, but we were too afraid and weary to find out. Uncharitably, we shooed him away, trying to avoid any undue attention. We got back to our apartment and wordlessly lit our few remaining pieces of coal. We would not freeze tonight.

PART IV

ESCAPE

12

PREPARATIONS

Somehow, we managed to survive that miserable winter. I turned 11 in February, and a new series of British air raids began again, as if in celebration.

We were experts now – air raid aficionados. Night after night that March, I headed down to the air raid shelter listening for the unique pitch of each bomb. "*Yes, that's a 500-pound bomb. And here it comes now, the anti-air-craft response.*" I sublimated my fear with these little tidbits of knowledge. It helped pass the time while we sat alone in our Jewish corner like the "untouchables." We averted our eyes that burned with jealousy and rage, as our German neighbors bonded over their shared fears, pooled their scant rations, and lifted their own spirits by sharing their contempt for us.

One night, Vati refused to go to the shelter. He stood in front of the door to our apartment, blocking the entrance, his two short legs set widely apart, his little muscular arms crossed obstinately across his chest. "That is it. I am done. I am not going to spend another night in the basement."

"Don't be ridiculous, Arthur; we'll be killed up here."

"Then I am going to finally say something to those so-called neighbors."

"No, you won't," countered my mother. "They will report you, and you know it." Back to the basement we went, in silence, my father looking deflated.

"The shelter is thoroughly useless," Vati announced to us a week later. "If a bomb were to hit our building, the whole structure would collapse into the basement. And then everyone who is in the basement would either burn or asphyxiate."

That is how my father finally convinced us to stay above ground in our icy-cold apartment. Facing mortal danger seemed a better option than feeling impotent around our neighbors. With the approval of our landlord Dr. Behne, we rode out the rest of the air raids in the living room.

Instant death is better than being buried alive. Those were the words of comfort I told myself every night. As we lay awake for two to three hours listening to the sounds of war, I prayed for the British to beat the Germans and somehow avoid destroying us. The explosions made the walls shake, and sometimes I was so afraid that I climbed into bed with my mother.

On March 31, 1941, we were granted Visa No. 5254 on the Polish quota, allowing us to enter the safety and protection of the United Stated of America.

Our new visa expired on July 31. We had to get to the US by that day and not one single day later.

That was it – our tiny window of opportunity. But what good was just a visa? A visa allowed us to get *in*. We still had to find a way to get *out*.

It seemed all but impossible, for we were stuck in a war that simply refused to stop on our behalf. In fact, it appeared as if Germany were trying to outpace us in a race for time. Hitler continued to invade Europe at breakneck speed. With victory after victory under his belt, Hitler became even more convinced of his own invincibility. The German Army had now turned and headed east. It had already successfully invaded Greece and Yugoslavia. So far, the only resistance it had met was from Britain. The British had received some support – aid and supplies – from the US which was strengthening its endurance. Of course, that made the United States another enemy of Germany. Roosevelt was now a target in Hitler's speeches, earning the moniker "Jew-loving capitalist." It made the crowds go wild.

We began preparing for emigration at a feverish pace. So much work was required to allow for our exodus! The temporary German Reich passports that we had obtained for our aborted emigration to China were set to expire in May. They would not be valid for our departure to the US and needed to be renewed at once.

Most importantly, we needed to arrange transport once again, this time locating an ocean voyage to America. That was going to be tricky, as the ship had to leave from a neutral country. By now almost all of Europe was at war, and there were not many neutral countries left. Where would we leave from? How would we get to our point of embarkation? We could not fathom it. It was so complicated, and we had so much to do.

Back we went again, reprising our trek to the Central Jewish Organization to find passage on a ship. Still a scene of madness and desperation, possibly worse than last time, with throngs of people trying to find means of escape, we walked back out empty-handed. There was not an available ship anywhere. "What happens now, Mutti?" I asked.

"We just go back, Wolf. We go back every single day, until something comes up."

Demoralized, we returned to Schillerstrasse and dragged ourselves up to our apartment. At the top of the steps, the ever-polite Dr. Behne was waiting in front of our doorway. "Good evening, Frau Schwersenz," he said, his eyes downcast, his voice low.

"I suppose there is no whitefish this time, Dr. Behne," my mother said, wearily.

"I am so sorry, Frau Schwersenz. That time has come."

"Dr. Behne, surely there is something that can be done," begged my mother. "With any luck we will be leaving in a matter of months. Please, just give us a little more time. I beg you, do not put us out on the street. Isn't there anything you can think of to keep a roof over our heads?"

Dr. Behne came through with a temporary solution to delay our imminent eviction. He found a young Jewish couple who was also facing eviction and arranged for them to share the apartment. They moved their few belongings into Oma Ernestine's old room.

The presence of the young couple livened up the atmosphere a bit initially, but any real hopes for friendship or camaraderie were soon dashed. My mother seemed oddly cold around the woman, and behind the closed doors of their bedroom, I heard my parents arguing again. "That woman is constantly flirting with you, Arthur. It's so unseemly."

I had to cover my mouth to keep from laughing out loud. The way I saw it, my middle-aged, now nearly bald father had been the one doing the flirting. I suddenly realized it had been months, maybe even years since my parents had argued like this. They had been too busy trying to survive than to be concerned about petty jealousies. As I held my head against their bedroom door and listened to my mother complain about my father's lack of character, I felt oddly comforted. There was no better testimony to convince me: she thought we all might live.

While Mutti went back to the agency each day to try to procure tickets for any ship to the US, I continued to aimlessly roam the streets with Heinz. We had created our own independent little world without obligations or responsibilities. When I was with Heinz, there was no war, no bombs, and no death.

That freedom came to a halt one day, when my mother gave me a most odious task. "You need to make a condolence visit to your former classmate," she informed me. "Karl Ludwig's father died.[1]

"How did he die, Mutti?"

"He killed himself. It's terrible. He was a pharmacist!" She shook her head pityingly.

It turned out the man's profession had no relevance to this tragedy. In fact, he had not taken a single pill. Karl's father had decided to end his life by throwing himself off the roof of his six-floor building. "Suicide by jumping" had become a growing epidemic of late. The fathers were either hopeless, or were trying to exert their last vestiges of control and dignity. Sometimes it was hard to tell the motivation. One thing I knew: I desperately did not want to make this visit. My father was alive, and I could not face my former classmate. "Please, Mutti. I don't want to go. I don't even see Karl in school anymore."

"Do not beg, and do not plead, Wolf. This is not a choice; it is a moral obligation."

I dragged myself to the apartment where they sat *shiva*, the seven days of mourning after the funeral. My plan was to make it brief. Say a few words and get out. "My condolences," I said to Karl, meekly. "I'm so sorry, Frau Ludwig," I politely conveyed to his mother, while I surveyed my plan of escape. But as if held to the floor by magnets, my feet would not turn and leave. Karl's mother began to converse with me and as always, the dialogue meandered to the one and only thing on everyone's mind. "What are your plans?" she asked curtly.

She did not mean weekend plans, or summer plans, or career plans. There was only one kind of "plans" people ever spoke of these days. "We finally got our visas to the United States," I explained to her, timidly. Then I waited for her to wish me luck.

"It is much too late," she said, shaking her head. "You will never get out."

In April of 1941, we finally secured three tickets for the *Ciudad de Sevilla*. Embarking from Barcelona, Spain on July 22, the ship would make its last European stop at the port of Cadiz and then would head to the United States. It was scheduled to arrive in New York on July 31.

"Grete, that is insane. July 31 is the *exact* day our US visas are set to expire. The timing is way too close; it doesn't leave us any room for a single mishap. Think about it, Grete, we are in the middle of a war. How can this possibly work?"

"Arthur, I invite you to go down there yourself and try to get a ticket *anywhere*, on *any* ship. We should count ourselves lucky." But even my mother knew this was going to be tricky. We could not allow any piece of the scheme to crumble, or our entire emigration plan – and our lives – would be finished.

Over the next few weeks, we secured the rest of the bureaucratic paperwork we needed to make it to Barcelona. From the police, we obtained permission for a one-time passage out of Germany through occupied France and Vichy France between July 9 and August 9. We had a three-week transit visa allowing us to pass through Spain, effective July 19. The only thing we had not yet received was the exact date we were leaving Berlin by rail.

Summer rolled in, and we still did not have a date set for when we would be leaving Berlin. It started to get dangerously close to our ship's departure date, we were all in a constant state of nervous agitation. We had to get to Spain in time to set sail and before all our other transit visas expired. In the meantime, Germany's Army had not stopped advancing. In the weeks since we had gotten our tickets, it had invaded Russia, its former ally. Would the US be next to join the war? It was offering aid and seemed to be taking baby steps toward involvement. If the US entered the war, we feared that all our plans would be scrapped for good.

On July 5, we were finally issued our departure date out of Berlin: July 12, 1941. After all this waiting, now we had just seven days to finish packing up our entire lives.

Each adult was allowed to take one suitcase and 10 dollars in US currency. My parents made a list of the most valuable, sentimental, or useful items they planned to pack. Sorting through linens, photographs, and clothing, they tried to condense their entire lives into two rectangular satchels. They submitted the list to the appropriate officials for approval. Then they withdrew their 20 dollars in US currency and closed their bank accounts forever.

We weaved our way between overturned headstones and dirt-covered graves. It had taken two hours by trolley for Mutti and me to reach the Weissensee cemetery. Ransacked by the Nazis for scrap metal, the graves had been robbed of their respect as well as their metal ornaments. "Over there," Mutti pointed. In that mangled maze she had finally found the graves of my grandparents, Ernestine and Hiller, as well as Manfred, my infant brother of whom she never spoke. She bent over, clearing broken branches and tendrils of disobedient ivy. She wiped the headstone with her bare hand and placed a small stone on top. Then she stood tall again and I watched her lips move as she murmured quietly to herself – a prayer, or maybe just goodbye – and we turned and left. We would take the trolley back and finish the last of our errands in the four days we had left.

Our few treasured belongings lay at a depot in preparation for packing. The scant clothes, linens and photographs were stacked on a table while a Gestapo agent reviewed the items and compared them to a list previously submitted for government approval. He watched closely as each item was checked off and then packed. The bags were then sealed and turned over to a freight forwarding company, where they would be embossed with our name and address in white block letters. All this watching and checking and sealing ensured we could not smuggle valuables out of the country. We would not see our luggage again until departure day.

Paperwork, bureaucracy, luggage, money. We did it all with steely speed as the week marched relentlessly onwards. But the emotional farewells? Those we intentionally saved for the very end. We needed the hearts of our treasured human connections to stay alive and beating for as long as possible. They would not be packed up, sealed, or checked off. Not yet.

We had experienced the ache of abandonment and knew the heartbreak of being left behind. Now our piercing sadness was laced with guilt. Our remaining family and friends were not getting passage out. We filled our thoughts with fiction – that our loved ones would be resettled somewhere in the east. It was a fantasy to be sure, but it was the only belief we could live with.

At the end of the week, we began saying our farewells. Vati and I visited Aunt Frieda and her tall, imposing husband, Alfred, the jovial man who had intentionally miscounted my buttons years ago. I spent long breathless minutes in Frieda's enveloping bosom, letting tearful goodbyes replace our previous precious laughter. Then I traveled with my mother to see her cousin Ella Hammer. I watched her weep with Ella, unable to recall having ever seen my mother share such unrestrained emotion. With each goodbye we held each other longer than we needed to, as if holding tightly would bond our souls together, would make us not forget. With each farewell, we felt drained and broken as soon as we parted.

The very last day before we left, I ran across Bismarckstrasse and the four more blocks north until I reached the apartment of my beloved friend Heinz. *Bang! Bang! Bang!* I pummeled his door with both my fists, fearful I would not find him, that I would miss our only chance to say goodbye. And then the door finally opened. "We're leaving tomorrow, Heinz," I sputtered, still catching my breath between words.

We stood in the hallway, neither of us crying; for we were men now. On the spot, I took out my pocketknife and we each ceremoniously cut our fingers, so we could bravely shed blood instead of tears. Then we mixed our blood and swallowed it, tasting the metallic saltiness. "We're blood brothers, now and forever," I cried, passionately. We swore to each other our undying friendship and loyalty, and our hope for each other's survival. "We'll see each other again, after the war, I promise."

I said these things to Heinz, and he repeated them back to me, but we did not believe them. We were only comforting our own souls with our false promises, our unlikely illusions. I left him, my legs too heavy to run, the lump in my throat growing until I could not swallow; the pain in my chest rising until it hurt just to breathe.

Later that evening, the very night before our departure, we all went to see Siegfried and Irma. We had saved them for last on our list of farewells. "Goodbye," we tried to say to them, but they absolutely refused to even hear us. "No, no, don't be silly," laughed Siegfried, interrupting our words, his good nature masking any underlying sorrow. "Why rush it? We still have one more day. We will see you off at the train station tomorrow and say our goodbyes then."

They would not even hug and kiss us, saving all their final embraces and good wishes for departure day.

July 12, 1941. The day we are leaving Berlin.

There was a calm in the air as we arose in the morning, but also a strange sense of detachment and disbelief. Our departure would not feel real until the train had left the platform.

The mad rush of activities was over, and only a few remaining chores were left. We split up, with a plan to reconvene at the Anhalter Bahnhof platform, not far from Potsdamer Platz. I was given the job of going to the freight forwarding company to find our luggage and make sure our bags were marked with our name and ready to be checked out. I took one last look at the skeleton of our treasured apartment, the view from the balcony, and the courtyard with its pear tree, trying to sear the image into my mind. Then I left for good. My parents busied themselves with a few errands, and returned their keys to our kind and generous landlord, Dr. Behne.

At 3 p.m. we found each other at the train platform, and together we watched it slowly fill with the ragged-looking Jews who would be departing, along with their friends and family who had come to see them off. As the hour grew later, the crowd expanded until we had become a mass of bodies instead of individuals. Throngs of people had gathered on the platform. Travelers, onlookers, family – you could not tell which was which anymore, and a crescendo of chaos was slowly building.

"Where are they?" my mother asked anxiously, her neck bobbing up and down as she scoured the busy platform for Siegfried and Irma.

We searched and searched for my uncle and aunt, but we could not locate them amidst the frenzy of people. Then one of the railway workers drew two white lines on the ground; he was trying to separate the travelers from the spectators. The police and railway workers started pushing back the anxious crowds to each side of the lines so no one could cross over. Suddenly we were on one side of the line, and relatives and friends were on the other. And there. Over there! We saw them. There they were!

We spotted Siegfried's distinctive limp, and right next to him was Irma. They were just 30 yards away, but they were being held back on the other side of the white line. They were so close, but we could not reach them. We could not run to them. We could not touch them. We could not feel the musty warmth of their skin. We could not hear their voices while making empty promises to see them again. We could not taste their tears or hold them just a little too long.

All we could do was wave.

13

ONE IF BY RAIL

We congregated on the plaza with our fellow passengers until we were about 85 people in all. What a spectacle we made, confused and frightened, shabby, and sad, standing on the street with our worn, marked-up luggage. We stood on the plaza, feeling exposed and exhausted and ashamed. No one could find a key for the room where we were supposed to have an orientation and review of our papers, so we just stood there, confused.

It was already approaching five o'clock, and a new crowd of German onlookers was forming across the street as the workday was coming to an end. "Filthy Jews!" they hollered. The large group started to close in and began spitting at us. We stood defenselessly, expecting to be attacked and beaten. Where were the railway workers now, who had been restraining all our family members? Gone. Disappeared, somehow, unable to hold back this mob. Just in time, the missing key to the orientation room appeared, and like a school of fish, we turned as a unit, and poured into the room. Temporarily far from the madding crowd, we shut the door and the mayhem behind us.

Here was all the information we needed: 85 of us were to be seated in a single, sealed railway car within a larger passenger train crossing war-torn, occupied Europe. A metal placard inscribed with the words "*Juden Transport*" would be nailed to the outside of our car. It would be terrible and frightening. Orientation complete.

It was not until 8 p.m. that the train finally left the Anhalter station. Eight of us crammed into the compartment along with our luggage and our heavy hearts as the train began its journey westbound. Packed with bodies, with a sealed window in the peak of summer, it was stifling hot. As the only child in the compartment, I was given a seat by the window, and I read the signs as we passed through each station out of central Berlin: Grunewald, Babelsberg, Potsdam. Soon we would not be in Germany at all, but no one was willing to let out a breath of relief yet, for we had over 1,600 kilometers (1,000 miles) to go through a war-torn Europe. We understood we were the lucky ones, for "*Juden Transport*" trains were traveling through Germany to the east, to a far different fate. Yes, we knew we were lucky, but we were not joyous. The car remained eerily silent.

The sun settled somewhere behind the square frame of my window. The sky dulled to a purplish gray, and finally we were enveloped in darkness. After an immeasurable distance, the train slowed and came to a halt. "Why are we stopping, Vati?" I whispered. "Do we need to show our papers?"

"No, Wolf, we are stopped for the night at a rail siding. It is just a precaution. The train's locomotive is powered by coal, and in the dark, the fire can be spotted by enemy warplanes. It is safer to avoid traveling at night. Try to sleep. In the morning, when daylight arrives, we will begin our journey again."

At dawn, the train resumed its journey west, zipping through tiny Luxembourg, and then into occupied France. We were out of Germany, but no one felt safe with most of Europe at war. We ate nothing; drank nothing. No one had tasted a bite of food since lunch the day before, but accustomed as we were to hunger and deprivation, there were no complaints. At nightfall, we were shunted into a siding again, and all signs of fire in the engine were extinguished.

Another night passed uneventfully. We slept upright in our seats, crammed so tightly against the bodies beside us that we did not even fall over. All these nighttime stops would extend a normally two-day journey to Spain to nearly four days.

The next day at dawn we started our journey again. By nine o'clock on the morning of July 14, we arrived at a major railway station in Paris and the first signs of civilization appeared outside our window. The station seemed to be bustling with life, but sealed inside our car, we could do nothing but sit passively and wait.

Finally, a group of Red Cross workers walked up to our car. *"Bonjour, bonjour,"* they called to us brightly, in sing-song French, with grace notes of enthusiasm and kindness. They had brought with them long, thin loaves of fresh French bread which they slid through the windows of our car like important mail. I had never seen a baguette before, accustomed to dense, chewy brown German breads. How graceful and elegant these crisp tan loaves were; the deceptively solid-looking batons that broke into soft and steamy white centers. They were simply marvelous. The volunteers passed us coffee and milk to drink, and in my hungry state, it seemed like the most delicious breakfast I had ever eaten.

Click. It was at that moment, at the Paris station, I felt a sudden change. It was as if someone had flipped a switch. I tasted the new food; listened to the exotic French language that I did not understand; I watched the hustle and bustle of the Red Cross workers.

Click. The switch flipped again. I could feel my anxiety abate. My earlier feeling of worried detachment dissipated. Something had rekindled my excitement and imagination.

Click. I am on a train. I am traveling.

Click. I am off on an adventure.

And although our third day passed without any food again and with no more exciting distractions, I felt neither bored nor hungry, nervous nor afraid.

By day four of our journey, we were nearing our last hurdle. In just a few hours, we were scheduled to reach the French border crossing point at Hendaye near the Pyrenees. This would be our last crossing out of German-occupied territory. All our paperwork would be examined. Each of the authorizations and permissions to leave Germany and enter Spain. Our luggage would have to be unsealed and examined as well. Everything would have to be perfect.

There was a nervous buzz in the air of our train car. I could see that everyone in our car was getting anxious. We all knew that the slightest irregularity in our papers or luggage would result in being detained, or worse – being sent back to Germany. And since none of us had German citizenship any longer – we had only been given permission for this one single departure from Germany – being sent back meant being sent directly to a concentration camp. Internment or death awaited us; of that we were certain. Of course, everyone was nervous.

The agitation and activity that were building in our car seemed unusually intense, however. Could this really be just a concern about paperwork irregularities? There were conversations and murmurs. Worried whispering. People were getting up and sitting down. Getting up again. They were pacing, anxiously. Suddenly, men started ripping open their clothing. And then we saw that a few passengers on our journey had hidden money, jewelry, and other valuable items that they had not declared to the Nazis. They had sewn these items into the lining of their clothes. And some people, we heard, had swallowed diamonds which they hoped to recover in their shit when they arrived at their destination.

I slowly turned to my father. I stared at him questioningly, beseechingly, and so did my mother. Vati shook his head. "Don't worry," he reassured us, smiling. This time, thank goodness, my father had not done anything foolish.

As we got closer to the border, the "smugglers" in our car began to really panic. Suddenly having second thoughts, some took the money and jewelry they had hidden and began throwing them out of the car window. The terror became truly contagious. Passengers started discarding their valuables and fellow travelers followed suit. As the train traveled through its last miles, the countryside became littered with a trail of clothing, jewelry, and money, like artifacts of a forgotten civilization.

We finally reached the Basque town of Hendaye. The train

stopped and we disembarked, solemnly carrying our suitcases to the inspection site. We declared what little currency we had. The French rifled through our suitcases while the Germans stood grimly behind them as back-up enforcers. The whole process took about two hours. We reboarded the train and waited in silence while nothing at all happened.

Our boredom was abruptly disturbed by the sound of a loudspeaker. It crackled at first, and then hissed with abrasive feedback. A series of announcements started. It was hard to make out at first, but then we realized that names were being called out. *What did it mean,* we wondered apprehensively? We knew it could not be good and held our breath with dread as about a half dozen names were announced: "Kaufmann, Eisenberg, Schwartz, Lieberman, Silverstein, Kahn." These were the people who were being detained. They got up and left the train and we did not see them again.

Only when we realized our name had not been called, did we finally exhale. Every single person on that train whose name was not called felt the same sense of relief. We hung our heads in shame and no one made eye contact. We had to conceal that we were happy, that we did not know what happened to those people who had left the train and at that moment, we did not care. We just thought, *thank God, not us.*

The train crawled out of the station and proceeded just a short distance over the border until it was on the Spanish side, at Irun. We stopped and disembarked once again to make sure we had appropriate temporary visas for Spain as well as visas to proceed to another country. As Jews, we could not stay in Spain permanently. The Spaniards were willing to facilitate our escape, but they didn't want us staying in their country either.

We remained at the station in Irun for an impossibly long time. Across the platform, General Franco's fighters, the "Black Brigade" were boarding a train headed east. They were bound for Russia, to help Hitler. The young soldiers were dressed in nothing but lightweight cotton uniforms. "How will they ever survive the Russian winter?" my mother asked aloud as she shook her head with a rush of concern. "They will get frostbite, like Siegfried."

We finally boarded a local Spanish train headed for the resort town of San Sebastian del Mar on the Bay of Biscay, along the northern coast of Spain near the French border. The moment the train began moving again, we felt as though a weight that had been with us for years had been lifted off us. We felt as light as mountain air; we felt giddy, we felt *alive*.

Our stay in the gorgeous oceanside resort town San Sebastian would be all too brief. We disembarked from the bus that had brought us from the train station and were greeted by a small cadre of Spanish-speaking volunteers. The eclectic assortment of do-gooders were there to help arrange for our hotel and travel. They included Quakers as well as former Jews who had been baptized and converted to Christianity – a requirement to be allowed to live in Spain. The volunteers had been working tirelessly with Jewish agencies to coordinate the exodus of Jews from Europe. We would come to rely heavily on these kind humanitarians in the days to come.

It was time to sort us out, arrange our transportation, and send us to hotels. But our little band of railway refugees seemed to have become possessed. It was as if the sudden freedom had overcome them. When it was time for hotel assignments, bedlam broke out, and all decency and kindness seemed to evaporate into the ocean air. Each person started jockeying for the best boarding situation for himself and turmoil quickly ensued.

My father became horrified by everyone's behavior. "Everyone, everyone!" he yelled out. No one paid him any mind; they were too busy arguing over their accommodations. "Settle down. Quiet!" he called out, louder, this time. Vati grabbed the bowler hat that had been inside his suitcase. It was a bit crushed, but he put it on his head anyway. Indeed, he looked more authoritative (not to mention, taller), but he still could not get anyone's attention. He needed some kind of platform, something that would give him even more height, so that people would finally listen. Vati looked around, and then he spotted a nice mound of mud and straw. It was perfect. He climbed on top and looking very smug, began his speech. "People!" he bellowed. "We must behave better than this. Where is our decency! Our camaraderie!"

The people were tired. They did not seem at all thrilled with this pedantic moral lecture. I looked at their faces and could practically see them thinking, "*Who does this guy think he is? Isn't he one of us? Who gives him the right to take charge and meddle? And what is that tiny man wearing? A silly crushed bowler hat? He is ridiculous!*" I knew that's what they were thinking, because that's what I was thinking too.

I looked around and I started to see people snicker. Then I looked down at the mud hill my father was standing on. Vati had somehow managed to mount a giant pile of manure. He was giving his speech of a lifetime on top of a pile of horseshit. I looked over at my mother, and she looked back at me, shaking her head. At that moment, I saw my father with open eyes. It was the first time, but not the last, that I was ashamed of him.

The group eventually got itself sorted out. With great luck, we were assigned to an elegant waterfront resort. Our room had a large terrace and a view of the shimmering turquoise sea. I stood on that terrace and breathed in the warm ocean air and thought I had never seen anything quite as beautiful.

There was still plenty of time to spare before the late Spain dinner hour. We cleaned ourselves up and walked along the promenade at the water's edge while watching the engorging summer sun begin to set in a pink evening sky. Later, we returned to the opulent dining room and feasted on a meal of beef, potatoes, and vegetables, served with red wine and fruit for dessert. It was the first full meal we could remember eating in years and to us it tasted like food for the gods. Returning to our room well-sated, we climbed into our soft, smooth beds, and descended into sleep.

We experienced only one night of luxury in our Spanish seaside refuge. The next day we all packed onto buses once again. The bus dropped us off at a local Spanish train that was much older and more arthritic than the German train that had transported us across Europe. It creaked and groaned across the neck of Spain, as it carted us from a beautiful Atlantic bay clear across the Spanish peninsula. Heading south, the scenery became progressively browner and the temperature warmer as we headed toward the Mediterranean to our port of departure in Barcelona.

We arrived in Barcelona towards evening and our group of refugees once again split up into different small hotels. There was no luxury this time; only tiny, austere hotels on the back roads of the city. And the weather hit us with all its weight. Such stifling heat and humidity! We had never experienced anything like it before.

The thick and heavy air seemed almost too tired to circulate. We settled in our tiny fan-less hotel room, salty sweat dribbling down our necks and gathering above our lips and on our chests. We greedily sipped from the one little bottle of seltzer water that had been given to us for drinking and brushing our teeth. "Do not drink the tap water in Barcelona," we had been warned. "It is not potable."

Exhausted though we were from our travels, we had every reason to be optimistic. So far, the timing had been working out with precision. We had arrived in Barcelona right on schedule, on July 17, and we would board the *Ciudad de Sevilla* on July 22. We would arrive in New York on July 31, the day our visa expired. Everything was still going according to plan. Like clockwork. All we had to do now was wait and wander.

We had four full days to explore this hot, exotic city of Barcelona, in the heart of the Catalan. Like leisurely tourists, Vati and I left our hotel in the morning and walked to the waterfront. We passed streets lined by elegant palms, each one slowly swaying back and forth in the tropical breeze, like a lazy metronome. We watched truck after truck drive up from the pier carrying bright green bananas transported from Africa. Young boys would wait for the trolley to come up the street and then hitch a free ride, hanging onto the outside with strong, spindly limbs. The scene gave me a pang of melancholy as I imagined Heinz and me hanging off the trolley car. I closed my eyes and could envision us hanging on and leaning back and feeling the warm, humid breeze in our hair... and then I shook the image away and snapped back to the present.

Just one block past the tourist thoroughfares – the hotels and the beautiful palms, past the tropical beauty and the ocean and the bananas – were telltale signs of war. The brutal Spanish civil war had ended just two years before, and Barcelona had been the center of support to the former monarchy, while resisting the current dictator of Spain, General Franco.

One had only to scratch the sparkling surface to see that homes and people were in ruins. Men stood with crutches, wrapped in bandages, missing the requisite number of limbs. Malnourished children with large, sunken eyes and swollen bellies lined the sultry sidewalks. Hollowed-out homes stood resting on their bare foundations, while the hulls of burnt-out ships filled the harbor. There was poverty on every corner, on every street.

Vati and I roamed the ramshackle roads until we grew too hot and tired; then we journeyed just outside of town into the surrounding mountains to find shelter from the sun. We came upon caves that were used as fortifications, or sometimes escape routes, during the civil war. The cooler air was a welcome relief from the stifling summer air of the city. We walked through the caves, making sure to avoid touching the walls that were still smeared rusty red with the bloodstains of slain soldiers.

My mother begged us to not take these excursions, but we did not heed her. We left her behind in the hotel where she continued to worry about our health and safety. Each day as we left, she admonished us, "Do not touch the sick people! Do not eat food off the street! Do not drink the water!"

We did as we were told. We only ate meals at the hotel when we returned at night. The food teased us with delectable looking, thinly sliced meat that was actually tough as leather. I chewed and chewed but my teeth could not get through it. But the fruit – how delicious it was! What a bounty of pineapple, oranges, bananas, plums! We had no complaints. We ate and we ate, and we ate.

We ate and we waited. We waited for our ship's departure as if in a state of purgatory, killing time in the tropical heat. And then one day, our luck ran out.

The bad news arrived as if on cue. The *Ciudad* was going to be delayed by one day. Its arrival in New York would now be on August 1.

It was as simple as it was catastrophic. *One single day*. Our visas to the US would be expired by then.

We would not be allowed to board the ship.

"*Mein Gott*, Arthur, what do we do?"

There wasn't much time left. As soon as our temporary transit visa for Spain expired, we would be sent back to Germany. And we were desperate.

"There is nothing we can do here in Barcelona, Grete. They don't even have a US consulate here. We must get a visa extension for the US on the Polish quota. It's the only option."

"But we will never be able to get a visa extension in time to board the *Ciudad*."

"That is correct, Grete. Not only do we need a new visa, but we need to find a new ship. And we must get ourselves to a city that has a US consulate. We've got to get all this done before Spain kicks us out."

It sounded impossible. We were citizens of nowhere, wanted by no one, with no place to go. How would we ever be able to pull it off?

Then came the smallest glimmer of hope. It was the only

remaining possibility of rescue. The local Spanish volunteers were able to find another ship headed to the United States, departing from Seville on August 6. There was a US consulate in Seville that might be able to help us get new, extended visas while we waited for the ship to set sail. The whole scheme would take luck and a prayer, but right now we had nothing else. Absolutely nothing. The industrious volunteer workers immediately started arranging for our travel to Seville, and passage for three on the new Spanish ship, the *Navemar*.

There was not a minute to think; this was our only option, our only hope. Quickly changing course, we haphazardly threw our few sweaty belongings into our luggage and converted our fear and uncertainty into action. With no direct routes to Seville, we boarded a train headed to Madrid for the first leg of a two-day journey. And we were off again.

If we had hoped to hurtle forward, we had to change our expectations entirely, for this train seemed to be taking the turtle's tour to Madrid. We creaked and crawled our way through the desert landscape and eventually settled into the sluggish pace. Gradually we became aware that we were hungry, for in the mad rush of our morning departure, we had not found time to eat.

Around midday, we pulled into a busy station. Out of my window I could see that numerous food vendors filled the platform. They sold Spanish foods that were unfamiliar; many looked frighteningly fishy. Eventually I caught sight of food that looked comfortingly recognizable: a huge roll with slices of slippery salami hanging generously over the sides. It was staring back at me enticingly and it looked delicious. I looked to my mother for approval. "Please, can we, Mutti?" I begged.

"Wolf, we only have 20 dollars. We must be very judicious about how we spend our money."

I turned to my more indulgent father. "Let's get it, Vati, please. It's loaded with salami, and it's big enough for all of us to share."

Vati was hungry too. Whistling between two fingers, he

beckoned to the sandwich vendor who quickly ran up to our train window. After Vati paid, he pulled the overstuffed sandwich through the train window just as the train began to roll out of the station.

How excited we all were to have familiar food to sate our hunger. Vati tore open the paper and even Mutti looked at the large sandwich approvingly; it was good value. The puffy white roll was enormous. Slick salami slices draped luxuriously over its edges. Vati opened the sandwich... but *¡Dios mio!* – we had been duped! Salami slices lined only the outside edge of the sandwich. On the inside, there was nothing but bread.

We stayed in Madrid overnight, and in the morning, transferred to another train. In our car, we were joined by two other couples who also had expiring visas on the Polish quota. Our new train headed southwest, through the heart of Spain. Seven restless refugees now stared out the window, watching the arid land turn more fertile. As olive trees, orchards, and fields of wheat emerged, the flat, lifeless color of the desert transformed to shades of gold and green. The train finally reached its destination, and we disembarked in the exotic city of Seville.

I felt as though I had arrived in an alien paradise.

Seville was a city awash with color and brightness, where tropical trees and red bougainvillea lined the streets and relentless sun shone in blinding whiteness. The beauty of my surroundings was only surpassed by the people, each one more glamorous than the next. Luxurious dark hair flowed like waves of liquid lava down the coffee-colored backs of the alluring women, while the handsome, tan-skinned men whistled and stared at them without restraint.

Once again, we found ourselves with time to spare, and Vati and I roamed the streets of Seville like tantalized tourists. Meandering through the maze-like streets, we marveled at the Moorish-style homes, dazzling in their painted white coats. Sometimes we were able to catch a glimpse of a secret inner courtyard that might house an elaborate tiled fountain, a lush garden, or a bird sanctuary. Along the neighborhood of Santa Cruz where the streets were so narrow that the buildings nearly touched, Vati explained how the once thriving Jewish neighborhood had been purged of all its Jewish inhabitants during the Spanish Inquisition. "Are Jews always being thrown out of their own country, Vati?" I asked.

"Yes, Wolf. When it comes to the Jews, history keeps repeating itself."

In the morning, we followed hordes of pedestrians and shoppers to the bustling center of town marked by its massive cathedral. White canvases hung between the buildings, shading the busy, narrow streets from the dazzling sun. After lunch, the streets suddenly went dead silent. Not a single soul was to be seen during the strictly observed siesta.

The city woke from its self-imposed slumber in the evenings. It aroused itself slowly at first, like a cat stretching its paws after a nap. Young men sitting on benches pulled out their guitars; they perched the instruments on their knees and began to sing. As if by magic, men and women appeared out of nowhere; they trickled out onto the empty streets, filling them with life. While the men strummed their guitars, the women began dancing expressively to flamenco music; the beat picked up and they fired their fan-like clacking castanets while they danced. A loosely formed audience clapped or joined in the dancing while throbbing, exciting rhythms reverberated throughout the city.

I was mesmerized by this sensory spectacle. It was like a drug. I wanted to linger on this alien planet and forget about everything else. Forget visas. Forget trains and ships and consulates. Forget all of it. I had had enough. But I had to snap out of my state of intoxication. We had to deal with practical matters. Each morning, we trekked to the US consulate in Seville. "Have our new visas to the US come through yet?" we asked.

Not yet. Enviously, we looked on as a dozen people on the

German quota got new visas within a day or two. Those of us on the Polish quota waited and worried. And all of us prayed, whether or not we had ever believed in God before.

There was only one person who could help us and that was the US consul in Seville. We knew we were completely at his mercy; we would live or die by his decisions. Yet we sensed something different about this man. He seemed unlike any of the bureaucrats we had ever met before. We could hear it in his voice, and we could see it in his eyes: he seemed to genuinely care about our welfare and was making every effort to help us. Each and every day he telegraphed Washington, D.C. Over and over, he said to us, "Do not give up hope."

But by Friday August 3, our visas still had not come.

It was a blistering hot morning, and we had returned from our daily trip to the consulate, frustrated and dejected. The *Navemar* was scheduled to depart the following Monday, August 6, and it looked as though it would be leaving without us.

We decided to visit the *Navemar*, as if simply staring at the ship could somehow compel it to take us aboard. The freighter ships in Seville were secured along the Guadalquivir River. We followed a single rail track as it wound its way to the riverbank. At its end, a solitary crane used for loading cargo stood like a giant heron balancing on one leg. Just across from it, we spotted the *Navemar*, sitting high out of the water like a colossal whale that had come up for air. Tied tightly to the stone embankment with thick, heavy ropes, it seemed like it was waiting to be set free.

My mother gazed at the empty ship. "So this is it," she sighed. "We have come all this way. So much waiting, so much traveling. So many days. And now, after all this, can you believe it? We will be turned back."

"There is nothing more we can do, Grete. If they send us back to Germany, it may still be okay. They'll probably send us east. Maybe we can even be with Siegfried."

I knew Vati was probably lying, but it was still comforting to hear those words. We stood staring at our last chance at rescue, but it was time to face the truth. After everything we had done, we had still failed. We would not be getting out of Europe.

Later that same day, the equally demoralized US Consul was unable to secure our extended visas. However, he had made a promise not to give up on us. He just needed to devise an alternate plan. Sitting down to his typewriter, he quickly drafted a letter granting us permission to board the *Navemar* despite not having valid entry papers. It was not really an official document, and he wasn't positive it would work. All he needed was for the crew of the *Navemar* to believe it.

"The *Navemar* will be making a stop in Lisbon, Portugal," he explained to us. "That gives us a tiny window of time until the ship leaves port to cross the Atlantic. During that time, I promise, I will work tirelessly with the State Department in Washington, D.C. to issue the visas necessary for all of you." He said all these words with the sincerity of a man who truly meant them.

This man – whose name I will never know – saved our lives.

14

ACROSS THE ATLANTIC

We now had something of priceless value – time.

It was only a first step, but at least the document that allowed us to board the ship would buy us valuable time to apply for a visa extension for United States entry. There were no guarantees, but finally, our desperation turned into hope again.

We were now three of the nearly 1,200 people scheduled to board the *Navemar* that Monday, August 6, 1941. Mutti was not going to wait until Monday. She wanted to guarantee that we had a place on that ship. She must have been imagining being turned away by the crew on boarding day. "Sorry, we're full," they would tell us.

"There is certain to be mayhem when everyone boards," she explained. She suggested we board on Sunday. After all we had been through, we wholeheartedly went along with her plan.

The day before we boarded, my father judiciously considered how we would spend our limited cash. He decided to buy a long, hard salami. "A smoked meat can survive the heat. It should last the entire journey."

That Sunday, holding tightly to our precious documents, our tickets, our two suitcases, and our one-pound salami, the three of us made our way to the *Navemar*. We climbed up the steep gangplank until we were just outside the ship's entrance. An officer checked and doublechecked our tickets. He took the hastily crafted document from the consulate out of our hands. We held our breath while he read it over and over again. Then he pointed to the entrance and allowed us to board.

As soon as we boarded the *Navemar*, we got totally lost. Since we had come a day early, there were no other passengers, and no organized "welcoming" committee. We had absolutely no idea where to proceed, and the ship seemed massive. Furthermore, we were not on a passenger ship and there were essentially no cabins. We were in a giant freighter with cargo holds. We suddenly wondered, where would 1,200 of us go? Where would we sleep, eat, go to the bathroom? We could not fathom it.

A Spanish officer passed by. He muttered something to us in rapidly fired Spanish, but Vati could not understand him. Another nearby sailor pointed toward a steep ladder. We nodded gratefully and headed that way.

Mutti and I cautiously climbed down the ladder. Once we had landed safely in the hold below, Vati proceeded down the ladder next. He was carrying both pieces of luggage in one hand, and managed to negotiate the ladder with the other. No sooner did his feet hit the floor, than a crew member in the hold shook his head vigorously. "No, no, señor," he said in heavily accented English. "You go back up. Is wrong place."

Back up the ladder we went. My mother led the way and I followed, with Vati again holding up the rear. "Señor, wait," the same crew member called out to my father. "I help you, I help you."

"No, no! Thank you," Vati stuttered, using his very limited knowledge of English. I knew he would be too proud to accept any help with his luggage, but I could see that he was struggling; it was much harder to climb up a ladder with one hand than to go down. I had made it to the top when I heard the crash below. The laughter came next. When I finally summoned the courage to look down, there was Vati, lying on the floor, arms flailing, our suitcases on top of him.

I shook my head in disbelief, and blushing with embarrassment, turned away. Vati must have accepted an offer of help, for he soon came up the ladder behind a crew member and we continued with our interior shipping "tour." This time, we were redirected down a different vertical ladder, and then another, and another. We kept descending until it seemed as though we must be nearly at the bottom of the ship in the bowels of the freighter.

"*Aquí,*" said the sailor. "Here."

Here it was at last. We had finally gotten to our hold, and Vati and I tentatively peered inside. The hold, which normally carried scrap iron, coal, and rubber – had been refashioned for its outsized human cargo. Rows of six-foot-by-six-foot plywood bunks were lined up as far as the eye could see. They were stacked three tiers high, and each had a thin straw palette and a straw-filled pillowcase. There were 280 berths in our hold, and there were three other holds just like this one on the ship. I looked around for any portholes or other forms of ventilation, but there were none, for we were well below water level.

"How much did we pay for our tickets, Vati?" I asked as I evaluated our dismal accommodations.

"For this luxury?" Vati answered, with a short laugh. "Our tickets cost 500 dollars each!"[1]

The *Navemar* was never intended to be a passenger ship. It had cabin space for just 15 passengers and about 25 crew members, just seven bathrooms and seven showers, and only one refrigerated room designed to store perishables for up to 40 people. There was no place they could store fresh food for 1200 of us. How they would feed us seemed incomprehensible.

By noon on Monday, all the passengers had boarded the freighter, and our luggage had been thrown into a hold in the hull of the ship. The moment had finally arrived for our departure. The crew untied the heavy ropes, and we began a slow glide down the mud brown Guadalquivir River.

I stood on the top deck as we floated lazily along the slow current. From my high perch, I imagined I was on top of my old apartment building and the building itself was floating to freedom. I peered down to the river. Narrow at first, it was flanked on both sides by rust-colored flat land speckled with intermittent islands of green vegetation. The river began to widen as we approached its mouth. Then suddenly we were on the open ocean. We sailed through the Gulf of Cadiz and then turned north and slid up the Portuguese coast on our way to Lisbon.

That first night at sea, Vati and I descended into the hold hoping for sleep. Vati's bunk was just next to mine, with bunks so narrow and so close together that our bodies were nearly touching. With 280 bodies piled together, no ventilation, and no air movement, it was brutally hot. The smell of other sweating human bodies was overpowering. I thought I could even smell the salami sweating. I tossed and turned, but sleep would simply not come. My mind was racing. "Where is the salami, Vati?" I asked, nervously.

"Do not worry, little Wolf. I have hidden it inside the mattress for safekeeping. This salami must last the entire journey. I will guard it with my life."

Morning came, with little sleep to show for it. Hot and exhausted, Vati and I waited in the endless line to use one of the seven bathrooms and then headed to breakfast. Out meals were served in a galley that was nothing more than another hold at the bottom of the ship lined with rows and rows of long wooden tables. Mutti joined us there; she had spent her own sleepless night in a hold for women. Together, we squeezed onto a long wooden bench and waited to be fed.

The hold was packed tight with tired, bedraggled-looking people. Almost all of them were adults; I saw almost no other children besides me. A few pregnant women, who looked supremely uncomfortable, sat with us at the tightly packed tables.

Every now and then, I heard the insistent cries of an unhappy baby.[2]

One Spanish-speaking crew member served our long table that morning. He wiped his sweaty forehead with his hairy arm as he passed out plates that were unpleasantly sticky. But the freshly baked Spanish wheat bread he served us was surprisingly lovely, fragrant and warm. We ate it with very salty butter – something we had never eaten before – and jam, and we drank strong black coffee with scalded milk. The freshly baked bread on board was always abundant and it would sustain us on our journey.

We went above deck after breakfast and watched as our freighter entered Lisbon harbor. Now our waiting time would begin again.

We sat in port in a state of limbo. No one was allowed to leave the ship. Yet sometime later that morning, six more scrawny passengers managed to board the ship. Like us, they were somewhat pathetic in appearance. And like us, our new passengers also had no valid visas for passage. But they weren't going to need any, for these travelers were never going to make it all the way to America.

"What are they, Mutti?" I asked. "What are they doing here?"

"Well, they have four legs each, and long curved horns," she replied. "I am pretty sure they're oxen, and I think they are going to become our supper on this journey."

Now we understood how the *Navemar* crew had solved its problem of inadequate refrigeration – by bringing our food on board alive. The animals would be slaughtered as needed. As the day progressed, the crew hastily built a makeshift pen and placed it in the most desirable corner of the outside deck. By the time they had finished, the oxen's accommodations seemed far more appealing than our own hold.

"Are you thinking what I am thinking?" Vati asked, turning toward me. I nodded in conspiratorial agreement. After such an abysmal night, we needed to consider new quarters. Staking out a little square of real estate on the deck, we surrounded ourselves with a canvas tarpaulin, and dragged our pallets, pillows, blankets, and bare necessities into our new lodgings. Many of the other passengers had the same idea. One by one they came out of the holds and claimed a little area for their family. Some even managed to claim a desirable spot inside the lifeboats. Slowly, the passengers filled each available space, until eventually the deck looked like a floating refugee camp.

We were to stay in Lisbon until August 16, after which the *Navemar* would set sail across the Atlantic. This stop was our final chance. If our new visas to the US did not arrive by August 16, this portside purgatory was where our passage out of Europe would end.[3]

That night, as I sat down in the galley to eat supper, I smelled something delicious. I looked at the tables near me; it looked like a delicious stew was being served family style. I was so hungry! I watched impatiently as the other long tables got their food and were already eating their first hot supper on board. Finally, the crewman made his way to us and the stew was served.

My father grabbed the ladle and scooped up a big helping of steaming meat, potatoes, carrots, and silken brown gravy. Just as Vati was about to tilt the ladle onto his plate, my mother grabbed his arm in midair. "Do not touch that meat!" she shrieked. She was practically shaking; and she said the words with such intensity, one would think our very lives were at stake. "It's the ox; they have slaughtered it! I don't like the way it looks, and I don't like the way it smells."

"Grete, enough already! We all need to eat. It's for our very survival."

I had to agree with Vati. I was salivating, the food was right in front of me, and everyone else at our table was eating. There was no holding me back. "Please, Mutti. Don't make us wait."

"I forbid you to eat it!" she yelled again. Those were strong words, even for my mother. But that night, while everyone filled their bellies with rich oxen stew, we listened to her as always and ate only buttered bread.

In the daytime, docked in port, we were prisoners of the ship, unable to leave without an official purpose. We sat idly, slowly baking in the feverish heat, feeling safer on that boat despite the awful conditions, than anywhere else we could be at that moment. On August 13, our sixth day in port, we were suddenly summoned, with no reason provided. Hastily abandoning our makeshift refugee base camp, we filed down the multi-stepped plank where a motorboat awaited us. We were transported under guard to the mainland, and – still chaperoned by soldiers – loaded onto a bus. "That's that," declared my mother in a whisper. "They are putting us on a train and hauling us back to Germany." She sounded unemotional; resigned to our fate.

A half-hour bus ride later, we stopped in front of a nondescript building. An American flag waved proudly in front. It was the US consulate! After passing a cursory physical (no hernia! no measles!), we were handed US Visas 80, 81 and 82 on the Polish quota.

On August 16, we pulled anchor and left Lisbon, beginning our cross-Atlantic journey to the US. All we had to do was stay alive, and it would be harder than we ever imagined.

We began our voyage across the Atlantic. The seas were calm, the heat relentless. There was no escape from the glare of the summer sun. My fair skin boiled and blistered, then finally burned. Large swaths of dead skin as sheer as moth wings peeled off my arms and shoulders in sheets, leaving behind a mosaic of raw pink skin. When numerous passengers on deck succumbed to sunstroke, the captain ordered canvas tarps to be strung above deck. This gave us temporary relief from our solar suffering, but the tarps created such wind drag that the already slow-moving ship came to a complete halt. The next morning, the tarps came down and we were destined to fry in the sun for the remainder of the journey.

Severe diarrhea struck the first of the ship's passengers almost as soon as we left port. There were circulating rumors that it was cholera, but the unrelenting cramps, bleeding and fever told a different gastrointestinal story. Dysentery, possibly typhoid fever.[4] Not as bad as cholera, but it could be deadly too.

On the fourth day of our voyage, we spotted land to the starboard side of the ship. Four green mountainous islands, the Azores, seemed to emerge right out of the water, like the humped back of a giant sea monster. The passengers headed starboard to delight in the change of scenery, but I eventually grew bored with the endless island greenery. I drifted over to the port side of the ship, where I saw a submarine – perhaps even a German U-boat – briefly surface. The sub tracked the *Navemar* for several miles, eyeing us like a primitive predator, until it seemed to lose interest and disappeared into the depths of the sea.

As our voyage continued, the seas remained placid, but on board it was anything but peaceful. Dysentery spread like wildfire, and hundreds of voyagers took ill. Passengers became so sick with diarrhea and dehydration that they could not get out of their beds in the holds. They lay in their excrement, day after day, getting weaker and slowly dying. The comingled smells of excrement and death hung in the air. To inhale it was overwhelming and no healthy people went into the holds anymore.

By now, everyone who was able to move, had relocated to the open deck or into the lifeboats. We were all packed in, over a thousand of us on deck. Refugee next to refugee, body next to body, with garbage and waste piling up in the spaces between us. The crew went on a cleaning strike and we became a mass of refugees and refuse. Steadily, conditions began to deteriorate until they became unfit for living.

How do we escape the dysentery aboard the ship? That became my parents' one and only obsession. Obsession turned to fear and fear to paranoia. Packed on board in the heat without sanitation, it would be nearly impossible. And what was safe to consume? Nobody knew. My mother's neuroses and some good common sense guided her, and she devised an eating plan for us. Handing out instructions like an Army colonel, she announced, "For breakfast, we will eat as much bread as possible, and we will steal additional bread and butter for later in the day. In mid-afternoon

Vati will distribute paper-thin slivers of salami so we will have some protein. The salami will have to last the entire trip. Whenever we dine in the galley, we will eat only vegetables and bread. Nothing else. Do you hear me? Nothing! We can only drink tea since the water is boiled, and we are to stay oxen-free, come hell or high water!"

The first death occurred on the fourth day on our voyage. It was on August 19, shortly after we spotted the Azores. One of the oxen had apparently died. We were told it was from "natural causes" and the beast was quickly thrown into the sea. It was not a human death. Still, it was a bad omen.

The next death occurred on August 20. This time, it was a human – a 70-year-old woman who had succumbed to dysentery. A burial at sea was planned, and Vati volunteered to be a makeshift pallbearer. A brief funeral was held in the dark of the night before the body was delivered into the ocean.

Vati's new role as pallbearer placed him at the hub of *Navemar* gossip and information. "You have no idea what I learned last night!" he boasted the following morning.

I hungered for any news to break the monotony. "Tell me, Vati."

"Where do I start. Well, Wolf, first I learned that some people paid up to 1,500 dollars for their ticket. That is triple what we paid! Some thought they were getting a private cabin! I also heard that the captain has vacated his own cabin and is charging 2,000 dollars per person to anyone who can fit himself in it. And, apparently, some poor souls who bought tickets found themselves with no place to sleep at all. They found that their berth had been sold and resold to three different people! It doesn't matter now, I suppose, since most of us are on deck. But I guess when all is said and done, Wolf, we should consider ourselves lucky. At least we did not get swindled."

Vati still had that excited look in his eyes.

"Okay, Vati, what else did you want to tell me?"

"I'm glad you asked. Well, this sounds crazy, Wolf, but I also heard about a conspiracy to seize the ship and turn it around."

"Why would anyone want to do that?"

"You know, Wolf, the conditions are terrible. People are dying. And some are saying that this old ship is not seaworthy. But I think they are just afraid. More afraid of what they are headed to, than where they were coming from."[5]

In the end, there was no mutiny, but there would be more dead before the voyage was over.

After the Azores, we saw nothing for the next nine days – no land, no ships, no submarines – just the monotony of the perpetual ocean. The calm sea offered a soothing visual contrast to the dreadful conditions on board, and I stared out at the vast nothingness from my place on deck. Every now and then, flying fish leapt out of the water like birds; I tried to count them as we slowly cut a path toward safety.

We had been on the open ocean for close to two weeks when there was a flurry of activity on deck. The crew, which until now had left us to lie in our own squalor, suddenly swung into action. They mopped and cleaned our filthy deck. The seven showers were scrubbed spotless. Fire extinguishers miraculously appeared on deck. In the holds themselves, there were about 50 people with severe dysentery in dire need of medical care who were simply too weak to get up.[6] They lay listlessly in their berths as the crew cleaned and mopped around their limp and lifeless bodies.

Early in the morning, dawn broke over the lavender sky. I sat at the bow of the ship and saw the first glimpse of land in the distance. It was Bermuda, our first stop. The *Navemar* had slowed to a snail's pace through the calm waters and I was impatient to reach the reassurance of land, but when I looked down, it seemed as though the ship was sailing cautiously through some strange-looking, floating aluminum tubes. They bobbed around like empty tin cans. Suddenly the *Navemar* came to a dead halt. I saw our crew waving red and yellow flags in strange patterns. The flag formations seemed to be sending some type of message to shore.

We had become entangled in a mine net! Mines lay across the ocean floor to protect Bermuda from a German submarine attack. The buoyant metal tubes that now surrounded our ship were attached to the mines via ropes. Our captain should have accessed the island via safe, mine-free lanes with navigational help from a Bermuda pilot, but somehow, there had been a miscommunication. We now stood trapped in between the mines, unable to go forward or back. The Bermuda navy was desperately sending the captain a frenzied series of semaphore signals – flag code – to alert the captain to the danger. The captain stopped the ship in time and was awaiting rescue.

At 10 a.m., a pilot from a small naval vessel finally boarded the *Navemar*. He carefully navigated our ungainly freight ship out of danger and into the harbor of Hamilton, Bermuda's capital. We passed the impressive US destroyers that idled in the harbor. They sat there, fine looking and strong, prepared to protect the British fleet from German U-boats, while still officially staying out of the war.

We eventually docked just along the main street of the city of Hamilton. The danger had passed and now I relaxed lazily in my pretend penthouse, enjoying the cooler, salty island breezes as I took in a bird's-eye view. Lush green islands surrounded me, with houses painted in pastel colors, their roofs tiled in bright red, green and blue terra cotta. The streets of Hamilton seemed to be abuzz with cyclists meandering back and forth, but I could not hear them from my distance. All I could hear was the serenity of the ocean waves lapping rhythmically against the hull of the ship.

There had been no plan for us to disembark in Hamilton, as no passengers were emigrating to Bermuda. Five of the most seriously ill people were taken off the ship and brought to a Bermuda hospital for medical care. British naval personnel came aboard to inspect our ship that had been made unrecognizably tidy for public viewing. The refugees on the ship were then interrogated by British officers. We were being debriefed for British intelligence. *Tell us what the morale is in Germany. How effective have the British air raids been? What were the economic conditions when you left? Describe the food shortages. Describe in detail the Jewish persecution. Tell us about the existence of concentration camps.* The British officers had a litany of questions for us that lasted into the night.

We slept in port. The next morning, I awoke bleary eyed to find a colorful tropical procession of pineapples, oranges and bananas marching up the gangplank. It was a veritable fruit parade! And thank goodness for that. For two weeks, I had been eating a diet of mostly bread – so much bread that I barely needed even one of the seven bathrooms. Fruit would be most welcome indeed.

And more good news was on its way. A philanthropic group[7] had arranged an unexpected afternoon of leisure for the scattered children aboard the *Navemar.* Our ragtag group of about 20 children was escorted down the gangplank onto a small excursion boat where we were given bathing suits and transported to another island for a few hours of fun and beach games.

That memorable day, we swam and tumbled in the warm aquamarine sea. We frolicked and splashed and ate treats and ice cream. We were legs and waves and salt and sand and sun and fun. For a few hours in Bermuda, we were carefree children in the teal ocean and the pink sand with war and death a world away.[8]

In the late afternoon, we left this slice of paradise with our moods lifted. It had not taken much: the sickest among us had left, the ship had been cleaned, and we had seen land. Although the passengers had nicknamed the ship, the "Nevermore," they said it with gallows humor now as we all prepared for departure. The next morning, the lines holding the ship to shore were loosened and we were escorted out to sea through a safe channel by a pilot boat. We were all still packed on deck, but now the smell of hope instead of death commingled with the ocean breeze.

The *Navemar* now headed due west. Three days later, we finally saw the coastline of the United States. It was in our view, so close we could almost touch it... and then the ship turned sharply left and began charting a course due south. New York would have to wait a little longer. Still, just seeing land – the coast of Florida – on the starboard side of the *Navemar* made me feel safer. We headed south, ships passing us in both directions, reminding us that we were near civilization. On the port side of the ship, a school of long-bodied barracuda hitched a ride and stayed alongside us for the journey.

Eventually we lost sight of the Florida coast and entered open water. Forty-eight hours later we entered a large half-moon bay containing a busy port lined with ships. Beyond the port I could just make out a mass of houses, with hectic streets and lively throngs of people. The soothing pastels of Bermuda had been replaced by the blinding, bright, primary colors of Havana. We dropped anchor just 30 yards from the shore where a few hundred passengers who could not get visas to the United States gathered their belongings and entered the safety of their new technicolor home in Cuba.

The Havana harbor was exploding with activity. Within minutes of our arrival, small boats swiftly left the harbor and raced towards us, parking alongside our unsightly ship. Everyone seemed to be trying to sell us something – fruit, food, souvenirs – even the shirts off their backs. It seemed as if our ship had promoted a whole pop-up economy. The problem was that no one could hear each other – not the vendors in their little boats down below, nor the buyers high on deck. They shouted back and forth trying to negotiate the prices in languages no one could understand. "How much? *Cuanto? Dos dolares.* What? *Was? Qué?* I can't hear you. I can't understand you. *Ich verstehe dich nicht. ¡No entiendo!*"

None of the passengers had much money to spare but somehow capitalism still reigned. Some of the more innovative crew and passengers quickly deployed a system of ropes, pulleys, and baskets. They pulled up the goods and wares in the baskets and sent their sparse money to the boats down below.

In the distance, I saw that a whole other industry had cropped up as well; a kind of scavenger industry. Along the shore, strapping, young, shirtless men had positioned themselves in a line and as soon as the coins in the pulley-baskets accidentally fell into the water, they dove in and swam to the ship to retrieve them. Everyone was benefiting from the ship's instant marketplace and it was raucous and wild.

We were only in Cuba for one night. In the morning, the *Navemar* came around and headed north for what would be the last stretch of our journey. Although only about 380 passengers had left, the ship suddenly felt capacious. We wallowed in our newfound breathing room as we headed up the east coast of the United States, within sight of land most of the way. Whenever we could not see land, the presence of sea birds gliding aloft always reassured us that America was not far away.

September 12, 1941. Our fourth day after leaving Cuba.

The vague outline of the southern tip of Manhattan slowly came into view. Buildings emerged from the morning fog like fairy-tale giants. They were taller and denser than anything I had ever seen. A few straggling passengers began to gather at the bow of the ship, and gradually, more and more passengers crowded toward the front of the deck, filling every inch of space. Together we all looked up. With our heads back and our necks extended we stared at the majestic steel. There it was: New York. A symbol of hope and freedom. Of life itself.

In the shadows of the skyscrapers, people began dropping to their knees. Some cried and kissed the floorboards on which they were standing. I looked up at those imposing buildings, and for the first time in the five weeks since we had left Spain, I knew with certainty that we would live.

Our ship was not destined to dock in lower Manhattan or on Ellis Island. With its yellow quarantine flag flying, it headed to the Columbia Street Pier in the great borough of Brooklyn. Photographers from all the major newspapers made their way to the ship to capture the story of the *Navemar* – the *"floating concentration camp"* – and its *"horror voyage"* from Europe.[9]

My parents and I stayed on the top deck, searching below. We had been there for hours in heat and humidity, awaiting the examination of passengers and lifting of the quarantine. The excitement of our arrival had decidedly waned, and now we wondered if anyone would be there to greet us; if anyone even knew of our arrival. There was a huge crowd on the dock and from our distance so high up, it was impossible to identify anyone's face. And then somehow, we spotted something familiar. Maybe it was a way of walking that we recognized, or the short, stocky, buxom body that once nearly suffocated me. But there she was, my Aunt Hede, with Uncle Arthur and my old playmate, Cousin Ilse. We pushed our way down the steep gangplank until we reached the dock, and we pressed through the crowds of people. And then we fell, crying, into each other's arms.

PHOTOS

Pauline and Salomon Arndt, Grete's grandparents, Wolf's great-grandparents, circa 1865.

Grete Schwersenz née Jacob (left) with a friend.

Ernestine Jacob, Grete and Arthur Schwersenz with Anita (age three), and Hiller Jacob, 1924.

Arthur and Grete Schwersenz, late-1920s.

Wolf with his father, Arthur.

Arthur Schwersenz (Vati) with his niece, Ilse (Elsa) Jacobsohn, Wolf and Anita, circa 1933, probably in Grunewald.

In Friedland, with Uncle Siegfried (from right), Aunt Irma, Grete, and two unknown women (possibly maids), 1934.

Dining out and people-watching while it is still permissible for Jews.
Grete, Wolf, and Arthur, circa 1935.

Damaged photo of the family dining table in Charlottenburg, Berlin. From left to right: Erma Ruschin (cousin who fled to Shanghai), Grete, Ho, Anita, Uncle Siegfried, Ella Hammer (cousin of Grete), Erma Ruschin's husband, Irma Jacob (Siegfried's wife) with Wolf in her lap.

Wolf (front) in lederhosen with friends (possibly Gladze and Achim) circa 1934-35.

Wolf's first day of school 1936, holding his Schultüte (cone of candy)

Wolf with friends second from the right, circa 1936-1937.

Family portrait (Grete, Anita, Wolf and Arthur) circa 1937.

Paula Kahnemann (Cousin Paula) with Hertha and Arthur Arndt and their daughter Lotte on the deck of the St. Louis, *1939 United States Holocaust Memorial Museum (courtesy of Lottie Brown)*

Arthur and Hedwig (Uncle Arthur and Aunt Hede) Jacobsohn and Cousin Ilse (Elsa), undated. The caption reads "Fangschleuse in Summer." (Courtesy of Helene Greenwald)

Photograph by Jeff King of the lifeboats on the S.S. Navemar *crowded with refugees. (Courtesy of The Center for Holocaust and Humanity Education)*

Deutsches Reich ReisePass (passport) allowing Wolf to leave Germany. Note the J for Jew on the left.

The original travel passport was valid from March until May 4, 1941.

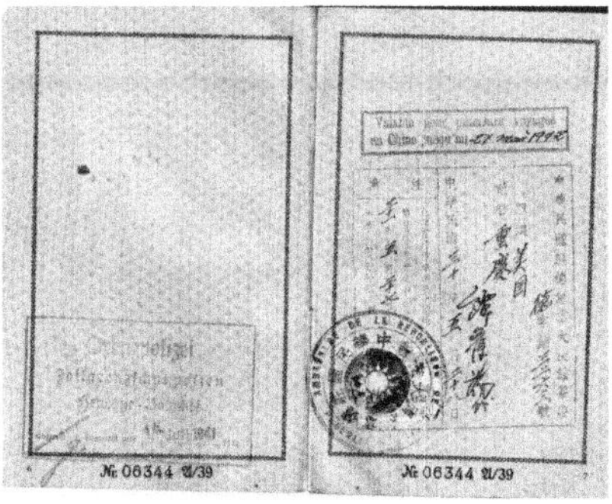

Permission was granted for a voyage to China that never came to fruition (right). On the left is a stamp from the border police/customs toll police at the Hendaye train station on July 16, 1941.

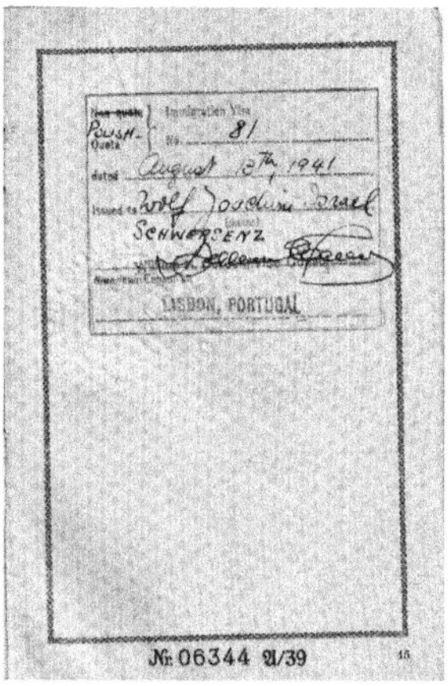

Visa to America on the Polish Quota. Just one of 81 granted by the American Consulate.

PART V

IMMIGRANTS

15

NO INSTRUCTION MANUAL

We were strangers in a strange land; exhausted and disoriented, but at least not entirely alone. With just nine dollars and ninety-eight cents remaining in our pockets, we gathered our two suitcases from a heap. Covered with mildew and smelling like a wet shoe, they were all we had brought with us for our new life in America. With our two bags in hand, we slowly made our way northbound towards the neighborhood of Washington Heights.

Uptown Manhattan seemed to be teeming with life. As everything whizzed by me – cars, buses, people – I remained in a distant daze, as if I were still standing in the early morning fog that had eclipsed the Manhattan skyline. An odd kind of dissonance overcame me. Although I could see and hear, every sensation felt strange. The foreign words that I could not understand made a constant, unfamiliar buzzing in my ear. The sensory overload and confusion were overwhelming, and the only thing that calmed me was the presence of family.

Aunt Hede's comforting German words finally aroused me from my stupor. She was making some kind of announcement.

"I rented you a furnished room at 90 Pinehurst Avenue," Hede explained. "And the nice thing is, it is not too far from our apartment on Fort Washington Avenue."

"But Hede, how much is the rent?" my mother nervously asked.

"Don't worry, Grete, it's only nine dollars a week."

I quickly did the math in my head, and I saw my father doing the same. "Perfect!" Vati exclaimed. "If we don't eat anything, we can survive here for exactly one week!"

There was snickering all around. I did not have to turn to look at my mother. I already knew she was not laughing.

At that point we split up. My parents went with Arthur and Hede to see the furnished room, and Ilse led me like a frightened puppy on a leash to Woolworth's.[1] "You must try the banana split, Wolf," she begged me, practically jumping up and down. "It is amazing! Don't worry, it's my treat, and it's only 25 cents."

We ordered at the cafeteria counter. I swiveled from side to side in my red vinyl stool and waited for whatever this "banana split" treat was. Shortly after, the waitress pushed through a set of double doors with her rear end, and when she turned around, I saw she was holding two dishes that were each the size of small boats. Flanking the interior of each dish were two bananas that supported three monstrous scoops of vanilla ice cream. A mountain of whipped cream blanketed the entire dish like a fluffy down cover, and a thick mantle of chocolate syrup rolled down the sides of the ice cream and dribbled over the ship-shaped bowl.

I had never seen anything like it. It looked like a replica of a snow-covered alpine mountain range. It was not just an indulgence; it bordered on the obscene. And I ate it, slowly, very, very slowly, with a very long silver spoon, as I tried to savor each swallow. With each bite I tried to capture and memorize the flavor of each melting mouthful of banana and ice cream and chocolate and whipped cream. I ate and ate, perfectly happy to make myself sick. After so many years of hunger, how could I be certain when an opportunity like this would present itself again? I did not leave one drop behind, and I would have licked the bowl if I were not in a public place. Nauseated and bloated, I rolled out of Woolworth's, eager to rejoin my family in our new furnished home.

What exactly would a "furnished room" in New York look like? I supposed I should have been satisfied with just a bed and shelter, but for my imagination started to run wild again. Here we were in America, hosted by our sponsor, Cousin Ellis – a man who was in fact, a wealthy benefactor. An upstanding businessman who was sure to be helping us out. We were finally settled in a rich country that was not actively engaged in war. I had every reason to be optimistic. I stepped up to our new dwelling and swung open the door.

My gaze was met by a spartan, square-shaped room. Two single beds stuck out from the wall; across from them, a small rectangular table with two chairs sat under a dimly lit hanging lamp. There was no kitchen. A sink stood in the corner, and next to it was a simple hot plate for cooking. I immediately swallowed my disappointment. I would have to adjust my expectations.

That night, my mother and I each took one of the beds and my father slept on the floor. I slept like a stone until the early morning, when the light was dim and purple and I could still feel the steady undulating of the ocean. At first, I thought I was still on the *Navemar*, but when I realized that I was in a bed, on land, the phantom rocking became a comfort. Slowly up, then slowly down, then slowly up again. After a while, I swung my feet over the bed where they landed lightly on the semi-solid form of my father. He was snoring softly on the floor, and I sat motionless while I got my land legs back and waited for daylight to come.

A tiny slice of light finally entered the window, illuminating a triangle of suspended dust until it shone like glitter. The prism of sunlight slowly spread to the floor, reaching my father and covering his body like a golden blanket. When the warm glow finally reached his face, he stirred and twitched. Then he opened his eyes, looked up at me and smiled, and said, *"Guten Morgen,* Wolf."

"Guten Morgen, Vati," I answered. And I reminded myself, we are alive, we have made it here; this horrid apartment is only the beginning.

On our second day, I saw New York and all its possibilities.

We descended the stairs of our building and emerged onto the hot sidewalk. And leaning against a sleek car right in front of our building, was a tall and impeccably dressed man with white hair and horn-rimmed glasses… who seemed to be waiting for us.

My mother walked right up to this stranger and embraced him. Then Vati stepped forward and began shaking the man's hand vigorously and every so often bowing. The tall man was not alone; he was standing next to an equally tall and striking-looking woman. My father shook her hand too. Eventually, my mother called me over. "Wolf, I would like to introduce you to my cousin Ellis Arndt. He is the man responsible for bringing us all to safety in this country and we owe him our lives. This is his wife, Bessie. Mrs. Arndt, to you."

Cousin Ellis said hello in a cheerful, deep baritone. He shook my hand, and I bowed, as I had been taught, but this seemed to embarrass him. So I turned and bowed to his wife. She was an attractive, mature woman with brown hair mixed with just a speckling of gray, who exuded elegance and carried herself with the grace of a dancer.[2]

Ellis spoke only English, for although he was our blood relative, he was as American as whatever I imagined America to be. Baseball. Cars. Big buildings. Speed. Money. We had all conceived some idea of America from the movies and photographs we had seen.

Yes, to me, Ellis *was* America. He had shed his Jewishness the way a snake shed its skin. Ellis: the least Jewish name I had ever heard, sounding more like a brand than a name. Unless of course, Ellis's immigrant father, Abraham Arndt, named him after Ellis Island. That would make "Ellis" the most immigrant-sounding name around. But somehow, I didn't think that scenario was likely.

The warm greetings over, Ellis and Bessie told us they planned to give us a tour of Manhattan and ushered us toward their white car. It was impossibly large, polished to a mirrored shine, with monstrous, white-walled tires and a sparkling front grill that seemed to be grinning. We climbed into the back and slid into seats of red leather and began our New York City tour.

We first drove down Broadway, leaving behind the walkup buildings of 191st Street. Passing under the elevated train tracks of Harlem, we made our way through the campus of Columbia University. Then the buildings soared in height and breadth as we approached the high-rise apartments of the west 70s and 80s. Stores began to appear at ground level, and pedestrians swarmed the streets of every neighborhood we drove through. Often, when we stopped at traffic lights, people peered into our car, wondering who could be driving such a fine automobile. I was too excited to consider how we must have looked to others in our humble clothes. Perhaps people assumed Ellis and Bessie were doing charity work and taking some impoverished immigrants out for a hot meal. But Ellis never appeared embarrassed by us, and so we did not feel ashamed as we continued to make our way southbound.

At last, we arrived at an area that was so unusually vivid, I did not know what to make of it. The street was overflowing with color. There were bright lights, and flashing, urgent signs on every building. "Coca-Cola! Camel!" the signs yelled at us, as if saying yearningly, "You must drink me! Smoke me!" Everywhere I turned, throngs of people were walking, running, and rushing about. I had never seen so many people in one place, looking so determined as they walked, scattering about in random directions and moving about in such a frenzy. Just as I wondered where we were, Ellis turned to the back seat and said to us, "Welcome to Times Square!"

I hardly remember what we did after that. At some point we headed back uptown, and on the way, Ellis and Bessie took a detour and stopped at their apartment on 79th Street. Their elegant building was just off of Central Park West and very close to the Museum of Natural History. Bessie kept pointing to the sky and saying "daughter," which I recognized because it sounded like the German word *Tochter*. Apparently, Bessie wanted us to meet her daughter upstairs. Ellis and Bessie's daughter would be my second cousin and although I realized she must be considerably older than me, I was still more than happy to meet any other relative who lived in New York.

A doorman ushered us into the entrance lobby. "Good evening, Mr. and Mrs. Arndt," he said, bowing obsequiously, as we crossed the high gloss marbled floors. We reached the elevators and ascended to the top floor, entering their penthouse apartment. "Yoo-Hoo. Dorothy! Come say hello, sweetheart," sang Bessie as we stepped across the threshold into a stunning luxury apartment with panoramic views of Central Park.

A young woman with long pigtails entered the living room. Wearing thick "cat's-eye" glasses, she was stout and quite short, looking nothing like her tall, elegant parents. I could not tell her age; she might have been in her twenties, but she was dressed like a child and had purple ribbons in her hair. "Hell-Low," she said, slowly, as though it were two separate words.

She waved from side to side with both hands, like they were windshield wipers. Oddly, a moment later, she ran to me with outstretched arms and hugged me, affectionately, as if we were old friends. She was very sweet, but something did not seem quite right. "Our daughter has Down Syndrome," Bessie finally explained to my parents. "Down syndrome," she said again much louder, as if raising her voice would somehow overcome the language barrier. My mother nodded and smiled. I looked at my mother questioningly, but she shook her head wildly as if to say, "Shut up, I will explain it later."

Ellis drove us back uptown, and we all sat quietly in the back seat. I suppose we were tired, but mainly we were each lost in our own reflections. What was my father thinking? That he could understand nothing, but would soon have to make a living in this strange country? And my mother, what was on her mind? That we owed Ellis everything, and we were grateful, but would Ellis help us going forward? He certainly had his own worries and responsibilities, not to mention a child with special needs.

And then, as we pulled up to our sad one-room "apartment," back to reality, we had to face the urgent truth: we were in dire need of money. The humiliating moment had come when my mother had to bring up our financial affairs with Ellis. As our sponsor, he was in control of an account containing 1,500 dollars put aside for our needs. All these months that my mother had been corresponding with Ellis via letters back and forth to America, she had also been slowly sending him our own money from Germany to put into this account.

Ellis took out a wad of American dollars from his pocket; then he licked his thumb and forefinger and peeled off a 10-dollar bill, and five singles. "Here you go," he said, a big, generous smile on his face, as he handed my mother 15 dollars of our very own money. "This should last you a week."

We walked up the stairs with leaden legs, the excitement of the day decidedly over, secure in our knowledge that Ellis would fulfill his obligations, and nothing more.

We turned on the dim light of our room. Suddenly, my mother let out a blood-curdling scream as hundreds of little brown insects scattered into every corner. It was the first time she had ever seen a roach.

And now I must share what I was thinking about in the back of that fancy car on the way uptown: *I must get a new identity. I must shed my German-ness and Jewishness as quickly as possible, just the way Ellis did.*

I must become an American.

Those first few days in New York were a dizzying whirlwind of activity; a montage of new sights, sounds and smells. Everything was foreign to us, but we were the foreigners. There was no time to get our bearings; no time to process what we were experiencing. We needed shelter, money, food, school. And we needed to find work immediately.

It was a good plan, with one minor catch. Not one of us was able to speak any useful English. I remembered a few English words from school but could barely manage to string them into a sentence. Anyway, I was reasonably sure that "how is the weather today," would not get me very far.

Uncle Arthur – ever a cheerful man – remained optimistic. Walking into our bare, dusty room, dressed ridiculously, but brightening our surroundings in his fabulous silk cravat and colorful clothing, Uncle Arthur sat in one of the two chairs in our apartment while he scoured the "Help Wanted" section of the *New York Times*. "Well, here's one for you, Arthur!" he exclaimed. "Pot washer at Sydenham Hospital. It pays 52 dollars per month. It even includes lunch!" The job was at 125th Street in Harlem and did not require a single word of English. In fact, it did not require speaking at all.

My mother looked for work that could be done from home and found the most menial of jobs putting elastic onto hairnets. It paid pennies per piece and could bring in a maximum of two dollars a day if she worked nearly every waking second. It was perfect.

Whether my parents explicitly told me to work, or whether there was just a tacit understanding that I would also contribute to our income, I really don't recall. But I found a job earning tip money as a delivery boy for a Chinese laundry. On my first day, a couple of Irish delivery boys beat me up. "Stay away from our territory!" they said. The laundry owner tried to explain it to me as I held a rag to my bloody nose. "Hey, kid, everyone here is immigrant, and every country has its own 'territory.' Every block is different country. You don't stand chance against Irish kids. I give you your own route, and I don't want you kids bother each other, you hear?"

As the week went on, I found there were plenty of ways to make money. You just had to keep your eyes open. A candy store on 181st Street had a sign in the window that read: "Newspaper Boy Wanted." Every day, a truck dropped off bundles of *The Daily News* at the corner of 175th Street and St. Nicholas Avenue, and the candy store needed someone to get those bundles up to them. I nearly gave up on the idea when I realized those newspaper bundles were way too heavy for an 11-year-old weakling like me. Then I spotted an abandoned, beat-up baby carriage that had been left on the sidewalk. Claiming the ugly, rusty rubbish for myself, I stacked the newspapers inside the carriage and wheeled them to the store as if they were my babies. In those days, I would have done anything for a dollar.

Somehow, at the end of our first week in New York, we had eked out just enough to survive.

However, something was glaringly missing. There were only three of us. We would not feel whole until we could hold Anita in our arms, until we were four again. Anita, our sacrificial lamb, had made her way to America nearly a year before us, completing her own journey west. She had, in fact, overshot just a bit, landing in some godforsaken place called Iowa.

How we missed Anita! And – let's be truthful – how we needed her again, now more than ever. Anita already spoke English. Anita understood this country and could navigate us through this maze of confusion. "Anita," my mother called on the telephone. "Can you please come to New York and help us?"

She did not hesitate. Within days of our arrival, Anita hopped into her own Model-T Ford and drove straight from Iowa City to Washington Heights, stopping only for gas along the way.

"Oh my God, I can't believe it. Let me look at you! How beautiful you are! How grown up!"

The last time Vati had laid eyes on his daughter, he was being dragged off a train, and Anita, a frightened teen, was headed for London alone. Now she was a married woman of 20. Did I say married? Yes, she was married to Ho. We had been all set to go to China last year, and Anita's marriage to Ho was one of the conditions of our Chinese visas. Well, our travel to China ended up falling through, but what was Anita to do? She couldn't just unmarry Ho. She was stuck with him.

Now my father looked as his grown-up daughter. He chose to see only the positive changes – more maturity, more womanly beauty – and ignore the subtle layer of weathered melancholy just beneath the cheery exterior.

"Stop, Vati! I know, I know. And you!" she said, turning to me. "Look how tall you are, Wolf. Almost as tall as Vati and me. Why you are practically a teenager!" I blushed, proudly.

"I cannot believe we all made it. I cannot believe it," repeated my mother. "I never thought we would see each other again. I really did not. For a while, I wasn't sure we would make it out alive."

We hugged; we laughed. We touched each other to make sure we were real. We were crying and laughing at the same time; we hugged some more and held on as if afraid to let go. After a long time, we finally released ourselves from the embrace, and then we began to talk. It was just details and facts for now. It would take weeks before we would all know the full extent of each other's sad stories. "Tell me about London," I asked, slipping my slightly longer, hairier arm around Anita's no longer slender waist.

"Ahh, Wolf. Let's see. Where should I start. Some of this you may know already. Well, it turned out the advertisement for the domestic job was in fact a ruse. That meant I did not have a place to live when I got to London. In the beginning, I was allowed to stay in a group home. As soon as I turned 18, my residence became a problem. The group home told me they could not let me stay on indefinitely. As an adult, I was expected to get a job, and not be a charity case. I eventually found a job as an au pair."

"What's that?"

"It's French for a live-in nanny. I was very lucky. It turned out to be a good job for a very nice family, but unfortunately my luck did not last."

"Why, Anita? What happened?"

"Remember my chest pain attacks? Well, they continued in London. I kept getting episodes nearly every month. They would last for days, usually with a fever, and I would be weak and sickly. Remember how useless I was during my attacks? The family I worked for was quite kind and tolerant at the beginning, but after a while, they lost patience with me. And who could blame them?

They had not signed up to take care of an invalid, and truly, I was unfit to care for children. So I lost both my job and a place to live.

"The group home allowed me to stay again, but they made it clear it was only temporary until I could find work. It was right around this time that Ho arrived in England, and somehow, he was able to find me. I was relieved – and at the same time, horrified."

"I don't get it, Anita. Do you like Ho or not?"

"Well, let me try to explain it, Wolf. It's complicated. On the one hand, Ho was a known friend, and a familiar face, which was a comfort. On the other hand, I felt like I was being stalked. I knew Ho wanted to marry me which put terrible pressure on me. And then I wondered, how could he have found me? There could only be one answer. Mutti must have told him where I was living. And that was infuriating."

"I thought you and Mutti could not write to each other because Germany and England were at war."

"That's correct, Wolf. But Mutti and I had figured out a system to communicate. We both sent letters to Ellis in America, and he was forwarding them to each of us. It was a painfully slow process. The mail was heavily censored so Mutti and I learned to write in a kind of coded language, but still our letters came with blacked out lines. One of the lines in Mutti's letters was never blacked out, however. 'Marry Ho, Anita! Save the family!' She was a broken record. I'm sure she was the one who told him where to find me.

"When he finally did, I was alone, frightened, and sick, running out of money and unable to keep a job. Ho started to provide for me. Then Mutti kept insisting that Ho would bring the whole family to China if we got married, and that it was the only way we would all be saved.

"So I agreed to marry him. In the spring of 1940, Ho got instructions from the Chinese government to go to America. Both of us were anxious to get out of London as soon as possible. The blitz had started that summer and staying in England had gotten quite terrifying. Ho was able to get a research position on road building techniques at the University of Iowa. We quickly left for the United States on diplomatic visas. And that's really the whole story. Now we are settled in Iowa City."

"Enough secrets, you two!" Vati cried, interrupting our private dialogue. "We all want to hear about your life in Iowa. Paint us a picture of your American life there, Anita. Is it wonderful? Exciting?"

"Okay, Vati okay! Well, overall, I can't say Iowa is bad," my sister continued, addressing all of us now. "It's flat as a pancake, but there are beautiful vistas and vast swaths of golden farmland. Maybe a bit like Spreewald. But everything is... bigger. Except for Iowa City, that is. It is just a small town of 10,000 people. If you blink you might miss it." She stood up now, as if she were giving a lecture. "Everyone acts very nice, friendly. I can't deny it. The problem for me is that the entire population of Iowa seems to be made up of white, Christian Americans. I am sure if I were a white, Christian American I would be very happy there. But just imagine Ho and me in this tiny, all-white town. I mean, think about it. It's almost funny: Ho, a Chinese diplomat, and me, a German-Jewish immigrant.

"When we first moved in, there was quite a bit of interest in us. We even got a write-up in the local papers. '*Chinese Diplomat! Nazi refugee!*' Iowa was very removed from the war, and no one had seen anyone who looked like us before, or who had our experiences. In the beginning, I admit it was a bit exciting. I was asked to give tea-time talks to some of the professors' wives. Foolish me, I thought I was making social inroads. It was only later that I realized we might as well be in a curiosity shop! The truth is, we are total social outcasts. It took me a while to realize how much prejudice there is towards Asians in this country. In Germany, we saw no such prejudice, but here, people are thoroughly shocked to see a white woman married to an Asian man. I see the looks we get. At least Ho can chat with some work colleagues at the University; it's not friendship, but at least it's collegial. I do not even have that luxury. And any initial interest in me as a novelty has dried up."

Now Anita's smile faded, and a look of sadness came over her face as she sat back down next to me. "The truth is, I feel completely isolated where I am. I have no friends and no family, I am married to a man I do not love, and I am living in a town that does not accept me. Frankly, I am completely miserable! I am just so relieved that you are here – that we are finally together." She squeezed me tightly and I pressed hard against her, without words to say how I felt. But somehow in Anita's arms I felt like someone had thrown a blanket of protection over me and I secretly prayed she would never leave us again.

I sat nervously in the Assistant Principal's office of P.S. 132, Anita and Mutti on either side of me. My foot was tapping uncontrollably, and my sweaty underarms were emanating a mild cardamom-like odor of early pubescence. My body seemed fully aware that I had not been in school for over one and a half years... that I did not speak the local language... that the school year had already begun weeks earlier. As I waited for my placement interview to begin, my imagination ran wild. What would they do with me? Would they make me do art? Turn me back into a lefty? But what they actually did was worse than I could have ever imagined.

A red-headed, freckled young woman with kind, bright green eyes walked in and sat behind the desk. "*Irische* [Irish]" my mother whispered to Anita.

The young woman began to speak. "*A gutn tog. Vos makhstu*?"

What exactly was she saying to us?

"I hope my Yiddish is similar enough to German so that we can communicate!" The Assistant Principal sounded hopelessly earnest. She held out her hand to my mother who look at first confused – the redhead was *Jewish?* – and then offended – she thinks we speak *Yiddish?*

Anita quickly replied in English. "We appreciate the effort. But I can translate English into German for my family." She did not have the heart to tell her that we did not speak any Yiddish at all.

The Assistant Principal looked me up and down and then she sighed in a way that did not seem promising. "Wolf, let us start with your name."

"What is wrong with his name?" asked Anita.

"The children will tease him mercilessly; I suggest you change it." Turning to me, the woman asked, "By any chance, do you have a middle name?"

Anita translated. Indeed, I did have a middle name. "Joachim," I replied, smiling. "Yo-achhh-eem," I repeated, more slowly this time, stretching it out phonetically, and making sure the second syllable sounded like I was hacking up a glob of phlegm – it would help her with the pronunciation. All right, the woman could call me Joachim if she preferred.

The Assistant Principal did not smile back at me. Instead, she shook her head. "No, no. That will not do at all. But I suppose we can use a bit of it. Why don't you pick Jacob. It's close enough."

Jacob was not only my mother's maiden name, but a name that was distinctly Jewish. No, no, *no*. I shook my head vigorously in protest.

"Jack, then? It's very American. Quite popular."

"Jack." I tested it out on my tongue. Short and direct. And then I finally understood – she was trying to Americanize me. It was not just a name change. From now on, Jack would be my new American identity. Jack it would be.

We moved on to size up my grade level and academic skills. "What level of math are you up to?" she asked.

"Fractions," I answered, confidently. I felt secure about my math abilities. She quickly handed me a piece of paper with a long division problem on it. Where was the fraction problem we had just talked about? Had she misunderstood me? Had Anita mistranslated? I could do long division too – I swear, I could – but I just sat there, waiting for my fraction problem. Was I supposed to do *this* problem? I was not sure. Was it a trick? The minutes rolled by, with the paper sitting in front of me. I did not do anything, I did not say anything, I did not ask anything. Instead, I sat in suspended silence as the minutes passed. I stared at the long division problem, and it stared back at me, unsolved, and before you could say "What is 1,480 divided by 23," she had placed me in the fourth grade.

Now I have always believed that if only I had done that one

equation, the course of my life would be changed forever. I had not even considered all those other teensy problems, such as my complete lack of English, my one and a half years of non-existent schooling and my complete lack of knowledge of American history that may have been factored in to the decision. I always thought being put into fourth grade was one giant mathematical misunderstanding.

So when my fate was decided, I expected Anita, my English-speaking advocate, to fight for me. But she just sat there. Not a peep out of her! A language barrier was not the issue, it was her cultural training. Both my mother and sister grew up with the dictum: never challenge authority. It was simply the German way. They quietly accepted the Assistant Principal's dreadful decision and did not say a thing.

And that is how I began school in America – an entire two years older (with a February birthday, no less) and a good five inches taller than my nine-year-old classmates. And wouldn't you know, at 11 ½ years old, I was already showing signs of puberty. A light moustache graced my upper lip, and dark hair had just started sprouting on my longish legs. And the two pairs of pants that I owned – bought over two years ago in Berlin when we were still allowed to purchase clothes – came down only to my ankles.

On my first day of school, I was *that* kid in class. The one that was too tall, too old, too hairy, with too short pants, and a heavy foreign accent. I could not have been a more perfect object of ridicule.

At least the name "Wolf" was gone. Now I had to make the rest of Wolf disappear for good.

16

EXTERMINATION

We lived in our furnished room until the end of October. By then, with our pooled incomes, we were able to rent a two-bedroom walkup on the fourth floor of 521 West 180th Street.

Technically, we were in Washington Heights, but we were on the outskirts. For one thing, we were as far east as you could possibly be from the Hudson River. Any further east and we would fall into the Harlem River on the other side of Manhattan. And we were avenues and avenues east of Broadway – the core of the neighborhood. Not only were we in the least desirable part of Washington Heights, but we were in the least Jewish part, too. Although we had found a working-class sub-neighborhood we could afford, we weren't near any of our countrymen. Nonetheless, this neighborhood of concrete and brick and metal fire escapes became my new home.

Jewish philanthropies came to our aid, providing us with used furniture for the empty apartment. But to our surprise, the apartment was not completely vacant when we moved in. We found it occupied by millions of tenants: an entire population of cockroaches, living there rent-free. They happily moseyed about in the dark – eating, socializing, and procreating. When the lights went on, they instantly raced about, scattering in all different directions, finding good hiding spots. I was desperately afraid of them. My mother did what she could to control the infestation. She sprayed all around the rooms with a kerosene-based spray called "Flit." When that didn't work, she spread "J-O Roach and Rat Paste" onto slices of raw potatoes, which she placed strategically on the floor around the kitchen. But it was no use. Right in the middle of the kitchen a dumbwaiter system ran throughout the length of our building. Using a manual pulley, each apartment used the dumbwaiter to send garbage down to the basement – and the cockroaches right back up. It was as if the roaches had a private elevator to our apartment. There was no way we would ever be rid of them.

No, we could not eliminate our apartment's cockroaches. Overseas in Berlin, however, the Germans had finally worked out its own efficient cockroach elimination program. By cockroaches I mean Jews, of course. That is what they called us. Or sometimes they called us parasites.

October 18, 1941, marked the end of legal emigration out of Berlin, just one month after we had made it to New York. That very same day, the Germans started mass deportations of Jews out of Berlin. There would be nine initial transports, each carrying about 1,000 Jews. They would be headed to Lodz, Riga, Minsk, and Kovno in Eastern Europe.

Relocation. Resettlement in Eastern Europe, perhaps to a Jewish ghetto. That must be the fate that awaited our loved ones we had left behind, we imagined. It would be years before we understood what resettlement meant: With little or no notice, Jews were pulled from their apartments and packed tightly into cattle cars, with no air, water, or food. Many did not even make it to their destinations alive. But those who managed to survive the trip were lined up at the lip of a mass grave and shot, execution-style, until they fell into the heap of corpses below them.

Maybe it was a mercy that we were spared this knowledge at the time. Maybe we could not have lived with the guilt of having survived. Aunt Hede had received two heavily redacted postcards from Aunt Frieda and Uncle Siegfried. They were our only pieces of information, and we held onto the few facts written on them. At least we knew *something*: that Frieda and her husband were on the fifth transport which left for Minsk (now the capital of Belarus) on November 11, 1941, and Siegfried and Irma were on the sixth transport which left for Kovno (Kaunas, Lithuania), on November 17.[1] But that was the last we ever heard from them.[2] Of Ella Hammer, and my dear friend Heinz, we never heard anything at all.[3]

Much as I wanted to be American, I was still in a state of culture shock the first few months after my arrival. My feelings about New York were hopelessly conflicted. On the one hand, it was hard not to be swept up by the contagious energy and optimism of the city; not to marvel at the speed of the subway, or the towering skyscrapers silhouetting the sky, their silver steel heights beyond my imagination. At the same time, I was overwhelmed by the contrast to my old life. I missed the quiet of the Berlin streets, its buildings no taller than 10 stories. I yearned for the softer sounds of classical music, the little butcher stores and pastry shops, the Linden trees, and the quaint trolleys.

I could not adjust to the graffiti, the dirt on the subway train and in the streets, not to mention, the rudeness of New Yorkers. How they dashed about, elbowing past one another! Loud, big band music played everywhere, sounding just like the city streets themselves. And how did I feel about the abundance of food, the enormous supermarkets, and the freedom that people experienced each day? I wasn't even sure. It was simultaneously wonderful and grotesque. Everything in America seemed big, bold, and brassy.

I'm not sure I fully recognized my feelings for what they were. I was homesick. Yes, I was nostalgic for a country that had kicked me out, a war-torn country of air-raids, rationing, and rubble. I was in awe of New York, but I was filled with longing for Berlin. Here, I was a stranger.

On December 7, 1941, Pearl Harbor was attacked by Japan, and President Roosevelt declared war on Germany, Italy, and Japan. It felt like a personal victory for our family. *Hitler will finally be defeated,* we thought, *and the Jews – and our relatives – will be freed!* We still thought our relatives had been resettled in some ghetto and we fantasized they could be liberated. I started tracking the war again, imagining I could control things by memorizing geography and hanging maps and pins in my room.

Just a month after Pearl Harbor, I finally could speak passable English. The fourth-grade teacher moved me up to fifth grade, and I was the new kid in class again. I was ready for a new round of teasing and bullying; heck – I was practically an expert at it! But with America now at war with Germany and Japan, I should not have been surprised at what happened next.

At the end of the school day, in early spring, a group of kids followed me and an Asian kid onto the school yard. I was about to head home when suddenly the children started chanting, "Fight, fight, fight." My brain said, "walk away," but the mob was like a magnet, drawing me in. Soon we were surrounded. We both knew we had no choice. The schoolyard demanded entertainment. It wanted blood and we would be its gladiators.

In a flash, we dropped our backpacks and began boxing with each other. I did not know how to box, nor did the other boy, but I was throwing out right jabs, and he was throwing out left hooks, and we were circling each other and punching each other, and dancing around on our toes, all to the roars and cheers of the gathering crowd. As we threw our blows, I was seized with hatred for this boy I did not even know. I found myself wanting to annihilate him, because it was the only way this drama would end; and his destruction was the only way I could save myself. And I wanted the crowd to root for me. That's what I really wanted. To hear them yell "Go, Jack, go! Jack you are amazing!"

The fight got rougher and rougher, and I saw with surprise there was blood on both of us; I was not even sure whose blood it was. By then I had chipped my two front teeth, and the Asian boy had a cut above his rapidly closing eye. Neither of us was winning and we both looked mangled and pitiful, but the crowd had not yet lost its bloodlust. The boys were still circling around us, goading us on, hailing us with names and epithets. I listened harder. Were they rooting for me? I tried to make out what they were saying in the commotion. "You dirty Jap!" I heard them yell out to the Asian boy, who I don't even think was Japanese.

And me? I could hear them scream out to me; yes, I could hear them clearly now. What was it they were yelling? Did I hear that right?

"You Goddamn Nazi!"

At least I was young. I would eventually adjust, trying and failing, and trying again to mold myself into an American. My parents were another story. They were both over 50; and although they were willing to work hard and do anything to earn a living, they neither knew how to adapt to, nor did they understand the American "system." "My sewing skills must be of some value," my mother declared, feeling confident in the one skill she had. With that in mind, she applied for a job at a garment "sweatshop."

She discovered her error soon enough. A sweatshop required no skills and no craftsmanship. My mother simply became a factory worker, a human machine in a place where speed superseded quality, standards were low, and the other workers had all learned their skills on the job.

"You might be a great seamstress, lady, but over here, we do 'piecework,'" explained the foreman. "This here's a factory, not a homemade dress shop. There's three types of workers here: an operator, a presser, and a finisher. We're gonna start you as a finisher. Ha, ha! That's funny – start you as a finisher, get it? Anyhow, alls ya gotta do is trim the excess threads and clean up the seams. That's it, easy-peasy. You see this tag on the dress with the serial number on it? When you're done with your garment, pull off that tag and hold onto it. Don't lose it, lady. Because you gotta turn over all your tags at the end of the week if you wanna get paid. The faster you work, the more tags you get and that's how you'll earn your money. Ya gotta hustle."

The foreman failed to mention a few things in his introduction. My mother learned soon enough that the "finishers" were the lowest paid of all the pieceworkers. And she discovered that some garments had a lower pay rate per piece than others. In time, she noticed that the foreman kept assigning these low-pay garments to my mother. "I'm sure he is doing it on purpose," grumbled Mutti. "Everyone is against me at the factory. The Jews there are all from Eastern Europe, and the rest of the workers are all Italians. I can hear the other Jews whispering to each other behind my back. They call me a '*Daitshe.*'"

We were used to my mother's oversensitivity, sometimes bordering on paranoia. Yet "*Daitshe*" wasn't a name she made up. It was nasty Yiddish word for a German Jew used by the Eastern European Jews. They didn't like the haughtiness and snooty attitudes of the German Jews who had always considered themselves more refined, educated, and sophisticated. Yup, it was finally payback time. From their perspective, German Jews were snobs and they had it coming.

Well, we had no choice, we needed the money. Mutti bit her tongue and did her job, and she would swallow whatever pride she had left. On the weekends, she cleaned homes in the borough of Queens, scrubbing other people's toilets until they sparkled like the fine porcelain figurines on our old mantle in Berlin.

We had said goodbye to a middle-class life and my parents had become laborers in middle age. Every now and then, I would hear a remnant of a dream rise to the surface. "Maybe we can open a dry cleaning store," my father would sometimes say aloud. "I can run the store, Grete, and you can do the alterations."

My mother would rarely respond. *Let him fantasize*, I thought. Even I knew my parents were too old to start over, and it was obvious we did not have a dime. We were living hand to mouth and our refrigerator had only enough food to last a couple of days. Every morsel of food was tightly measured. I had to ask permission for everything, even a glass of milk.

"What is this? I asked for pastrami on rye! You gave me salami on white!" the deli customer screamed at my father.

Vati was trying to work evenings as a waiter, but it was not working out well at all. His linguistic deficits led to too many sandwich debacles, and when a wrong order was sent back one too many times, he was not so politely dismissed.

It seemed safer to hole up in the hospital basement, where he could just put his head down and wash pots with the other non-English speaking immigrants from all over the world. Down in the basement, he never saw the light of day and his command of English did not have a chance to improve. At home, I tried to teach him some English, but he could not wrap his head around the seemingly senseless syntax of the language. Worse, the sentence structure was completely reversed from German ("You mean, in English the verb comes *right* after the subject and not at the *end* of the entire sentence? That's crazy!") Without language, his career and social opportunities were hopelessly narrow.

Formerly so boisterous and light-hearted, my father gradually started to become quiet and moody. I had never seen his disposition so dark. Even when his own life had been threatened on Kristallnacht, even when he was doing forced labor in Germany, Vati had always maintained his sense of whimsy and adventure, his boundless optimism, and even his goofy sense of humor. Here in America, nothing he did seemed to be taking root. He could not improve his work situation and he seemed socially isolated. Providing his family with a decent living wage was at the core of his pride as a man, and he was not cutting it.

Once again, Uncle Arthur came through with a decent idea to improve his prospects. "Why don't you try working as a busboy?"

he proposed. "It's not the classiest job, but at least you'll get out of that basement."

Le Ruban Bleu was a well-known, somewhat swanky night club on East 56Th Street. Vati became the only busboy for the entire club, clearing tables for a staff of four Italian waiters including Carlo, the colorful headwaiter. Overall, the waiters appreciated my father's helpful hustle every evening, and they treated him well, despite the occasional ribbing for being Jewish (all in good spirit, of course). Vati got 10 percent of the pooled tips and had to simply hope the waiters were being honest and fair. On average, he pulled in about eight to 10 dollars each night, his pay entirely in coins.

But from that point on, I almost never saw him. And while Vati might have gotten out of the basement, he still did not see the light of day. By 4 p.m. he was gone, and he did not return until nearly 5 a.m. When I awoke to get ready for school, he was usually asleep. But sometimes, when he could not sleep, I would find him at the kitchen table counting his hard-earned money, and I would give him a kiss good morning just as I left for school.

17

ROOTS

When the summer of 1942 arrived, we had been in America nearly one year. I took a quick inventory of how far we had come. My mother was working in a sweat shop, my father was a 50-year-old busboy, my sister was married to a man she hated, and I was a solid year behind in school. We were a real immigration success story.

Loneliness was my biggest problem. It was all I obsessed over. I had made no friends among my diminutive younger classmates. Yearning for age-appropriate companions, I thought it might be time to look for friends in my own neighborhood. My block was teeming with American kids my age who hung out on the street; and I figured there had to be someone willing to talk to me. I just had to build up my nerve.

One scorching summer day, I made the decision to head outside where young people were gathering on the stoops in front of their buildings. At least I would catch some fresh air, I rationalized, even if I did not make any friends. I opened the double wood and glass doors of my building and stepped out onto concrete landing where a smattering of kids stood against the railing. Several more sat scattered on the six stone steps below the landing that led down to the sidewalk. Up and down the block as far as the eye could see, the scene looked the same: different children on different stoops of nearly identical buildings.

The sun's blaring heat reflected off the concrete steps and brick walls, creating a virtual oven. A truck rolled down the street, swirling exhaust fumes into a simulated breeze; otherwise, the air was still. I immediately began to perspire, the heat and my nerves combining into one sweaty stew.

At first, I thought the kids were just hanging idly, but then I realized they were waiting. Waiting for someone to start a game. How comfortable the kids around me looked, safely tucked into their little groups of three of four. Standing by myself on the landing, I felt so alone, so exposed. There seemed to be nowhere to hide my accent and my foreignness. Even my poverty seemed to be on full display. Still, I took one step down off the landing. Mustering all my courage, I said, "Hello," into the thick, soupy air. Right away I realized I had sounded way too formal, and I immediately closed my mouth. Then I sat down and waited.

That was the beginning of my first American summer. Day after day, I just sat on the hot stoop and watched the American kids play. They played touch football, street hockey, stick ball, baseball. I absorbed the rules of all these American games while I watched and waited, and waited and watched. I grew accustomed to nobody speaking to me until it was starting to feel oddly comfortable. And then out of the blue, a disembodied voice broke the silence. "So what's your story?" the voice asked.

The words were coming from a boy a couple of steps below me. I instinctively looked behind me to see who he was addressing but there was no one there. "No, *you,* stupid," the boy said. "I'm talking to you. Who are you?"

"Um, I'm Jack," I said. "Jack Schwersenz."

The boy laughed. "Jack *what*? What the hell kind of name is that? Wait, is that Polish? I'm not even gonna ask how you spell it."

I flinched, momentarily annoyed, but mostly embarrassed. "It's

German," I said, unsure what bothered me more – the misidentified ethnicity, or just being called out as a foreigner in general.

"Oh," he said. "I thought it sounded Polish. Because I'm Polish. I'm Teddy. Teddy Jerz." He put out his sweaty hand and I took it eagerly, not knowing that I was about to meet someone who would soon become my closest friend.

"You're Polish?" I said, poorly masking my disbelief. "You don't have an accent, though. I thought you were American."

"Well, technically, I'm American; yeah, of course. I mean, all of us guys were born here. But that's not how we think of ourselves. Everyone here is from somewhere. You see those guys sitting over there?" Teddy pointed to the stoop across the street. "Yup. Those two brothers. That's Charlie and Emanuel Cassimatis. Charlie and Manny are Greek. And Johnny Locilento?" Teddy pointed to an olive-skinned boy sitting on the bottom step. "He's Italian. And Armando Pobleto, the guy over there pretending that fuzz over his lip is a moustache? His family is from Cuba."

That is how Teddy introduced me to our ragtag group. They were a bunch of poor, hard-working, unprivileged kids, and together we would soon become a stickball team. Teddy's father had died in a coal mining accident, and his mother was supporting the whole family as a waitress. He had three sisters and yearned for male companionship, so he was outside all the time. He became our shortstop. Every evening, as soon as Charlie and Manny's dad donned his tuxedo to wait tables in a Greek restaurant, the two brothers would join us outside. Charlie was a great stickball hitter and Manny was our regular first baseman. I did not know what Johnny's father did for a living, but Johnny could throw a mean fastball. And Armando couldn't hit a ball to save his life, but he could sure run like the wind. Not one of my new friends was Jewish and they didn't seem to care that I was. But we sure represented a lot of countries. In fact, our little group was a veritable League of Nations.

Every evening after dinner, we played right on 180th Street. The street was full of heavy traffic. There were so many cars that we could only play when the light was red. So that is just what we did. When the light was red, we hit the ball. When it was green, we stopped. Red light: run to base. Green light: Wait. Play. Stop. Play. Stop. It was a miracle we ever finished a game.

My learning curve for American sports was steep, but if that's what was needed to have a social life, I was all in. I would have done anything to have friends; I would have played any game, I would have even caught a ball in front of a moving car, which I sometimes did if there were any girls watching.

This became my new life. I understood these friends were not blood brothers. How could they be, when none of us had been through a war together? I knew they were relationships of fun and convenience, but I was still satisfied. All I wanted was some sort of childhood to replace the one that had been taken away from me.

One evening, after a game of touch football, I came home and found my mother sitting in the living room. She was not cleaning or sewing or doing any kind of work. She was just sitting and waiting for me, and that was ominous. I closed the door quietly, and tiptoed inside but there was no getting past her. "*Vas* is all this hanging out on the *shtoop*, Wolf?" she asked me. She had been practicing her English lately, and her accent was heavy.

"What's the big deal, Mutti? We were just playing."

"*Vy* aren't you hanging out *mit* any Jewish kids? Your new friends are going to lead to trouble!"

The panic in her voice! She made it seem as if I were hanging with a group of gun-toting American mobsters. It was abundantly clear she was not happy about my new-found social circle. True, my friends were not the best students – I couldn't argue with her about that. I suppose they were also not the most ambitious kids – she had me there, too. But they were my *friends*, and that was worth a lot to me.

Yet that seemed to be *exactly* her fear. These new American friends would not only corrupt my future academic ambitions but cause me to lose touch with my roots. Not only with my Jewish heritage, but even my *German* heritage. For a while now, she had been nudging me with this repeated request: "Go to the YMHA, Wolf – the Jewish Y. It's where all the other German-Jewish children play after school."

Retaining my German-Jewish culture was absolutely the last thing I wanted to do. Didn't she get it? I was trying to become an American as quickly as possible. But how could I say that to her face? I would never have had the nerve. I tried instead to say something less threatening, while still attempting to stand my ground. "Mutti. I have been here a year, and I like playing stickball in the street with my American friends. And by the way, from now on, I'd like you to call me Jack."

Right after the New Year in 1943, my parents suddenly had an epiphany. Or maybe it was more of a panic attack. They woke up and realized that I was turning 13 in February. This should not have come as a surprise to them as I had been 12 the entire previous year. Turns out, the surprise was on me. "Jack, you absolutely must become a Bar Mitzvah," they insisted.

They had to be kidding! After all, we were barely practicing Jews. We did not go to synagogue. I had never gone to Hebrew school. I loved ham! I didn't even know the difference between saying Kaddish – the mourner's prayer for the dead – and saying kiddush, the blessing for the sabbath. Okay, maybe that was the point, that my Jewish education was sorely lacking. But a Bar Mitzvah? It did not fit in with my plans to become American one bit.

Mutti tried every tactic she could think of to persuade me. "Vati will be heartbroken if you do not go through with it," she implored.

I was unmoved. Then she tried this one: "Think about all the times Oma Ernestine took you to synagogue when you were a child. How can you so easily just throw away your Jewish identity!"

I remained steadfast. Until she dropped the last guilt bomb: "Jack, we all nearly perished just for being Jewish. You cannot turn your back on your religion. You owe it to all the Jews of the world to keep your heritage and culture alive."

All the Jews in the world? Yes, Mutti, they were all my responsibility.

It was an effective guilt campaign, nonetheless, and I finally folded. But I had less than six weeks to prepare and we had no money to speak of. This was going to be a shotgun, economy class Bar Mitzvah to be sure.

My parents somehow put the event together at breakneck speed. They found a "rent-a-rabbi," Dr. Hanover, who was willing to officiate even though we had no synagogue affiliation. With my completely absent knowledge of Hebrew and only weeks to prepare, the frustrated rabbi had to teach me the abridged version: I needed only to memorize the *Aliyahs* – the prayers before each Torah section – and one short *Parshah* (the actual Torah section). The congregants and rabbi would do the rest to see me through.

On February 27, 1943, I woke up with a pounding heart, prepared for only one thing: total humiliation. That dreary, cold Saturday, I donned my very first suit – with pinstripes an inch apart, shoulder pads that would befit a general, and lapels the size of airplane wings. I combed back my greased hair into a high pompadour. I was as ready as I would ever be.

Looking like a 13-year-old gangster, I walked with my parents completely across town through soot-covered slush until we finally reached Broadway. We stepped inside a discount furniture store and left muddy footprints as we walked across the entire showroom, passing couches, EZ chairs, dinette sets, and plastic-wrapped mattresses. At the rear of the store, we found a staircase, and just at the top of the stairs, on the second floor, was a set of double wooden doors. Vati swung open the doors. Behind it was a sanctuary filled with a sea of unfamiliar faces.

"Here we are. Finally!" announced my mother. "The Temple Gates of Hope."

Bar'chu et Adonai ham'vo-rach!

I said my lines unsteadily and then looked around the congregation. At first, I didn't see anyone I knew. Then Aunt Hede and Uncle Arthur smiled and waved to me. That was a relief. But where were Cousin Ellis Arndt and Aunt Bessie?

Evidently, they would not be coming. My mother had ended their somewhat tenuous relationship. As the story went, Mutti asked for 50 dollars instead of 15 dollars for her weekly allowance, but Ellis kept giving her 15 dollars, week after week. Was it a misunderstanding? The language barrier? Or an *intentional* effort on Ellis' part to withhold our money! My mother was certain it was the latter. She finally requested the entire balance be given over in a check, and Ellis, hurt and angry, agreed, but not until he deducted each of the expenses he had incurred in preparing the many affidavits for the consulate over the years. It was a tit for tat. They closed their "business arrangement" and never spoke again.

Baruch Adonai ham'vo-rach l'o-lam va-ed
Baruch Atah Adonai, Eloheinu Melech ha-o-lam,
a-sher ba-char banu mi-kol ha'a-mim,
v'na-tan lanu et Torah-to.
Baruch Atah Adonai, no-tein ha-Torah.

Where were my peers? The truth is, I hadn't invited any. With no Hebrew school classmates – since I never went to Hebrew school – and no Jewish junior high school friends, I had not felt comfortable inviting any children my age.

Despite the small numbers of relatives in the congregation that day, and my absolute butchering of Hebrew, I managed to get through the service. The rabbi was able to give a fill-in-the-blank generic speech about me and my parents despite not knowing us at all. He made us sound wonderful! All I had to do now was get through the little luncheon my parents pulled together.

So far, it felt like the day had been just a chore to get through. I couldn't honestly say it had any meaning. After lunch I made a speech that was uninspired and perfunctory. In the sing song style of a careless pre-teen, I read from my handwritten notes. "I want to thank my parents... and Rabbi Hanover... for all they have done for me..." At that moment, I looked over at Vati and saw him beaming with pride. The day was not meaningless, at least not for him. It was the first smile I had seen on his face in several months. I felt my voice shake and immediately felt the sting of hot tears rising. I paused to catch my equilibrium and swallow. Then Vati winked, and that was the moment that nearly broke me.

At the end of the day, I managed to walk home with pride and a prayer book both tucked away under my coat. Later that evening Vati and I sat at the kitchen table. For the first time in quite a while he looked happy. Timidly, I asked, "Now that I am a man, Vati, may I have permission to smoke?"

Vati put his hand in his jacket pocket and pulled out two cigarettes. He lit them, drawing on both cigarettes; then he passed one over to me. We sat together, smoking in silence for a while. Then he reached over and squeezed my hand, and I felt his pride pass through his fingers and into mine.

I suppose I had only one motivation to smoke, and that was to look cool. My confidence, already low, had dropped to a negative number now that I was in the full throes of puberty. Examining myself in the mirror, I noted the emergence of my signature large, somewhat aquiline nose, a genetic gift compliments of my mother and Oma Ernestine. Then there was the hair. It was everywhere! Hair on my back peeked out from beneath my shirt collar and climbed up my neck like ornery ivy; hair on my chest and legs had thickened into a furry coat suitable for hibernation. And did I just spot even more hair taking root inside my nose and protuberant ears? Yes, it was a good thing the name Wolf was dead and buried.

Yet even without the name, I was destined to be teased. Everyone in our friend group got taunted about their looks. It was a tradition, supposedly, all in good fun. One kid was "shorty," the other "fatty" (cleverness was not our strong suit). Then there was me. My friends could not decide on one feature to mock, so they decided to pick on all of them. They teased me wildly about my accent, my hirsuteness, my big nose, my prominent ears. By the time they were done with me, I was convinced I was a monster.

One day I just got sick and tired of the teasing. That's when I thought, maybe it *was* time to search for new friends. Maybe I needed some Jewish friends who also had big noses. Perhaps Mutti had been right all along. It was time to check out the Jewish "Y" on 178th Street and Fort Washington Avenue.

I walked into the Y with a game plan. I would go slowly at first, look around a bit and get my bearings. Find the basketball court and maybe see where some kids were playing ping pong. *Somebody* had to want to hang out with me. But no sooner had I walked inside, than I was hustled into a gym room. About 30 other boys were already inside. A man holding a clipboard in the front of the gym had us sign in. "This must be some kind of mistake," I muttered. "I haven't signed up for anything." Well, I guess I muttered so softly that no one heard me, and things just kept on moving. The man quickly placed us into pairs, and before I knew it, he had handed each of us a set of boxing gloves. I had never intended to sign up for boxing, but I fleetingly thought, *I suppose it could be useful to know how to box for real*, as I recalled my involuntary German-Japanese battle on the fifth-grade schoolyard.

We sparred for two to three rounds, while another man who seemed to be the coach walked around and gave us pointers. After we were done boxing, we were told to gather around in a semi-circle. For another hour some guest speakers came up to the front of the room and gave us talks about Zionism. *Israel, Israel, Israel. We must establish the state of Israel!* Yawn.

"How was it?" my mother asked when I returned home.

"Um, okay, I guess. Not as social as I had hoped," I replied. "I learned to box. But some of it was a bit boring."

I described the activities to my mother. "Well, it sounds like good exercise, good discipline, and good Judaism. You should go again."

I could practically hear my mother's invisible exclamation points. Good exercise! Good discipline! Good Judaism! It checked off all her priorities. If I had said it was fun, she would have made me quit.

I went back several more times, and each time we followed the same routine. Boxing, Zionism. Boxing, Zionism. Israel, Israel, Israel. At the end of my fourth week, just as I thought we were done, the group leaders made a big announcement. "We have some exciting news, boys. We will be meeting outdoors in New Jersey next week for weapons training!"

I was confused. Had the YMHA become a military organization? I went home and discussed this new development with my mother. "Weapons training? What did you sign up for, Jack? Think hard. Retrace your steps that first day. What did you do?" my mother asked me.

"Let me think, Mutti. I walked into the Y, I passed the ping pong room and the basketball court and the social room. I passed the snack room. No, I might have walked into that one. But then I walked into the boxing room, and I signed an attendance sheet that was on a clipboard."

"Go back and find out exactly what you signed," instructed my mother.

I humbly retraced my steps through the Y all the way to that clipboard. "Son," one of the organizers asked me, while looking at me incredulously. "Did you really *not* know that you have been recruited to Betar?"

"What's Bitard?"

"Betar is a military Zionist youth group. What did you think all that talk about Zionism was about? We are enlisting teens to fight in the Jewish underground in Palestine, with the goal of pushing out the British and forming the state of Israel. All this training has been preparation for war. Are you in, son?"

Hell, no! I was not going to Palestine! I was staying right here in Washington Heights.

18

DIMINISHING RETURNS

After my Bar Mitzvah, everything went downhill.

It was as if we were surviving, but we were not really living. Comfort and security still eluded us. And the blanket of protection I had hoped for, now that Anita was back in my life, had somehow been pulled out from under me. How could Anita take care of me when she was barely surviving herself? Her war traumas were quite possibly bigger than mine, but I didn't know it then. I didn't know anything about her problems at all, until the day she fell down the subway stairs. Or to be more accurate, the day she threw herself down the subway stairs. Not one flight, but two.

I should have realized that things were not okay with Anita or with her marriage. I was just happy that we were all together again, and I was blind to everything else. Those first days, when Anita abruptly left Iowa and came to New York without Ho, I just thought she was excited to be reunited with us. And when she stayed in New York to help us get our bearings, we encouraged her; after all, we needed her assistance desperately. But as the months went by and Anita did not show any signs of returning to Iowa City, we greedily kept her for ourselves, without ever worrying about Ho's feelings and the state of their relationship.

At first, Ho waited. He had always been an exceedingly patient man. Then, he finally had enough. He was not going to let Anita just leave him, and he was not a man to be humiliated. He packed up his things, left the University, and followed Anita to New York.

For a while, Ho was back in our lives again, and it seemed for a moment as though we had managed to rewind the clock to the days before the war. On Sundays, we would all go hiking together. We'd pack a picnic lunch, a thermos of water and some cookies, and Anita and Ho would pick us up in their car. We would drive to a park not far from the city – the Palisades in New Jersey, or Van Cortlandt Park in the Bronx. Sometimes we would venture as far as Westchester County, just north of Manhattan. My parents were trying to emulate our weekend walks and picnics in Grunewald, yet somehow, nothing felt right. We seemed like imposters; actors playing our former selves. We had all changed; we were damaged in some way, and I was older, my innocence lost. On our dreary and joyless walks, we realized the old days were gone and we could not bring them back.

Adding to the gloom was the fighting. Anita and Ho's marriage seemed to be dissolving. They fought vehemently on our hikes, in the car, in our apartment. They yelled in English words I could not understand. I did not need to know the words; I knew that tone of voice from witnessing years of bitter arguments between my parents. The feelings spoke for themselves: unhappiness and disappointment, rage and resentment, scorn and contempt.

Anita's tumultuous relationship with Ho went through dizzying periods of deterioration alternating with repair, talks of separation, and an unexpected move together to Boston where Ho got a job as a civil engineer. Finally, in 1943, right after my Bar Mitzvah, Anita moved back to New York leaving Ho behind in Boston. She bravely tried to petition for divorce. The hurt and enraged Ho quickly followed Anita back to New York. He tried to do everything legally in his power to block her petition and swore he would never grant Anita an uncontested divorce.

"Mutti, I don't think Ho is ever going to let me leave him. He is like a man obsessed," she shared with my mother one day. "And he frightens me."

"Anita, we will find a way, somehow. Hold on for a while longer until I think of something."

"I'm afraid I will never be free of him. You don't understand how he looks at me. The intensity, the anger. Even if we found a legal angle, there's no guarantee that he won't continue to stalk me, to interfere with my life. I am going to have to take things into my own hands and solve this my own way."

Shortly afterwards, Anita announced that she had resolved her dilemma with Ho. They had negotiated some kind of arrangement and he promised to grant her a divorce in return for a favor.

After six weeks, the promised divorce never materialized. The only thing that *was* borne from Anita and Ho's "negotiation" was an unexpected embryo.

"What did you do, Anita?" my mother lamented, her head in both her hands. "What did you promise Ho when you met with him?"

"I told him I would be intimate with him one more time, Mutti. Those were his terms. One encounter, and he would grant me a divorce. He gave me his word."

"Well, now we know what his word is worth. Ho can never know about this pregnancy, Anita. Not ever."

It was 1943, and a termination of pregnancy would not be legal in New York for another 27 years. That's when Anita took her leap down the New York City subway stairs, her intent known only to her alone. Anita's pregnancy did end sometime after the fateful fall. I was told she had a miscarriage, and I have no reason to doubt it. But if any other road was taken, that secret was buried long ago.

With my mother's diligence, Anita's marriage to Ho was annulled due to her young age and the extenuating circumstances that forced her into marriage.

Legally speaking, her marriage to Ho never happened at all.

And then I experienced déjà vu.

We were all living together again, Ho was out of the picture and things seemed as normal as they could be. Until Anita woke up one morning with chest pain, shortness of breath and fever. I thought it was a fluke, and then the next month it happened again, and I realized she was back to having her "attacks." After a third episode lasted four days and left her practically incapacitated, my mother finally said, "Enough. There must be a diagnosis, Anita. The New York doctors are certain to find a cause. I am making an appointment for you at Mount Sinai Hospital."

This plan seemed overly drastic to me. "Why can't we just go to Columbia Presbyterian Hospital. We can walk there. Mount Sinai is all the way on the east side of Manhattan. It will take forever to get there. Plus, we will have to pay for transportation."

I expected my mother to be pleased with my thrift and logic. Instead, she looked at me as if I had two heads. "Mount Sinai was once known as Jews' Hospital," she replied. "Haven't you learned anything, Jack? We will go where we are welcome."

Anita began an extensive work-up for her mysterious symptoms. Over a period of several weeks, she underwent detailed bloodwork, numerous consultations and imaging, until the climactic moment when we were brought together to hear the final pronouncement.

"The news is wonderful," the attending physician declared, directing his attention to my mother. "I am happy to report that we found nothing wrong with your daughter."

"There must be something," said my mother. "She is suffering with pain. Debilitated. Short of breath. Unable to get out of bed."

"Have you considered that the chest pains may be psychosomatic?" another doctor piped in. He gazed compassionately at my mother and added, "You know, these episodes do look a lot like panic attacks."

My mother stood up and smiled politely. She went around the room and, while shaking the hands of each of the consultants, thanked them. Then she put on her coat. "Anita, Jack, come. We are done here."

"We will be happy to see your daughter in the clinic regularly.

Something might turn up," the doctor quickly added as my mother's hand turned the knob of the office door.

"Mutti, how could you be so polite?" said Anita, after we had left. "Not only wasn't I diagnosed, but I was not believed! They just think I'm hysterical. They were so condescending."

"We know they are wrong. I believe you, Anita. And you will keep coming back here until they have answers."

The doctors did not dismiss her entirely, whether out of politeness, or genuine scientific curiosity. Anita trudged back regularly to the outpatient clinic, often during an episode, when she would require my mother or me as a traveling companion. Winter visits were brutal, the wind wickedly fierce and blustery behind the large Fifth Avenue buildings across from Central Park. After one of Anita's appointments, we walked towards the 96th Street bus stop, where we usually took our crosstown bus across the park to the west side of Manhattan. It was an unusually cold day, and I pulled my scarf over my face as we pushed against the stinging, fierce gusts. "Why do we even bother to make these trips, Jack?" Anita yelled to me above the sound of the screaming wind.

We reached the corner of 96th Street and Fifth Avenue and waited for the bus. "It's always the same," Anita continued. "They take my blood and examine me, but I can tell that no one really believes me. There's no one here who is fighting for me."

I did not know how to reply, so I stood dumbly at the busy 96th Street intersection feeling cold and bored, as I watched the traffic light change from red to green and back again. The cars started moving, when suddenly Anita broke away from me and leapt right into the oncoming traffic. I instantly reached for her and jerked her back to the sidewalk. "Anita! What are you doing!" I screamed.

Anita looked up, but the expression on her face was dull and flat and she did not seem to be focusing on me. She simply said, "What difference does it make, anyway?" Her voice was devoid of emotion, and she said it into the air, as if I wasn't there at all.

I was at a loss, unsure what to say or do. I only knew that the blank look in her eyes frightened me. But I did not know how to recognize depression, despair, and hopelessness back then. I did not see it in my sister that day.

And not long after, when it happened to my father, I missed it entirely.

During all this time, while Anita was divorcing Ho, going to the hospital, and trekking back and forth to the clinic, my father had become a ghost. He was there, yet he was not. He was slowly diminishing, and gradually disappearing.

We had already grown accustomed to barely seeing him since he worked the night shift. In his physical absence, we simply did not notice how much his mental health was declining. He was self-absorbed, he was detached, and we did not recognize these signs as being emblematic of depression. What we did notice is that physically, he seemed to be falling apart.

It seemed like he had aged 20 years! Undoubtedly, the three years of hard labor under the Nazis had served to accelerate the process. He developed a bone spur in his heel requiring special orthotic shoes. Chronic lower back pain pestered him, and he started walking with a hunch, staring at the ground as his feet shuffled forward in their clown-shaped shoes. A bronchial cough from heavy smoking became a constant hacking. He barely slept during the day due to the noise from the busy street and the daylight, and a prescription for sleeping pills barely had an effect on him. The chronic fatigue was of no help to his disposition. Worst of all, my father seemed to have lost all his confidence. He was isolated in a country he did not understand. The last time I had a glimmer of his old self was at my Bar Mitzvah, but since then, his spark seemed to have gone out completely.

My parents' lives seemed to be contracting. Not only had my mother made no friends at the factory, but she was a social outcast. And how could my father call the Italian waiters at the club his "friends" when they did not even speak the same language?

Their only close ties were with Uncle Arthur and Aunt Hede.

Then, one day, Uncle Arthur came to my parents asking for a loan. My mother behaved true to form. She expressed outrage and distrust. She convinced my father of the folly of lending money to Uncle Arthur. "Your brother-in-law is a spendthrift," she said. "Look at all those fancy clothing he wears." She denigrated Arthur's general character. "Look how he flits about from job to job. Why does he keep changing jobs? Is he stealing from his employers?" She maligned his behavior. "Do you see how flirty and touchy-feely he is with Ilse, his own daughter. Why, she's already a teenager? It's inappropriate!

"Absolutely not, Arthur! No loan! We cannot expect to ever see our money again!"

And just like that, Hede and Arthur – my *only* surviving aunt and uncle; Hede and Arthur who had met us at the dock when we arrived in America; Hede and Arthur, parents of my only first cousin, Ilse; Hede and Arthur, who had procured our furnished room, helped us find jobs, and been through *everything* with us – never spoke to us again.

19

ATLAS

It is all up to me.

That was the epiphany I had the day I entered P.S. 115 on 177th Street. I had started Junior High with the terrifying feeling that it was entirely my responsibility to pull my family out of poverty and despair.

We had taken 50 steps backward. We worried about money all the time, for my mother's piecework was seasonal, and my father's tip money went up or down (along with his mood), depending on the night. I could see now that my parents would never catch up; they were simply too old to start anew. And Anita could not help, afflicted as she was with a mysterious illness. It seemed abundantly clear: the whole family's well-being was on my shoulders.

I had to be Atlas. And I could not fail.

My parents did not ever have to verbalize that I must go to college or become a "professional." I already knew what was considered important and valuable. My mother's cousins had been doctors, lawyers, businessmen. The value of education was undeniable. But what job could I do? I had no real passion for anything. Become a doctor? Way too squeamish. A lawyer? Not slick enough.

Just then, a searing pain in one of my molars offered an answer to my career conundrum. Having not seen a dentist since 1939 in Germany, it looked like I could avoid the chair no more. But I did not have a dentist, and neither did my parents. In fact, they never thought they would need one.

Before leaving Germany, rumors had circulated that we would not be able to afford the expensive dental care in America. Friends and neighbors offered my parents sage advice. "Get all your teeth pulled before you get to America!" Now, both my toothless parents wore full dentures, which they kept in a glass on their nightstands at night. I was not so lucky, I suppose, since I still had my own teeth, which hadn't been tended to in nearly five years. I needed an "honest" (read: *cheap*) dentist right away.

Dr. Alterman was the answer to my dental dilemma. He found no fewer than 20 cavities among my pearly not-so-whites. And while the visit was torturous, it was enlightening as well. The thrifty Dr. Alterman had no receptionist or nurse, so while he drilled each of my cavities with his right hand, he answered both the phone and his door buzzer with his left. It was a fascinating business model – the height of streamlining and efficiency. And at three dollars per filling, payable at the time of the visit, he had to be making a fortune!

Yes, dentistry! That was the career for me. And since I was practically ambidextrous, I could see myself easily drilling with one hand while writing up the bill with the other.

Once I made my career choice, everything else started to fall into place. I chose Latin to fulfill my language requirement in junior high school – a very useful language for a medical or dental career. Next, I took a job as a delivery boy at a local pharmacy for some practical pharmaceutical experience. I decided the 50 cents an hour I earned would not go into the family coffers this time. The money would be my own, and it would have to be my "allowance." There was no way I could ask my parents for an allowance. If I was going to have any spending money, I was going to have to pay myself.

My pharmacy delivery job was the perfect way to pick up some extra cash... for the short time it lasted.

Along the wall of the pharmacy, countless pills of various colors and sizes sat like penny candy in large glass bottles. The white-coated, white-haired pharmacist moved with slow but steady confidence as he handed out simple advice like a medical practitioner. When he was not with a customer, he slipped behind the counter to count out pills. I waited on the sidelines as he poured the oval, circles, and square pills through a metal funnel into small bottles. Once the bottles were labelled and bagged, I ran with them to the nearby apartment buildings to make my deliveries, hoping for a generous tip. A nickel would be good. Fifteen cents would be a dream.

Just a couple of months into the job, I was really getting the hang of it. The buildings and the faces in the doorways were beginning to look familiar, and stairwells were no longer menacing, even in the dim lamplight.

One afternoon, as I bounded carelessly down the stairs after a delivery – with my mind focused on my earnings and my tip money jiggling optimistically in my pants pocket – an arm suddenly jutted out from behind me and grabbed me around my neck. A voice in my ear said, "I've got a knife."

My abductor's voice was deep and gravelly; his arm was large and muscular, and he was gripping me firmly. I had no reason to doubt his pronouncement about a weapon – I didn't care if it was a switch blade or a butter knife – and I made no move to escape. The big arm dragged me out of the stairwell into an empty apartment and threw me into a chair, where I finally came face to face with my captor.

I immediately had a jolt of surprise. I recognized this man! In truth, he was not a man at all, but an older boy from my school. Way older. Having been left back a few times, the adult-sized "boy" in front of me was well past puberty, scruffily bearded and had a reputation in school for being "crazy." Maybe even violent. Any initial relief soon relapsed back into panic. There was no solace in the thought that my abductor was just a student. The student in front of me was the school sociopath and a budding felon to be sure.

"Hand over your money," he ordered. This demand alone felt catastrophic. That money was my allowance. My future ice cream and candy money! As I handed him the change from my pockets, the loss felt devastating. But I did not know my torture was just about to begin.

The juvenile delinquent lit a match and threw it at me. I instinctively ducked. As he watched my terror mount, he joyfully lit another and another, the matches flying past me like mini-Molotov cocktails, burning out just before they landed on me.

Soon he grew bored with the activity. He lit a cigarette and took slow and silent drags, his cheeks hollowing with each inhale, his face blank. Was he calculating his next act of cruelty? Or was he just taking a break? I squinted my eyes, trying to pierce his crazy mind, but I could not tell. "Stop looking at me like that or I'll put this lit cigarette out on your face, you little wimp," he finally growled.

I sat there for what seemed like an eternity, speculating what he really planned to do with me. In my mind – the one with the overactive imagination – he was not improvising. He had a plan leading up to something far more portentous. *This kid is far past bullying,* I thought, certain he was the type of boy who hid mutilated cats in his basement. But even if I was wrong, and his endgame was only to take my money and scare the heck out of me – well, on those fronts he was already turning out to be a very successful criminal.

Truly fearing for my life, I decided my only means of escape would be to talk my way out of captivity. If he had any compassionate side at all, maybe I could appeal to it. I had to try to come up with a sob story on the spot, and so I started to ramble without any pauses and without any obvious punctuation. "I am really truly sorry but you have to let me go I'm so very happy you took all the money here you can have all of it but my mother she is very sick she has a heart problem and if I don't get back home in time she will get so worried and then she will have a heart attack which could kill her and then she will die so please PLEASE you have to let me go."

Just then, I stopped to take a breath and saw that the boy was laughing. I was so relieved. I thought, *wow, I just cleverly talked my way out of a kidnapping and certain execution! I am a hero! And an excellent storyteller! Not to mention, my English must be really improving!*

Then the boy abruptly stopped laughing. His brow furrowed and he leaned his face so close to mine that I reflexively pulled my head back to avoid the noxious stench of cigarette smoke and onion breath. "I'll let you go," he gnarled, "on one condition, and one condition only: that you won't squeal."

I swore to him that I would never! Never, ever, ever. I went straight home, my pockets no longer weighty with the comforting clang of collected coins. Still shuddering with fear and adrenaline, the first thing I did was tell my parents. Yes, I squealed like a pig.

Perhaps I hoped for sympathy; possibly I needed a hug. But that is not how things worked with Mutti. "*Ach, mein Gott!* How could this happen? Such behavior cannot be tolerated!" she yelled instead.

Outrage was what I got – it was my mother's version of a hug. Action too, for that was her style of caring. My parents dragged me right away to the school authorities. Appropriate punishment for the boy was expected: they would be okay with forced labor (in Arctic Canada, for it was closer than Siberia); but if that could not be arranged, then a jail sentence would do (tried as an adult of course). At the very least, my parents expected expulsion from school and an apology.

We sat down with my junior high school principal to discuss an action plan for the budding criminal. But the principal just looked at us and said, "Just let it go."

My parents were stunned. Speechless, at first. After the shock, my mother finally spoke. "You are not punishing the boy? And us? What about us victims?"

The principal shrugged his shoulders and smiled weakly. "What can you do, these things happen," he said feebly.

We went home exasperated. "I cannot believe this," spat my mother. "What kind of a country is this, where crime goes unpunished?"

Yes! In her beloved Germany, people followed rules. There was law and order. Everyone listened to authority. Just look at the Nazis. The system had clearly worked to perfection.

With the boy tyrant still on the loose, I felt I had no choice but to leave that prized pharmacy job. But I still needed to provide my own allowance, so I looked to my immediate neighborhood for any job I could do with lousy command of English and not a single useful skill.

On the corner of Audubon and 180th Street was a busy Irish pub that would overflow onto the street, especially on payday. By nightfall, there was usually raucous fighting among the drunk patrons. No, there would be no job for a 14-year-old kid like me in there.

Two doors down from the mayhem was a beloved candy store, Sam's, known for making the biggest and best chocolate malteds and truly superior egg creams. Sam's candy store was our destination whenever my friends and I had enough money. Skinny Sam Lubowitz and his corpulent wife were a notably mismatched pair of Russian immigrants. They were non-practicing Jews who were devout in their communist beliefs. The one drawback to our visits: you could never go into the candy shop without getting a Russian-accented political lecture on the corruption and inferiority of capitalism. I was pretty sure Sam kept his own profits and didn't share them with the proletariat, but I kept these thoughts to myself and nodded attentively while I sipped my malted. Despite these issues, I imagined Sam's would be a phenomenal place to work. There would be free egg creams! Candy samples! It was worth a Marxist lecture or two. But my hopes were dashed because the candy store was not hiring.

Further down the street, I was finally able to find a shop with a "help wanted" sign. A small photography store was in need of a delivery boy right away. "Take the rolls of film down to the processing lab on Fulton Street. Can you do that, son?"

I sure could! I would just need to take a 45-minute train ride down to the South Street Seaport, wait at the lab for the film to be processed and return uptown with the negatives and prints. This became my new after-school job. On the weekends, I was also the attendant for our not-quite-automated photo-booth. I took the patrons' quarter, sat them on a barber-style chair which I pumped up or down with a foot pedal, and snapped their photo. Then, I ran into the darkroom to process the film and minutes later handed them their strip of four pictures.

On busy Saturdays, groups of teenage girls would often come in for their photos in dress clothes and makeup looking preternaturally mature. As I positioned the giggling girls in their chairs, and raised them with the foot pedal I would become self-conscious and flustered. And then I would run into the darkroom where the overhead red light hid my blushing, ugly face.

In time I got to know the owners of the processing lab on Fulton Street, and they offered me a job delivering prints and negatives to their customers – drugstores, mainly. My new route went from 34th Street and Third Avenue to Chatham Square, right in the heart of Chinatown. Before long, I was servicing 15 stores. In addition to my pay, the photo lab fronted me 30 cents to cover the multiple train rides I would need to take along the Third Avenue "El" – the elevated train line – to reach all the stores. In those days, each train ride cost a nickel.

It would be far better to pocket the extra 30 cents, I decided. Briskly walking the streets of lower Manhattan, I tramped from drugstore to drugstore, delivering prints and picking up rolls of film. My walking route took me along the Bowery, where it looked like all the homeless people in the world – the flotsam of humanity – congregated. It seemed like thousands of people were living under the El. There were alcoholics, panhandlers, and other afflicted human beings, devoid of family or safe havens. Men lived in boxes or covered themselves in newspaper blankets. They pushed all their belongings in shopping carts or wandered up and down the streets with nothing more than a bottle and their shame hidden in a crinkled paper bag. They held out their dirty hands hoping for loose change, or they stared vacantly, while coughing into their ragged sleeves or talking to some invisible voice inside their heads.

As low as we had fallen, I could see there was always something lower. Poverty and suffering seemed to know no bottom. I walked past the homeless vagrants, wanting to help, but at the same time feeling the comfort and security of my spare nickels jiggling safely in my pants pocket. I touched each of their sharp edges with my thumb, confirming they were still there, while I prayed that I was on my way up.

On August 10, the day after the US decimated Nagasaki using the second of our atomic weapons, the Japanese agreed to the surrender terms of the Allies. A formal surrender document was signed on September 2, 1945, and World War II officially came to its bloody conclusion.

It was not until the war was over that images of concentration camps began to circulate around the world. Only then did the full atrocities committed by the Nazis and the horrors of the death camps finally penetrate the international psyche.

Those images felt deeply personal. *That could have been our fate,* we thought. We felt relief along with the guilt of survival. At the same time, we hungered for any morsel of news. Had our relatives ended up there, in those camps? Did they ever make it to the ghettos? Or were they shot when they got off their transport trains? The incomplete answers, the vagueness of the information, left us alone with our imaginations to fill in the horrible blanks. We were well past any fantasies of happy reunions, but we yearned for some closure. Instead, our friends and family were simply missing persons, lost and never found again, leaving behind just a void of confused longing.

There was only one person whose fate we learned. Anita's

former love, Fips, had been in a labor camp, rather than a concentration camp – only a slightly less horrific internment, possibly because he was half-Jewish. Miraculously, he survived the war. A US Army truck liberated him, but while returning from the camp, it skidded in a rainstorm, and crashed into an oncoming vehicle. Fips suffered a severe head injury and died just days after his liberation, having never experienced freedom.

We moved on, pretending the trauma was behind us. And we kept living and tried to look for good news wherever we could find it.

In the spring of 1946, I found an unusual item in our mailbox: an envelope addressed to me. I ripped it open and unfolded the single sheet of paper inside. "Congratulations," read the unassuming piece of parchment. "You have passed the entrance exam for Stuyvesant High School."

I reread the letter. Was this even real? When I had taken the exam for Stuyvesant the previous fall, it was only on a whim; I had no expectation of passing. In fact, until the very moment I opened that envelope, I firmly believed I was a moron.

Stuyvesant was the well-known, prestigious, and highly competitive science and math high school in downtown New York City. Attending the elite public school was one of the few ways to level the playing field for us poor city kids. It was as close as I would ever get to going to private school. This was my ticket to my future as a dentist; I was sure of it.

This small success was my first achievement here in America, and I felt it was deserving of a celebration. Ninth grade graduation was coming up too, giving me two special occasions to commemorate. Suddenly I had a grand idea: I would celebrate both these small victories with my father. My thought was to take him to a Yankee game. I didn't know for sure if he would love it, but I knew I would! I fantasized that the game would lift Vati right out of his bad mood, and we would bond over our new shared passion: baseball. Who could not enjoy America's favorite pastime?

We sat in the uncomfortable bleachers for a double header, looking out over a sea of blue-painted wooden chairs. What a game we were in for, and what a team, with Yogi Berra catching, Joe DiMaggio in the outfield, and Phil Rizzuto on the infield. I mean, c'mon, we were unbeatable!

The organ played its spirited tunes over the loudspeaker as we waited for the game to start. Leaning over to my father, I explained, "Vati, this is how to fill out a scorecard." He stared at the card blankly while I kept on talking, reviewing each player and his stats, but I could see I was not engaging him at all. Finally, the game started. Baseballs flew up in the air, but my father's eyes did not seem to follow. "There! Look Vati! A double play!" The crowd roared! They stood up in a ripple and raised their arms in the air. My father did not move an inch. He sat glued to his seat and did not utter a sound.

Now the Yankees were on base and the pinstriped Aaron Robinson was at bat. The audience went wild as DiMaggio slid to second. I screamed, "Look, Vati, 'Joltin' Joe' just stole second base!" as the whole stadium jumped up in a giant wave of excitement. I looked down at my father. How was it possible that the excitement had failed to penetrate him? Vati just sat there, bent over and staring blankly at his feet, showing no joy or interest. Was he unable or *unwilling* to smile? He was right there next to me, but I felt like I could not reach him. I felt helpless and frustrated and sad. And I could not help but feel angry too.

Somehow that day was a turning point. I knew my life had to keep moving forward. I had tried, but I could not lift my parents up. Was my only option to leave them behind? I had to look for a chance at happiness without them, outside my home.

One day after school, Teddy Jerz found me moping on the stoop. His timing could not have been more perfect. "Hey, Jack," he asked. "Do you want to come up with me to the Lake Spofford Hotel this summer?"

I knew very little about the resort where Teddy had worked each summer as a glass washer, but I jumped at the opportunity. I could not think of a better way to be with my best friend, make a little cash, and get away from the heat and depression in the city.

"*Depêchez-vous*, 'urry up, move faster."

I was trying to do an adequate job as a pantry assistant, but Leon, the second pantry chef, was quickly losing patience with me. And he was well within his right. I was slow as molasses, and I did not know a chef's knife from a paring knife. In his strong French accent, he made his unhappiness with me loudly known to the entire kitchen.

Yup, I had zero experience, but I was somehow working in the kitchen of a top Jewish resort. Situated on a five-mile lake in the Green Mountains, the Lake Spofford Hotel boasted 275 guests, a golf course, multiple tennis courts, water activities, a night club, and all the amenities of a first-class resort. Somehow, the finest of Catskills-like hotels had gotten off at the wrong exit and ended up right here in New Hampshire.

And here I was, nestled in the kitchen with an international cast of characters. The all-male staff included Gene, the head pantry chef from Italy who was my boss and mentor, and Leon, the fancy Frenchman and number two pantry man who had taken a strong dislike to me. In the far-left corner was an ancient Jewish bread baker who was as dry, thin, and crusty as a Passover matzoh. The large central dessert area was run by a magnificent Italian pastry chef with a giant Toque hat; he was a veritable da Vinci of dessert, whose artistic billowy creations I would often dream about. Manning the glass washing area on the American side was Teddy, and right beside him, on the far-right wall, were four alcoholics with ruddy cheeks and bulbous noses who were operating the dishwashing area. Those sorry souls had quite literally been dragged up from the Bowery earlier in the summer and had been detoxed and deloused before the guests arrived.

The only woman in the entire operation was "Aunt Sarah," the widowed sister of the hotel's owner, Abe Jacobson. Square, squat, and downright scary, she stood like a sentry at the doors separating the dining room from the kitchen. As the "kitchen supervisor," she examined each tray coming back from the dining room and scavenged it to see what items could be retrieved, recycled, and reused. Rolls turned into croutons, lettuce leaf garnishes became salad, and as for that untouched meatball – "Well it looks perfectly fine to me. Put it back!" If it lacked a bite mark, it was headed for another meal or onto the staff's plates. When she was not recycling food, Aunt Sarah's job was to prevent chaos from erupting in the hectic, crazy kitchen full of colorful, intercontinental personalities.

I had expected the summer to be a breeze, but I was sorely mistaken. In those first few weeks, I found the job as pantry assistant unexpectedly challenging. It did not sound like high-skilled work: I was to keep the coffee urns topped off, fill the pitchers with various juices, and cut up the grapefruit, melon, and other decorative fruits. It was also my job to set up the "medicinal" gastrointestinal counter, i.e., the prunes and figs. I also cleaned the vegetables and lettuces and put the requisite Jewish food – the pickled herring, lox and whitefish – into their respective showcase dishes.

It soon became apparent, however, that I did not have the first inkling how to use a knife. All kitchen work in my house had been handled by my mother and sister, and I was a pantry imbecile. In that first week, my hands were covered with thousands of little knife-cuts. Then, when I would grab a tomato or a lemon – MOTHER F---ER – how those cuts would sting! I would drop the fruit on the ground like an idiot and it would simply roll away, cutting a circuitous path through the pastry area, or between the legs of the dishwashers, and invariably landing at the feet of Aunt Sarah. Sometimes an unattended tomato would simply roll off the counter and smash on the floor beneath me, and I would run to get a mop for a "clean-up in aisle five."

After the first week, Gene pulled me aside. With my head bent, I stood in front of him, expecting to be packed up and sent home. "Jack," he said, with a strong Italian accent and a soft smile, "I like you, and I wanna give you a chance, but I'm gonna have to fire yer ass if you don't wake the f--- up!"

When I showed Gene my bloodied hands, he immediately stopped berating me. "Aha!" he cried, as he passed me a pair of rubber gloves. Then, like a proper mentor, mixed with the touch of a caring parent, he taught me a few clever tricks with a blade and I was on my way.

From that moment on, I started to really hustle. I zoomed through the kitchen as if the Hitler youth were after me. I could practically juggle the fruit while I zigzagged from station to station. No one was firing *me*!

A few weeks into the summer, Leon, the French second pantry chef who disliked me, was fired. Apparently, Gene thought he was lazy. Now Gene had no choice but to take me under his wing and show me his craft. I learned how to make canapés, dressings, salads, and other artful delicacies. By summers' end, I could cut a tomato into a rose and whittle a radish into a tulip. My cucumber slices were as thin as fine silk lingerie, and I splayed them out like a deck of cards in a magic trick.

After dinner clean-up each night, I ate with the staff in our own dining room right off the kitchen. We got leftovers from the prior day's meal thanks to Aunt Sarah's parsimonious recycling service. While the rest of the staff complained bitterly about the food, I thought it was delicious. I always found food to be delicious, simply because it was there. I did not have to ask permission for any of it, and I ate ravenously.

I worked non-stop from 7 a.m. until 9 p.m. every single day. By nightfall, dead on my feet, I dragged myself to our sleeping quarters. Teddy and I shared a room in one of the staff buildings. It looked like an Army barracks, and was hidden away from the guests at the edge of the wooded property. On our first day of work, a white-haired woman wearing an all-white uniform, handed us freshly cleaned all-white linens which we carried to our all-white room. The only color in the room was the red rust of the bed frame.

Hanging on the wall was a broken mirror, below which was a rickety worn-out white chest whose drawers I could never get to slide open. Every night I threw myself into my creaking, rusty bed and lapsed into a coma-like sleep. It was uncomfortable; it was ugly; it was awful.

And I loved it.

In the fall of 1946, I returned from a magical summer full of optimism for my future. I was about to start tenth grade at Stuyvesant High School, my first step of the grand plan that I succinctly referred to as "rescuing my family out of poverty and economic disaster." A fabulous opportunity lay ahead of me to attend an elite school for the gifted and talented. After coming to this country speaking no English and then being "left back" almost two years, I had a dream that Stuyvesant would advance me toward my imagined future. Success! Prosperity! Dentistry! My triumph was all but predetermined.

But as soon as I walked through those doors on 15th Street and First Avenue, I sensed I was in trouble. The imposing school was enormous. There were four floors of identical-looking classrooms and labs. I was practically guaranteed to never find my class or homeroom. And with a student enrollment of over 2,600, the school was the size of a small town. Did I mention that enrollment was 2,600 *boys*? It suddenly hit me that I would really feel the absence of girls in this all-boys' school. I was already 16, and I could "feel" absent girls all over my body, all the time now.

Tossed into this Stuyvesant "village," I roamed the hallways like a lost soul while I noticed with some consternation and confusion that not everyone looked quite as lost as I was. Throngs of boys my age already seemed to know each other. They were chatting, and ruffling each other's hair, and punching each other playfully on the shoulder. And when I arrived late to my first class after getting totally lost in the giant maze of a school, I found most of the boys already neatly seated. "I don't get it," I whispered to a boy beside me. "How come everyone knows their way around? Did you all get a floor plan? Isn't everyone here new, like me?"

"No, stupid." I made a vow never to ask him another question, but the boy continued. "Obviously, some of the kids have been here since ninth grade. You knew that, didn't you?"

I didn't, but I pretended to. "Oh, sure," I said. "Duh! So that's why everyone seems to know each other!"

"Well, don't you have friends from your school here? There's a whole bunch of us here from P.S. 6, and a group from–"

"Oh, yeah, sure, sure." I cut him off and groaned internally, my confidence crumbling as I started to understand how things worked; how "behind the eight-ball" I was already. There were kids here who knew each other; some had been here a whole year. Only one other kid from my Junior High had come to Stuyvesant and I barely had said two words to him. Ever. Suddenly I felt like a transfer student from an outer borough. Another planet even.

Suffice it to say, school was hard, and I wasn't ready. Not psychologically, socially, or academically. Maybe I couldn't see how easy it would be to fail without support or resources. And especially without a circle of friends who knew the ropes. Getting in was not my ticket to success; there was a lot more to it. What was easy in a big place like Stuyvesant was to be lost and invisible until you crashed and burned.

And that is exactly what I did.

The old building that we inhabited, built in 1904, was inadequate to house our monstrous class size. The solution was to divide us into a morning and afternoon shift. I got the afternoon shift from 11 a.m. to 6:45 p.m., returning home at nearly 8 o'clock each night. Did I come home and dutifully pull out the books? Not a chance. I had every intention of seeing my neighborhood friends after school. I was going to keep my social life alive come hell or high water.

My grand plan was to wake up early to do my homework *before* school. But in those first few days, in the wee morning hours, as I stared at those endless pages of Latin and intermediate algebra, I completely crumpled. Everything felt way beyond my ability. And why did I take Latin? Now the idea seemed idiotic. "I just can't do it," I said to myself, as I yawned. I felt thoroughly defeated.

For about two weeks, I tried to do my homework each morning. And then I just stopped. It was way too hard. And besides, I was way too tired. Who needed Latin anyway? Or algebra, for that matter. It was sleep that I needed, more than anything.

One day, the teacher started going over the math homework in class. That was new. He started calling out names. "Schwartz!" he yelled.

No one answered. There was an embarrassing silence. "Schwartz!" he repeated.

How could I possibly know that he meant me? Then everyone in the class snickered and started staring at me. "Umm, it's Schwersenz, sir," I finally volunteered.

"That's exactly what I said. Schwartzends. *(More snickers.)* Get yourself up to the blackboard and write out the solution for number three on the homework. Don't forget to show your work."

Panic. "Umm. Umm... sorry. I couldn't do it sir."

"Couldn't do it, or didn't do it?"

"Ummm, both?" *(More laughter.)*

Well, that sealed it. It was obvious what I needed to do. I could not keep going to class. How could I allow myself to be upbraided by the teachers for not knowing the work and then laughed at by the other kids? No, it would be far better not to show up. At first I started "cutting" Latin and algebra. Then, I stopped going to school altogether.

Each morning I took my nickel meant for train fare, and instead of going to school, rode the bus all the way down to City Hall. Then I rode it back home. After this three-hour time-killing ride, I tiptoed into my apartment, inching past my snoring father who was sleeping off his night shift. I crawled under my bed, lay as still as a statue, and waited there until Vati left for work.

I lay under the bed every single day. I waited for *something* to happen, but what? Did I secretly hope for the fateful call home? I would get in trouble of course, but some kind teacher or guidance counselor would say, "Where is Jack? Why isn't he in school? Is anything the matter?" Mutti would scream at me and I would be punished (cruelly). I would wallow in self-pity, and then we would sort out what to do next.

No call ever came. I waited and waited, but no one seemed to even know I wasn't in school; that's how invisible I was. At home, no one found me under the bed – I was invisible there, too. No screaming, hysterical mother found me and punished me. And I became stuck. There was no dramatic conclusion in sight.

I could not figure out a solution. As I lay under that ugly mattress each day, the fear and panic that had grown from my initial school avoidance had somehow dissolved. Fear had been replaced with boredom, and the boredom supplanted by confusion about what would come next. Finally, I decided I simply couldn't do it anymore. Twenty-eight days later, rather unceremoniously, I concluded that I had better go back to school. One month of collecting dust bunnies was more than enough.

How hard it was to slide out from under that mattress. I had to basically *will* myself to do it. Like Lazarus, *I arose*. Or, like Frankenstein's monster, *I awoke*. Yes, that was more like it. With every ounce of courage, I exited my apartment one morning, stepped onto the correct train headed to Union Square station, walked down 15th Street to the corner of First Avenue, and walked through the double doors of a school that seemed to hate me.

Of course, the school was completely indifferent to me. It didn't hate me; it did not even know me. It didn't give two beans if I was there or not. It was just a building, after all.

When the yellow envelope arrived in the mail, I knew this time it would contain no words of congratulations. It was certain to contain evidence of my failure. My mother's English was not great, but she knew the letter F.

Slowly, I pulled the report card from its envelope. This was unbelievable! How could the teachers have *passed* me in all my classes? Had they failed some other kid named Schwartz by mistake? Oh, my grades were quite awful, but having not actually failed, I would be spared my mother's punishment again. I would not even have to repeat any classes. I was home free!

It would not be long before I would recognize the disaster of my first semester. I had missed all the critical foundations in math and science and those educational deficiencies would follow me for the rest of my academic life. By the next semester, I could already see the writing on the wall. I would never catch up. I could kiss my future, my family's future – and my fragile self-esteem – goodbye.

I was not Atlas. I was a moron, after all.

20

FOUND AND LOST

Looking for relatives and friends in the United States. Bakker.
call 555-777-1212

"Arthur, Come look at this."

It was so unremarkable one could have easily overlooked it. A plain little advertisement sat inconspicuously in the back of the *Aufbau* [Reconstruction], a German language newspaper created in 1934 for the scattered diaspora of Jewish refugees. My mother read this paper religiously, for it was her only connection to her lost culture. Little ads appeared all the time in the paper as displaced war and concentration camp survivors tried to reunite with family members, and this nondescript ad was no different. What caught her eye was that it was placed under the code name[1] of our Dutch Red Cross smuggler, the one who had taken our jewelry back to Holland. Mutti saw the name and momentarily caught her breath. "Arthur, is it possible? Come take a look."

My father came and looked at the ad, but he couldn't be sure either. The name was a common Dutch surname.

"No. Forget it, Arthur. It can't be. It has been six years since we have heard anything. It probably does not mean a thing. But just in case... "

Mutti picked up the phone. She nervously dialed the phone number on the ad, and someone picked up immediately. On the other end of the line, a woman with a pleasant voice spoke. "Yes, you are correct. I am looking for several families who smuggled jewelry out of Germany. Can you identify some of the items?" she asked.

My mother had no difficulty recalling the precious possessions that were seared into her memory. She described them over the phone in detail. They quickly made an appointment to meet.

We squeezed into a booth at a coffee shop, waiting to meet either a savior or a swindler. It was already 1946, and we had long ago given up hope that we would ever see our valuables. So far, no one had shown up at the appointed time. The hour was passing, and my mother was getting progressively more nervous. "I don't think it's real, Arthur. It might be a scam. The woman placing the ad is probably a charlatan looking for money. And I described the jewelry to this woman in detail. How foolish of me. I should have made her describe the jewelry to *me*, shouldn't I?"

"Grete, why always so negative? Let us meet with her and see what the lady has to say. Maybe there are still some good, decent people left in this world."

"Not in my experience, Arthur. Not in my experience."

The door to the coffee shop dinged repeatedly, and each time we strained our necks to see who had entered. An old married couple, arm-in-arm... an elderly lady with her little tan teacup Chihuahua tucked under her elbow... a young woman with a toddler in tow. Each time the door swept open we felt a combination of hope and anxiety, and each time it closed, our hearts sank. It did not look as though anyone was coming.

Just as we were about to leave, an impossibly tall woman stooped her head in the entrance and walked into the coffee shop. Her eyes settled on us immediately, and she nodded and walked over to our booth. "Hello, it's very nice to meet you," she said. Her English was nearly perfect, with barely a trace of an accent. She sat down in the booth next to me and across from my parents. "Well, let's get to it, then," she added quickly, and proceeded to search inside her bag. Moments later, her long and graceful hand emerged holding a folded white handkerchief and she placed this neatly on the table and slowly unwrapped the corners of the cotton fabric.

Lying inertly in the middle of the white cloth lay a diamond brooch, a diamond ring, a diamond necklace, and a heavy gold bracelet. They were perfectly polished and looked as though they had just woken from a long hibernation.

My mother picked up the gold bracelet and held it tightly in her hand, pulling it against her chest. "This had once been my father's watch chain," she said, her voice quivering. She handed the chain to me across the table, while she wiped her eyes with the heel of her other hand. "Your Opa Hiller's."

A few awkward minutes passed. Eventually, the lady touched her swan-like neck and cleared her throat, disrupting the sentimental moment. "I'm sorry to interrupt. I just want you to know how apologetic I am for the long delay in bringing these items to you. You see, the Red Cross worker who brought this jewelry from Germany to Holland gave them to my father for safe keeping. When the Nazis invaded Holland, my father quickly buried them in his backyard so they would not be seized. Unfortunately, my father died suddenly just before the end of the war. He had left no written information, nor told anyone where these valuables were buried. My brother and I have spent over a year digging up the entire backyard. We were only recently able to find where the jewelry was hidden. Again, I'm so deeply sorry."

"Please," my mother exclaimed, "do not apologize. This jewelry, these few rings and chains, are not of great monetary value, but their connection to our past is immeasurable. To us, they are priceless. The risks that your father took for us are beyond words. We do not have very much, but we would like to offer you some reward. It is the least we can do to thank you."

My father raised an eyebrow and stared across the table at me with a look of amused disbelief.

But the woman shook her head. "I want no reward," she replied. "Your happiness is thanks enough."

"You see, Grete," my father said, after we had left the diner. "There *is* decency in the world! People are good, most of them, at least." How nice it was to hear a hint of my father's old optimism peek out, if only briefly.

My mother did not respond to him immediately. She seemed lost in the emotions of the day, and appeared to be pondering a serious question. Finally, she spoke. "Arthur, do you think we should contact Hapag-Lloyd, the shipping company that transported all our furniture to Rotterdam before the war broke out? Maybe some of our furnishings survived the war."

"Now I like your optimism, Grete. Yes, we should!"

"We are sorry to inform you, Mrs. Schwersenz, but the warehouse was bombed by the Germans in 1940 during an aerial raid on Rotterdam. All its contents were destroyed. I'm afraid there is nothing left."

"What about the insurance? We had all our furniture insured. It was very costly. Is there any recompense?"

"I'm very sorry again, ma'am, but if you read the fine print, you would know that your policy excluded 'acts of war'."

"Well, there you have it, Arthur. You believe there are good, honest people in this world? Hah!"

Was it naive of us? Presumptuous, even? For a moment we held out the unrealistic hope that somewhere we would find our possessions. The grandfather clock, the prized Persian rugs, Anita's piano – they were gone, our former lives forever lost to us. If we had forgotten, we were reminded again. Germany was over. It was the past. America was our future.

I was not as convinced as my mother of the global evil in the world. Sure, there was plenty of wickedness in the universe, but here were plenty of good people too. Right now, I happened to be standing next to one of them.

"Look over there, Jack. That's Gemini, the Twins, and over there is Ursa Major." Anita's new boyfriend, Lou, made some incomprehensible squiggles with his index finger in the air that I pretended to follow.

"Where's the North Star, Lou?" I asked. He didn't answer me; didn't seem to acknowledge the question. "Lou?" I asked again. I tapped him on the shoulder.

He turned to me, cupping his left ear. "Sorry, couldn't hear you, Jack. What did you say?"

Anita was gradually putting her life together. She had taken a job as a collection agent at Finlay Strauss, a jewelry retail chain. This job, while way beneath her potential, seemed to suit her personality. Anita had refined the art of telephone intimidation and turned out to be a maestro at getting people to pay up.

At the store, Anita had befriended the assistant manager, Lou Molatto. For the past few months, they had been dating, and it looked as though they were getting quite serious. Lou had been an Air Force officer and navigator in the South Pacific in World War II, experiences that gave him an air of worldliness and sophistication. After numerous bombing missions originating from New Zealand, he was finally discharged just before the end of the war due to a ruptured ear drum that caused hearing loss in his left ear.

On that clear, star-filled evening, Lou was showing me the constellations just as my father used to do. We gazed out together over the Hudson. "Those tiny lights in the sky aren't just millions of light-years away," he tried to explain to me. "Their light left millions of years ago. Can you believe it, Jack? You are looking back in time."

I had no idea what Lou was talking about. I only knew that I had never met a kinder, gentler soul than him. I watched the stars twinkle faintly and thought that Lou was just the kind of calm person Anita needed in a husband and all of us could use in this family.

My mother and Anita began to make wedding plans, and I started to imagine what it would be like to have an older brother.

The wedding was just weeks away, when I came upon Anita and my mother embroiled in a serious discussion. Anita seemed consumed with worry. Was she getting "cold feet?" In an unusual role reversal, it was my mother who tried to be encouraging and reassuring. Lou seemed to be the kind of man who could provide for Anita, and Mutti was on a mission to put Anita's concerns to rest and get her settled down.

"Anita, what is the hold-up? You have found a nice man, he loves you, he has a good job."

"Well, I'll tell you, Mutti. There are a lot of problems, as I see it. First, Lou is a Sephardic Jew, from Salonica[2]. We are Ashkenazi Jews from Europe. It's a mixed marriage! It will never work!

"Jews are Jews, Anita. Next?"

"All right, Mutti. Well, this is my other concern. Lou's last name is Molatto. And I was thinking, with his dark olive skin, and his dark and curly hair, people will think he's *mulatto* – meaning, they might think he is racially mixed. And if we have children, people will think *they* are racially mixed."

"Because of his name? That's ridiculous, Anita, and I won't even address it."

"And what do you think, Mutti, of the fact that he's only an assistant manager at the store. That's not very impressive. Do you think he can support me?"

"Assistant managers can eventually become managers, Anita. You have a role to play here. You can push him a bit, encourage him. Like I used to do with Vati. I don't think you need to worry about this now, so long as Lou has potential."

"But wait until you hear this, Mutti: Lou is supporting his entire family in the Bronx, including his three adult brothers and his parents. And not one of them seems to be employed."

At that, my mother took a gulp and paused for a minute. "I see, Anita. Now that could be a problem!"

Yes, perhaps there were some "red flags," but Mutti was going to make sure that Anita got married. There was no denying that Lou was handsome and decent, kind, and amiable. The fact that he was not brimming with ambition (a family trait, apparently) was, nonetheless, exceedingly worrisome. Financial security was imperative! Any suggestion of sloth – even the desire to relax – would not be tolerated.

They had to quickly come up with a remedy to improve Lou's professional prospects before this marriage could proceed. Anita hatched the plan: Lou would take courses in watch repair and diamond cutting on the GI bill which would eventually allow for a career change. Then he would be the ideal spouse. Now that she had organized his continuing education, career advancement, finances, and future, Anita could marry Lou. She decided he could keep the name "Molatto." After all, it was spelled with an *o*.

I listened to all the shenanigans and realized that Anita had turned into a replica of my mother. I wondered when exactly it had happened, and how I could possibly have missed it.

At least Anita's happiness seemed all but assured. But as my father sank ever deeper into a pit of darkness, I became increasingly miserable at home.

School offered no respite as it was a never-ending source of anxiety. My disastrous first semester had left me with huge learning gaps. I couldn't get a grip on anything; it was all slipping through my fingers. As nonsensical trigonometry equations appeared on the blackboard, I stared at them in confusion and horror. SOH CAH TOA. Was that English? Latin? A mnemonic? A corn and lima bean side dish? I honestly did not know. I was living every human's worst nightmare – that I had appeared in the wrong classroom and was being given a test on a subject about which I knew nothing. Only this was not a dream, and I would not wake up in the morning, relieved that it had all been a figment of my vibrant imagination.

I had no understanding of how to get help. No confidence to go to a guidance counselor. No support network to help me navigate a forbidding, intimidating system. I did have old-fashioned parents who assumed that every bad grade was my fault, and naturally, I believed them.

Escape. This was my only solution. Every day I dreamed of summer. I would disappear to Lake Spofford. I would become someone else. I would temporarily leave my parents and Stuyvesant and depression and failure behind.

In May, those dreams started to unravel. After dinner one evening, I was studying in the living room when I heard the unusual sound of moaning. It was coming from the kitchen.

I went into the tiny room where I saw my mother, holding her abdomen and bent over the counter. "What is it, Mutti? What's the matter?"

"Nothing, Jack. Just a stomachache. Probably something I ate. I have my annual physical with Dr. Schneider in a few weeks. I'll mention it to him when I see him. Go, study. Harder. Work harder!"

In just a few weeks we were sitting in Dr. Schneider's office as I watched the kind, elderly German refugee palpate my mother's abdomen. Using the fingers of both his hands, he pushed deeply into the top, and then the bottom, as if he were kneading dough. Then he placed his left middle finger on her abdomen and tapped that finger with the middle finger of his right hand, moving it from place to place to place to place. My mother's abdomen sounded like a hollow drum when he tapped. Was that normal? Then the doctor took my mother's hand and patted it reassuringly. "Frau Schwersenz, *keine Sorge*, don't worry, I'm certain it is indigestion."

When a similar but more severe incident of pain recurred a few weeks later, my mother seemed more concerned. We traipsed back to Dr. Schneider for a repeat tap-tap-tapping. "Indigestion again," said the doctor. "It must be stress. Or gas, perhaps? Gas can be very painful, Frau Schwersenz. Imagine your intestines stretched out like a giant, tight balloon." He put the fingers of both hands together, then slowly pulled them apart, the gap widening between his fingers. "How excruciating! We don't want it to pop, now, do we! No, no, no," he laughed. "Make sure to sit on the toilet, Frau Schwersenz. Perhaps take a little bicarbonate. But please come to the office if you are not better in a day or two."

I walked out of his humble office with my mother, not reassured in the slightest. Intestines, like a balloon, ready to pop? Intestinal linings were pretty darn thin, as anyone who ate sausages or hot dogs could attest to. It sounded ominous. More importantly, I had often heard my mother complain bitterly about things or people, but never about pain. She was quite stoic. But maybe Dr. Schneider was right. Gas could be painful. These were not things my mother and I spoke about anymore. We were well past fecal examination and bowel conversations, thank goodness.

At 11 p.m., agonizing screams emanated from the kitchen. I raced in and found my mother holding her distended abdomen. *A baby?* No, that was absurd. Immediately switching to panic mode, I realized there was no way I wanted to be responsible for this. Vati was at work at the club and could not be reached, so I dialed Anita. She was a married woman, and a responsible adult, and would know what to do (I hoped). Anita lived at the edge of Harlem with Lou and arrived at the apartment within half an hour, and as soon as she saw my ashen, swollen mother, she swung into action. "We must find a doctor who will make a nighttime house call!"

I recall that we stood on the street, ringing the doorbells of doctors in the neighborhood. Did we find their names and addresses in the phone book? Was there an ad in the Yellow Pages that said, "I Make House Calls?" My recollections are fuzzy now. Why didn't we call an ambulance right away? Maybe we felt we did not have the authority without doctor's orders. Perhaps between her moans, my mother cried out, "Whatever you do Anita, don't call an ambulance, we might have to pay for it!" Those bits are hazy now, but what I can recall is the doctor who finally answered our incessant ringing.

He lived on 178th St. and Audubon Avenue and he followed us to the apartment with his mysterious black satchel in hand. Once inside, he sat next to my mother, set the bag down and fumbled through its contents until he found the right vial and syringe and gave her an injection. While we all waited for the narcotic to set in, the doctor held my mother's hand and spoke to her in gentle German. "Yes, yes, I'm from Berlin," he told her. (This was not surprising, as we were in Washington Heights, practically a German-Jewish ghetto.) "Yes, of course, I know your hometown Lobsenz in Prussia," he continued. "Yes, yes, and I knew your cousin Dr. Arthur Arndt. I used to cover for him."

Well, now, those handy coincidences were sure adding up. How comforted my mother was. Not only capable hands, but a kinsman. *How unbelievable*, we thought! It was like a miracle. *He knew our relatives!* Sent from God, Himself. We never doubted him, not for a moment, not for a lifetime.

Did we really know some people in common, or did the doctor provide the perfect illusion that we needed to believe in that night? I will never know. The wise and kind doctor diagnosed my mother with intestinal obstruction, and quickly arranged for an emergency admission to Columbia Presbyterian Medical Center just a few blocks away.

We were headed to the Christian hospital this time, and not a moment too soon.

"Please, sit," requested Dr. Self. "I'm afraid it's cancer."

We tried to absorb the significance of the words we had just been told. The finest of doctors proceeded to describe my mother's diagnosis and care plan with the utmost of clarity and kindness. *Dr. Selfless*, I thought briefly. *Of course, that should be his name*. But even that brief mental interruption did not cushion the harsh reality to come.

"Your mother's tumor is enormous, and it is obstructing her colon. I am sorry to tell you that it is in fact malignant. However, it is not all bad news. Malignancies vary in their aggressiveness. This tumor is very slow growing and has likely been there for years. For now, we will do surgery just to relieve the blockage. We will delay the major cancer resection until July."

The doctor had left us a bit of room for optimism, but we still left his office shell-shocked. Mutti was the family's anchor and without her, we would all be afloat. I was devastated. I hoped and I pleaded. I bargained and I begged. I promised that I would be a better student, a better son. "Please, God," I prayed. "Please, let my mother live..."

And I must sheepishly admit that I added a small addendum to my prayer. I asked God in a very small voice this one tiny additional request: "God, while you are listening, and after you take care of my mother of course, is there any chance that I could still go to Lake Spofford this coming summer?"

God listened. By the time the summer had passed, things were not nearly as bad as they had started out. My mother underwent a successful surgery and was considered cured of cancer. Lou was promoted to store manager. I made it through another wonderful summer in New Hampshire and was now hunkering down in school as a junior and was getting decent grades. And as the coup de grace, Anita announced that she was pregnant with twins.

Yet all these nuggets of good news did not seem to lift my father out of the doldrums. His old self had completely collapsed inward. He seemed to be in a permanent state of misery from which he could not emerge.

That fall, my mother suggested I start working at Le Ruban Bleu with my father. What was her real motive for wanting me there? Was I there to help him with his work so he wouldn't lose his job? Was I supposed to keep up his spirits, or to make sure he made it home unharmed? Maybe she just had a growing feeling of unease that he was not okay on his own. Whatever the reason, I began to accompany him to the club every Saturday night.

The club was another world; an underside of New York that I had never seen. It was loud and trashy. The audience was drunk and crass. There were married couples and overdressed tourists. There were rich old men, who sat with girlfriends barely older than me, their wrinkled thick fingers touching the soft ivory skin of the girls as if they owned them. It was America alive at night, and it was just where I wanted to be.

Now I had a first-hand view of my father working at the club as its one and only busboy. How hard he worked clearing tables; making empty glasses disappear from view like a sleight of hand and behaving obsequiously using only elementary English. As I watched Vati labor, I felt deep compassion for him; but I could not help myself – the feelings were tinged with embarrassment.

For me, working at Le Ruban Bleu had its perks. As a glasswasher, I had ample time to hang around the bar area and mingle with the famous (or almost famous) headliners that were waiting to go on stage. Sometimes I stood on the sidelines behind the curtain, coughing amidst the thick smoke, my shoes stuck to the liquor-spilled floor while I watched great comedy and music.

All the acts were first-rate, or so they seemed to my inexperienced ears. Sometimes we would get a big-name headliner, like Pearl Bailey, Imogene Coca, Carl Reiner, or the Ink Spots. On those days, the line would gradually grow outside the Club until the street looked as busy and frenzied as Times Square. Then the pace of my father's work picked up even further, as the manager tried to pack as many patrons as he could fit into the little club. My father had to haul out extra tables and chairs, running back and forth with the heavy wrought iron tables hoisted over his head, filling a tiny empty space in a corner; then circling back and returning with two chairs, until no empty space remained. It was hard not to be reminded of his days hauling train tracks on his shoulders; only now, with his scoliotic back bent, his head sunk low, and his orthotic shoes shuffling, his little body seemed drained of all dignity.

In time, I got to know all the waiters, including Carlo, the headwaiter. "These are my Italian friends," Vati told me, beaming with pride as he introduced me to everyone as "*my zohn who goes to Stuyvesant.*" But late at night, when I stood near the cash register where the waiters entered their checks, I overheard them imitating his speech and hobbling around like a hunchback. Then I knew with certainty what I had always suspected: these were not really friends, not in the true sense of the word. My father did not have a friend in the world.

At the end of the night, it was Vati's job to clean up and shut down the club. During those two hours, while we worked together unharried – with no one giving orders and no onlookers – I found my embarrassment miraculously gone and my fondness returned. We slid from table to table, collecting the sticky glasses and emptying the stale ash trays. We worked in silence, enjoying the peace, while we leisurely slid back the tables and pushed in the chairs until everything looked just like it had before the club opened. Then we headed to the kitchen. We found the club sandwich that the chef usually left us, and we shared it, both of us famished after the long night. I pulled on every cabinet door and refrigerator handle in the hope one was left unlocked. No luck – they were all locked, as usual; but somehow, I miraculously found the ice cream bin left open. I helped myself to a huge scoop, then scrounged around for some other leftover dessert, which I wrapped up like a delicate treasure to take home for the next day.

Sometime between 3 and 4 a.m. our work was done, and by the time we finally made our way up to Washington Heights, dawn was just starting to break. We silently took in the emerging beauty of the apricot-tinted light, a perfect background for the silhouetted, graphite-colored skyline.

On May 12, 1948, Anita gave birth to healthy twins. Lorraine and Ronald Molatto arrived just two days before Israel was formed, as if heralding the birth of the nation. We were speechless with emotion. These were not just two healthy newborns; their birth symbolized that our family would go on. The Nazis had not destroyed us completely.

If the birth of his grandchildren bolstered my father's

disposition, it was only fleetingly. It was as though this last bit of joy required fuel, and now his tank was on E for Empty. Vati's mood sank to an even deeper low and he seemed practically moribund. He started talking about overdosing on sleeping pills, but he would say it threateningly, as if he were trying to garner sympathy from us. After a while, he started to speak of this so routinely that it seemed almost habitual. He had always been dramatic, and we did not take him seriously.

Every day, it felt more insufferable to be at home. My brief tastes of summer freedom somehow made things worse, as if heightening the contrast with my sorrowful confinement at home. I felt like I couldn't breathe; the very air in the apartment felt toxic and claustrophobic. And I was never alone; my parents were always there, there, there. My father would be sleeping off his night shift, and my mother was now doing her own tailoring at home, for she had left the factory job and was back to having her own sewing clients. But even though they were always around, my parents no longer spoke to each other; on the rare occasions when they opened their mouths, it was only to argue bitterly. Otherwise, there was silence.

I had to find refuge from the suffocating feeling in our tiny flat. One summer evening, I simply left. My feet seemed to move automatically as I trekked down a lonely section of Broadway and continued past a dimly lit cemetery. I passed the Audubon Terrace on 156th Street which housed the Museum of the American Indian. Usually bustling during the day, the museum was closed for the night, and the surrounding street was deserted, the air completely still. I kept on walking through the stagnant, humid air, gradually finding some peace as I relaxed into the rhythm of my shuffling shoes. *Crash*. Like the clatter of a cymbal, the sound of a fallen garbage pail lid interrupted the silence; the offending clumsy kitten meowed as she scampered across my path in the darkness, then all was quiet again. The empty streets, noiseless as they were, still felt less desolate than the suffocating bleakness of my own home. I walked briskly down the abandoned section of Broadway, listening to the soothing sound of my own breath, and following the path of my elongated shadow.

Unconsciously, my feet led me to the outskirts of Harlem until I had reached Anita and Lou's apartment on 147th Street between Broadway and Riverside Drive. I rode up the caged elevator of their once-upon-a-time luxurious building and rang the bell again, and again and again. Anita answered. She had a twin in each of her arms, but she saw the sadness on my face along with an urgent need for love. She handed the babies to Lou and held me tight, rocking me the way a mother would.

After that night, I started going to Anita's apartment several nights a week. She lived about a mile and a half from our apartment, and if I walked briskly, I could make it there in under a half hour. I subsisted on the noise and commotion in that apartment, the raucous cacophony of crying babies, the arguing between Anita and Lou. The chaotic sounds of family life were far more comforting than the deafening silence of my own home. I ate freely from Anita's full refrigerator while we sat in the kitchen, and I listened to her complain about Lou; apparently, he was still financially supporting his parents and otherwise able-bodied brothers. Listening to her grievances was the small tax I had to pay for Anita's kindness and encouragement. After we both unburdened ourselves, Anita surreptitiously slipped a dollar into my pocket before I made my way back to my hopeless home in Washington Heights.

"Jack, it's your third summer at Lake Spofford. Now you are a rrrregular." Gene had taken me under his wing like a true apprentice and was teaching me all manner of culinary skills and rolling R's. "So why you don't wanna become a pantry chef like me, Jack? After all, you tell me you don't like school so much."

Gene was a true craftsman – an expert at edibles – and I was full of respect for him and his trade. He also had a successful career when the resort was closed working as a pantry chef on the cruise lines. I truly loved my summer kitchen work, but not for a second did I seriously consider it as a career. How could I explain this to Gene without hurting his feelings? How could I tell him that being a pantry chef did not fit into my plan to "pull the family out of poverty and economic disaster?" Perhaps I should have followed in Gene's shoes. Maybe then I would have avoided all the debacles that followed.

Another glorious summer ended, and I returned to high school, finally a senior. I started the school year working like the devil to pull my grades up. I had worked out a plan for my future but it was going to take a miracle to achieve it.

In late Autumn, my entire plan fell to pieces.

Teddy was the first to find out. "What's up, Jack-o?" he said, in his cheerful way. "You look like your pet hamster died." He plopped down on the stoop next to me where I had been sitting alone, wallowing in self-pity, and looking quite despondent.

"It's my transcript, Teddy. I'm absolutely ruined."

"Ruined? Did you fail out of school or something?" Teddy asked.

"No, Teddy, it's my GPA. It's a 78!"

"Oh, whew. That's not so bad, Jack. I mean, that's a *Stuyvesant* 78. If I got a Stuyvesant 78, I'd probably be the valedictorian at my school!"

"No Teddy, you don't understand. This is a disaster. You see, I had a plan. Part one of that plan was that I go to the City College of New York."

"You are going to have to explain this to me. What's the big deal about City College?"

"Teddy, you know they call City College the Jewish Harvard."

Teddy burst out laughing. "The Jewish Harvard? Seriously?"

"Teddy, I'm not kidding. City College is extremely hard to get into. It has amazing professors. It's tuition-free. And maybe you don't know this, but we Jews can't just go anywhere we want. All the top schools, like the Ivy Leagues? Everyone knows that they don't want Jews. Oh, sure, they're willing to sprinkle in a few of us, but there are strict quotas to limit Jewish admissions. So bottom line, City College is the most prestigious school for someone like me, and the only one I can afford. But here's the problem, Teddy. To qualify, I needed a minimum GPA of 80. So that's why my 78 is a downright disaster. Now I'm at a dead end. I don't know what my next move will be. And I'm already 19! I'm ancient!"

"Well, I'm so sorry Jack. I have every confidence in you, and I am sure you'll figure something out. And now I have some news of my own to tell you. Because I already know my next move. You know that I have never been much of a student. So I've decided to enlist in the US Army."

"The Army?" I paused for a long second. "The Army!" I said again, letting it fully sink in. And then, I completely flipped out. "Don't do it! Don't do it, Teddy," I begged. "Please, anything else. Please."

"C'mon Jack," Teddy laughed. "Don't be so dramatic. You're like a dramatic baby. Nothing's gonna happen. It's 1949 and the whole world is at peace. Besides, I am absolutely done being cooped up in a house full of women."

"Teddy, seriously, think about it. When has there *ever* been such a thing as lasting peace? I'll answer that myself because I kind of know history. NEVER. Please don't sign up, Teddy. I don't want to see my best friend become cannon fodder!"

"Aw Jack-o. I'm honored that you care. But the deed is done. The fact is, I've already signed up."

Teddy was right. I was being a little over-dramatic. What I could not dare to say out loud was, "Teddy, you are my best friend. I have lost enough people in my life. I could never bear to lose a friend again. Promise me. Please. Promise you will never leave me."

Teddy had made up his mind and there was nothing I could do to change it. But I was still uncertain about my own future. One day, Anita spotted an ad from the Department of Labor.

FREE APTITUDE TESTING and FREE CAREER GUIDANCE SERVICES.

It seemed like just what I needed. Where did I stand? I honestly did not know. It was time to find out if dental school was a pipe dream. Three grueling days later, I completed testing on intelligence, aptitude, and abstract reasoning. Anita and I now sat down with an advisor to review my results.

"I am happy to inform you that you are eligible for an academic scholarship," the advisor told me.

"And why is that?" asked Anita, her eyes squinting, suspiciously.

"Because your son scored in the top one percentile."

"Wait," I interrupted. "Do you mean I can pursue my dream to become a dentist?"

"Yes," he assured me, "absolutely."

Anita stood up. "Thank you, he is my brother, if you must know. But we don't want or need your scholarship. We will not accept any government help." Then she practically dragged me out of the office.

"What do you mean we won't take a scholarship, Anita? Isn't it an honor? Shouldn't I accept it graciously?"

"Absolutely not, Jack. We will not take any handouts. Not from the government, and not from private charities, for that matter. We will not be turned into welfare recipients!"

"But Anita, this isn't welfare *or* charity; it's a scholarship!"

"Jack, you must learn not to be beholden to anyone in your life. You are just going to have to pay your own way through college."

The summer after high school graduation was my first at Lake Spofford without Teddy. I upgraded from a pantry assistant to busboy and the tips start rolling in. When the hotel guests found out I was a pre-dental student, they tipped even more, as if they felt obligated to fund my education. *How's that, Anita! I created my own little scholarship!*

That summer, I met another busboy, Sid Aliber, a super nice

guy from New Hampshire. Sid offered to give me driving lessons in his brand-new Model T Ford, became my new summer stand-in for the absent Teddy, and turned into a truly good friend.

As busboys, I suddenly found myself with time to socialise. I was even allowed to mingle with the guests. Some of the bolder busboys dated the daughters of the guests. However, I learned quickly to sidestep those entitled rich girls. Their world seemed complicated and frightening. Instead, I set my sights on the sweet simplicity of the female staff who expected nothing from me but kindness and friendship.

It turned out to be a fabulous summer, and I felt truly happy.

21

NEW BEGINNINGS, SAME OLD ENDINGS

Autumn ushered in a new beginning, a fresh start. The pre-dental program at Washington Square College – the liberal arts college of New York University – was willing to bet on me, and at least I could envision a future. At the NYU freshman orientation, I befriended another freshman named Melvin Tiger, who in turn, introduced me to his friends, and in just a few weeks, I found myself part of a social group. These blossoming college relationships were something entirely new. What had changed? Was America finally opening its arms to me? Did I finally belong?

Our college friend group grew quickly, and soon we were 25 liberal arts students, most of us pre-med or pre-dental. We hung out in Washington Square Park between classes, studying and socializing, believing ourselves to be big shots instead of the nerds that we really were. We decided to form a house plan – a fraternity-style social club – with the thoroughly ostentatious name "Epicurus." Our goal was to party every Saturday night with a female house plan. Partying was the pretext. Losing our virginity was the endgame.

Everything seemed to be falling into place. Money was not a problem; I had saved enough tip money from the summer to cover tuition, books, and lab fees. Just before school started, my mother surprised me by announcing she and my father would be paying for my education. I did not protest. Even the college curriculum did not seem too daunting. I was getting my work done easily and had the good grades to show for it.

A fragile confidence was gaining traction and it was pulling me further from home, psychologically speaking. I began to feel almost lucky.

Yet, there was always something that sucked me back into my old life. It started with my mother. One day she asked for my counsel. "Your father's mood is weighing me down so much," she confided in me.

Over the last few years, while my father was floundering, Mutti had become increasingly independent. She had worked on her English, developed a whole clientele of sewing customers, and managed to stash away money. I could almost feel her boosted confidence as she explained her finances and how it was that she was able to afford my tuition. There was one downside to her independence, however: she did not need my father anymore. "I am considering divorcing Vati," she finally said out loud. "What do you advise?"

I gulped. "Well," I said, uncertainly, "I think it might be very hard for Vati to be on his own."

"I don't think you understand my question," Mutti explained. She was not asking for moral guidance; she was asking for financial advice.

That is when I found out that my parents had saved nearly 20,000 dollars.[1] It had taken ten years, but they had turned pennies into what seemed like a small fortune to me. Like Rumpelstiltskin, they had spun straw into gold. How had they done it?

There was no magic involved, no fancy investments, no luck, even. Just painful labor and sacrifice. Everything made sense now: why there was never food in the house, why I had to ask for every morsel. It was not because we did not *have* the money. No, that is how we *made* the money. It was the same playbook my parents had used to accumulate their modest means in Berlin: work like crazy, scrimp and save every penny, even if that meant using only one square of toilet paper or one-ply of a two-ply napkin (apparently, they separate). Walking, instead of spending a nickel for the train. I was speechless.

And it wasn't only my mother drawing me back in; Anita was playing her role as well. "I am so frustrated with Lou," she complained to me. "That man has no ambition whatsoever!" She also fretted endlessly over the twins. "Do they seem normal to you, Jack? Are they delayed? Shouldn't they be crawling by now?" she asked me, as if I had any idea whatsoever.

I felt a seismic shift. I was becoming an adult and was now the de facto "man of the house." I had tried to separate, to really immerse myself in college with my peers, but my family wasn't having it. Somewhere along the line I had been handed the role of confidante. It was not a role I had volunteered for, and hearing the chronic discontent of both the women in my life was, quite frankly, exhausting.

"I am going to jump! I can't take it anymore."

Vati was the last to draw me back in. I ran home to find him standing on the windowsill, looking out over the ledge. This was something new. Someone had to take care of Vati. Would that role be left to me, too?

"Do something, Jack," my mother pleaded.

"I am going to jump. Really," Vati cried again.

"Vati, calm down," I begged, gently. "Come down from the windowsill. Come inside. We all love you. We need you. *I* need you. Come down from there."

After his third or fourth time on the windowsill, we started to become inured to it. *Which is it going to be, Vati? Pills or jumping?* Surely, he did not have the nerve to do either. These were idle gestures. They were designed to get our attention and pity, weren't they? In the recesses of my mind, I remembered the boy I paid a *Shiva* call to in Berlin – Karl – whose father had jumped to his death from their apartment building. Could my father be like him, planning to jump out of despair? Or was my father the Vati of my childhood memories, standing high on the dung heap back in Spain, puffing himself up, begging us to listen, and trying to hold onto his last vestiges of control? Yes, of course, *that* was my father. Ever the dramatic actor.

Yet there were times when my father seemed as hopeless and dispirited as the bums on the Bowery. I would start to worry that his threats weren't idle at all. And just as I would begin to panic, his "dark mood" would lift ever so briefly. At those times, it was as though the sun had suddenly come out from behind a cloud. His eyes would sparkle – glow, even – but he would be talking nonsense, filled with fiction and fantasies. "You know, Jack, I have many contacts at the club. With my connections, I can start my own clothing store." *Sure, Vati. Your own clothing store. Sure.*

Then, out of the blue, my father's nightclub, Le Ruban Bleu, shut down for good. The head waiter, Carlo, graciously helped my father get a job at another nightclub. It was located at the Hotel Shelburne on Lexington Avenue and 37th Street. The pay was lower, and the club was smaller and far less swanky. There were no headline stars, and nothing at all to feel proud of.

In June of 1950, the Korean war broke out. All those things I had muttered to Teddy about war being inevitable, and peace being ephemeral – all those warnings I had proclaimed out of my own selfish desire to keep Teddy home – turned into grim reality. It had been only five years since World War II had ended, and we were at it again. When I had uttered to Teddy, "there is no such thing as lasting peace," I had not intended to be right.

The Korean peninsula was split in half, with China backing North Korea, and the US putting all its military weight behind South Korea. The US reinstated the draft. My friends and I were all draft eligible and we were terrified. Our only protection was to stay enrolled in college with 12 credits or more and pass a deferment exam. If we were lucky, we could defer the draft until graduation. I was not ashamed of my desire for deferment. I had lived through war and I knew enough to be afraid.

That summer, while the Korean war was raging on another continent with my friend Teddy in its sights, while my mother contemplated divorce, while my sister contemplated her chronic discontent, and my father contemplated the value of his life, I dared to contemplate the seeds of my good fortune. I felt the success of school, and the weight of solid friendships.

It turned out to be a diamond of a summer. I bussed a table with the famed pianist Rudolph Serkin[2], and convinced him to give the staff a private concert of Beethoven sonatas. That summer I tried to make out with a waitress in the backseat of Sid Aliber's car. I was not successful, but I heard rumors that girls found me attractive. Something about my blue eyes, I think they said.

That summer, I did not know how fleeting good fortune could be.

The one bit of science I retained from high school was Newton's third law of motion: simply put, all things that go up must come down. And in late 1950, after a fabulous start to my sophomore year in college, that is exactly what happened.

I was trudging through my homework in the early evening when the doorbell rang. I hoped it was Teddy's sister, and I was more than happy to put my work aside for her regular visits. She was due to bring me his latest letter, and together we would read it and share his military escapades. I opened the door, and there she was, with a letter in hand, just as I had hoped. But I looked up and her tear-stained face said all I needed to know. "Don't say it. Please don't say it," I kept on repeating, as if these words could change Teddy's fate.

She said it anyway. "He stepped on a land mine, Jack. It was instantaneous."

We held each other and cried, each of us comforting the other. "It's okay, Jack," she whispered in my ear as we hugged. "Teddy is in heaven now. He is in a better place. You don't have to be sad." I didn't believe in heaven, but I found comfort in the tangibility of the idea. A place. Not nothingness.

Teddy's body was flown back from Korea. Despite all the losses I had experienced in the past, I had never had an opportunity to mourn them. Loved ones had simply disappeared. Aunt Irma and Uncle Siegfried were gone, but where was the proof? Heinz Spiegel and Cousin Ella had both vanished into thin air. It was like a magic trick. No bodies, no funeral. Not even a date to mark their deaths. Here and then not here.

Teddy's death was so tangible, the weighty evidence in front of me. Everything seemed heavy. The coffin, mahogany in color, was polished and hard. An American flag lay on top, like a dense blanket. There were black dresses and intense perfume. Tissues and tears. The agonizing wails of his mother. So many senses were sparked in me. But inside, I felt only quiet, empty desperation. Suddenly, I felt nauseated and dizzy, as random thoughts rushed through my head. *Why didn't I try harder to convince Teddy not to sign up? I was right about peace never lasting! Is there some higher power who is testing me? Taking away anyone whom I have been close to? First Heinz Spiegel, now Teddy.*

I leapt from guilt to anger to self-righteous indignation to self-pity and back again. I could not make sense of it. Because the death of an 18-year-old cannot possibly make sense. It should not be allowed to happen to one of my friends. Certainly not because of war. It should not be allowed to happen, period.

In the spring of 1951, my mother's loosely formed idea turned into a tangible reality. She told my father she wanted a divorce.

Soon after, I was parenting my parents again. It occurred stealthily, and I barely realized it. I was advising my mother on divorce and her finances while I was simultaneously reassuring my father that everything would be okay. "Don't worry, Vati. Divorce will be best for everyone all around. I promise you will never lose me, Vati. I will always be there for you, and of *course,* I love you."

How could I have really thought that divorce would be good for him? It could not have been further from the truth. He was struggling. He was helpless and dependent and alone. But I was far from neutral. Heavily influenced by my perpetually unhappy mother, I tended to see only her point of view. And I must also admit, we were worn out. We had grown tired of the depression and the drama, the antics and the instability. Divorce seemed like a new beginning. A kickstart.

Perhaps my father felt it too, for despite all this talk of divorce, he did not seem more depressed. Quite the contrary; on May 19, just a week after the twins' first birthday party, I found my father waiting for me in the kitchen. How excited he looked! His eyes were unusually bright, his cheeks seemed flushed, and there was a thin line of sweat above his lip. Bursting with anticipation, he blurted out, "I have some great news, Jack," and he began rambling, almost without pause. "I'm going to be back in business soon! I'll be selling pants and men's outerwear. Well, it will be on consignment at first, but the manager of the Shelburne has promised me space in the lobby this fall. And then I will have my own clothing store!"

"Wow! That's great news, Vati, but slow down, slow down for just a minute, will you? Take a breath! What is all this about? Tell me what is going on."

Vati proceeded to tell me in detail the secret business dealings he had been involved with over the past few months. "One night," he explained, "when I'm closing up for the night, I meet a woman at the club. Her name is Bella Dodd. Bella speaks a little German, and we start chatting. What a charming woman she turns out to be! We have become such good friends and confidantes over these months. I've told her all about our immigration to America and all our hardships. Anyway, in our conversations, I mention how I have been wanting to start a business again. And as it happens, Bella knows the club manager, Mr. Kissel. Kissel is a serious entrepreneur with multiple businesses. One of them is a limousine service – he has a fleet of 10 airport limousines!

"Mr. Kissel is not only the manager of the club, Jack. He also happens to be the manager of the entire Shelburne Hotel. So Bella introduces us. Since then, we have been talking and negotiating. Kissel has promised me lobby space in the hotel for my own men's clothing store just as soon as one of the current tenants vacates the space. In the meantime, he is going to help me sell clothing on consignment. And I have made another deal. I have extended to him a one-year loan for 3,000 dollars to obtain an 11th limousine for his limo business. This is a great investment. The interest on the loan is 10 percent. Bella Dodd is a lawyer, and she brokered the deal. Here is the contract."

My father now pulled the signed contract out of his jacket pocket and displayed it to me proudly as if it were a trophy. He had moved through this complicated story very fast, but I got a sick feeling in the pit of my stomach. Something just did not sound right. *My father just made a three-thousand-dollar loan.* That was a great deal of money – a fortune for us. I could not understand how this worked. How did Mr. Kissel end up with our 3,000 dollars while my father ended up with a "promise" of lobby space for a store. Something seemed fishy. Yet I could see my father's excitement. He could see it all before him, a store owner again! A resurrection of his dignity. "Do you have a signed agreement for the store in the lobby?" I now asked him.

"No, it was an oral agreement, over a handshake," my father admitted. "Your generation doesn't understand! This is how it's done. It's a gentleman's arrangement." My father sounded exasperated with me, while my own anxiety was building.

"Okay Vati, but just explain to me why making a loan to Mr. Kissel was necessary for starting the clothing business. I'm sorry, but something about this does not seem above board."

He had no real explanation; he just kept defending the good reputations of the people he was dealing with. Mr. Kissel was no stranger, he reminded me – he was the hotel manager. Still, Vati had handed over our money with nothing but a promise and a handshake. "Why did you do this on your own without discussing it with us, first?" I asked him. Our roles had become so reversed that I spoke to my father with the authority of the head of the household, and as the de facto family financial advisor.

"I wanted to surprise all of you," he sighed, his enthusiasm already crumbling. The look of doubt and distrust in my eyes had already killed his joy. I realized that as his son I had overstepped, and we ended our discussion.

Instead, I told my mother. Within minutes, she was certain my father had been swindled. "What have you *done*, Arthur?" she shouted, the panic rising in her voice. "Don't you realize you have become the victim of some con game!"

"No Grete. You just have no faith in me, as usual, and are being suspicious of other people, as you always are."

"And so... what are you telling me? That you liked this Dodd woman, and she smiled and spoke three words of German to you, so you thought it was perfectly fine to take thousands of dollars of the hard-earned money we have saved and saved over 10 years, and simply hand it over to a stranger? And for what, Arthur? For what? For a worthless piece of paper?"

How distraught we became. Irrational. We proceeded to call Anita, who came over right away. All three of us went a bit crazy. We were screaming at my father, we were frantic. We became outright unhinged.

How could my father not have understood the rules we lived by? Money could not be simply *spent*. Money was not to be enjoyed. And certainly, money was never to be given away. Money had to be preserved, maintained, counted, and socked away for any emergency, foreseeable or unforeseeable. How would we know if we might need to flee our country again? Money had become a kind of god. Losing it felt catastrophic.

"Please talk to your boss, Arthur. Talk to Mr. Kissel." My mother was begging him now. "Tell him you've changed your mind. If Mr. Kissel is honest, as you say he is, I am sure he will have the contract nullified and he'll return the money."

"No, you are *wrong*, all of you!" My father was shouting now; his face was red, and the veins on his forehead were bulging. "These are honorable people. I am a capable businessman. I know what I am doing!" He punctuated his words with a bronchial cough that left him choking.

That evening he went back to work, demoralized. Both Mr. Kissel and Bella Dodd were at the club. Sheepishly, he asked for his money back. "We're so sorry, Arthur," they exclaimed, "but the money is gone. We have already invested it in a brand-new limousine, just as we promised."

In the morning, my father came home upset and agitated. He explained that the money could not be retrieved. "What a foolish and gullible man you are," one of us said. It no longer matters who said it, since no one spared any words in berating him. Vati went to bed, drained and dispirited, and I packed up my things and went to school, simmering in rage.

In the early afternoon I returned home. "Where's Vati?" I asked.

"He is still sleeping," my mother replied, curtly.

Vati was in my parents' bedroom snoring unusually loudly. "Go check on your father," Mutti instructed me, but I did not go in right away; I was still fuming, and I tried to bury myself in my homework until eventually, the whole apartment quieted down.

Only later did I go into Vati's room to wake him for work. There, like always, lay my father, his toothless mouth open, his dentures placed neatly in a glass at his bedside table. I touched his motionless body, and I felt his arms and legs, the pale skin lifeless and cold. What I had heard earlier was not snoring. It was his death rattle.

The official report from the Medical Examiner declared my father's death a heart attack. But my mother, Anita, and I knew better. We found his bottle of sleeping pills lying open and empty at the bottom of the medicine cabinet. And although we could never prove that he overdosed, in our hearts, we all felt that we were complicit in his death. In our minds, we knew we had killed him.

We held a graveside funeral for my father at Cedar Park cemetery in Paramus, New Jersey. My mother had presciently reserved a plot at the cemetery just one year before, choosing a spot on a hill just below a majestic maple, with a clear view of the horizon. She informed Aunt Hede that my father had died, but Hede did not come to the funeral; she had been too wounded by the rift between us, and we never heard from her again.

On the morning of the funeral, the sky was overcast, and rain fell on the gravesite and its sparse attendees. Just as the rabbi gave his sermon, the sun's rays escaped through the clouds, casting a bright golden light on the grave and the stately tree. I looked up at the sky; it looked like a religious painting, and for a moment I tried to believe in a deity that would forgive me.

Vati's "business partners" called with condolences and met with us in person, promising a first loan payment in three months. They seemed so very sincere and kind that we started to doubt our own suspicions about their integrity. *They were honest businesspeople all along!* This made us feel even more sick with remorse; we had bullied my father to his death and been totally and completely wrong.

Three months came and went, however, and no payment came. Uncertain what to do next, we turned to the owner of the Shelburne Hotel. "I'm sorry to break the bad news to you Mrs. Schwersenz, but Mr. Kissel[3] had been embezzling money from the hotel and I had to fire him. In the process of our investigation, we uncovered that he had a big rap sheet: Brace yourself. He has a record of bigamy and impersonating a doctor and he has done jail time for grand larceny. Your husband got involved with a notorious con artist and a career criminal. Kissel fooled all of us, including me."

"What about Bella Dodd, the lawyer?" I inquired. "What is her role in this?"

"Bella V. Dodd is in fact a bona fide lawyer.[4] She also carries the designation 'top woman communist' in the United States. Why she was working with such a shady character as Mr. Kissel is unclear. It is possible that since she has been blacklisted by Senator McCarthy, she is unable to make a living reputably, but that is just conjecture."

The kind owner of the Shelburne referred us to his attorney, an experienced prosecutor who was as anxious to get Kissel as we were. After the lawyer reviewed the signed contract between my father and Kissel, he suddenly paused. "The loan contract is usurious," he explained. "That is going to be a legal problem for you."

"What does usurious mean?" my mother asked.

"It is illegal in New York to lend money with an interest rate so high – higher than six percent to be exact. This makes your husband's loan contract null and void; therefore, legally it does not have to be repaid. I suspect that Bella Dodd intentionally wrote up the contract this way. Very clever of her! Unfortunately, you will have to desist with your lawsuit; however, I will do my best to help you negotiate new terms of good faith repayment with Kissel's lawyers."

The lawyer was able to negotiate new terms for repayment of the loan, interest free and without penalty. Mr. Kissel sometimes sent us 100 dollars per month and often missed his payments entirely. In the end, he did finally pay us back. It took him nearly three and a half years.

Emotionally shattered, I didn't even have the spirit to go back to the Lake Spofford Hotel that summer. Frankly, I didn't have the heart to do much of anything.

"You need the money and the diversion," my mother suggested. "Why don't you take a friend with you. It might be comforting to go with someone you know." It was, in fact, one of her better ideas. I decided to ask Melvin Tiger, my first acquaintance at NYU, who by this time had grown into a close friend.

Mutti's instincts were spot on; being back at Spofford was a welcome distraction. During that summer, Anita and I wrote to each other often; we had become very close in our shared grief.

Dear Anita,

I am starting to gradually enjoy the summer. I have become good friends (and a little romantic) with a waitress, Ellen. Even though I miss Teddy greatly, I am getting along very well with Melvin. He is also on a draft deferment, only he is classified as 4F on account of his asthma.

I'm glad you and Mutti pushed me to come up this summer. It was much better than staying home and wallowing in self-pity. There is another NYU student – a pre-law student, Elliot[5]*, who is a busboy, and we have all become good friends.*

Yours, Jack

By the end of July, I had settled into the familiar rhythm of the resort that had become my second home. My work, my friendships with Ellen and Melvin, and my social life helped stave off the tendency to self-indulgent sadness.

It had been a hot summer so far. There seemed to be no respite from the heat except for the lake; a quick swim offered a cooling reprieve. One afternoon, after bussing the main dining room, Ellen and I tried to play volleyball on the main field. Melvin and Elliot had been bussing the lunch service at the outdoor lakeside area and were relaxing somewhere by the lake; we planned to join them there later and hopefully take a dip.

It was too hot for volleyball and Ellen and I gave up, plunking down on the grass. Everything was still; butterflies sat motionless on leaves that refused to quiver in the thick, summer air, and we both felt lethargic and heavy.

Suddenly, a movement out of the corner of my eye jolted me from the heat-induced languor. I heard a hum of voices, and noticed a wave of people moving towards the lake and the boat house. Ellen and I stood up and began to walk slowly with the crowd. Something was amiss, but we could not make it out.

Our walking became a trot as the pace of the people picked up. A trot turned into a jog, and snippets of words reached my ears.

"Pulled out of the water" and "boathouse." The crowd broke out to a full run, and I started running, too, and as I did, that sick, nauseous feeling began rising from my stomach again. I heard the word – did I hear it right? – "drowned." Who exactly had drowned? A guest? That would be terrible. Then the word "busboy" floated in the air, and I started to panic. It had better not be. It could not be. Not this time.

I kept running until I got to the boathouse. That's when I saw him lying there. The lifeguards were trying to resuscitate him, but it was no use.

Melvin was dead.

There were no tears this time; I was simply numb, in shock. The police were called to investigate the incident and they pieced together a semblance of a story that became their initial theory: *Melvin and the other busboy Elliot take out a canoe and paddle to the boat house. The canoe tips and the boys stay in the water horsing around when Melvin suddenly goes under. Melvin cannot really swim well. Elliot tries but fails to pull him up.*

Their story was so full of holes and fictions that conspiracy theories naturally followed. By the time the newspapers had gotten a hold of the story, rumors had been circulating that both boys were dating the same girl, and that Elliot, "knowing Melvin could not swim," had tipped the canoe intentionally.

The next day, local headlines read "NYU Student Drowns NYU Student," and the DA charged Elliot with manslaughter. Elliot – a budding lawyer – pleaded not guilty. By his account, both boys agreed beforehand to tip over the boat, believing they were in shallower water. The DA lifted the charges and Elliot was exonerated.

Of course, I could have told them who was responsible for Melvin's death. It was me, obviously. After all, I was the one who had brought Melvin up to Lake Spofford in the first place.

It was my third death in a year, and my culpability was stamped on each one of them. With that, I suppose I went a little crazy. My own conspiracy theories became a salve for my guilt. I had to find out why Melvin really died. "Nothing makes any sense, Ellen. I know that Melvin could swim just fine. I know that Melvin was not dating anyone. The police, the papers, the DA – they know nothing! This is a suspicious death. We must investigate!"

I became obsessed, fancying myself an amateur sleuth. "Read the medical examiner's report, Ellen. No water in the lungs... watermelon in the throat. Maybe it's *not* a drowning, then? Perhaps it's a choking incident? Or was it his asthma?" I searched for other witnesses, I rounded up staff and guests. I interviewed people who had been at the adjacent public beach – anyone who might have seen something. I did this after working hours with Ellen, who had become my de facto roommate. I was up night after night, sleuthing, and staying up later and later until I stopped sleeping entirely. I was busy, so very busy, too busy to feel anything.

Towards the end of the summer, I finally started to feel something. However, I was not feeling the repressed emotions. "Ellen, my throat hurts like the devil."

"Jack, I think you have a fever too," Ellen noted, as she put the back of her hand on my forehead.

"Just find me some aspirin; that should keep my temperature down."

"Jack, honestly, you look terrible. You are obviously sick. Maybe you should go home early." Ellen looked at me with wide-eyed fear, the way someone might look at a rabid dog.

"Ellen, not on your life. It's almost Labor Day and I would lose the summer tips that practically make up my whole salary. Anyway, I must solve this mystery. I'll manage."

A bottle of aspirin later, and no closer to the truth, I was on the train heading back to New York having just barely made it through the holiday weekend. I got off the train at Grand Central Terminal and dragged my luggage and my tired, feverish body up the stairs to the main terminal where Anita and Lou were supposed to pick me up. Indeed, there they were, standing at the circular information booth with its distinctive clock top. They were waving at me vigorously. "Welcome home, Jack!" I heard them yell, but their voices sounded almost as if they were under water.

I lifted my free arm to wave back. Then everything went black.

"It's tonsillitis. Strep," the doctor declared definitively. After I fainted at Grand Central Terminal, Anita and Lou had taken me to a clinic right away for a proper diagnosis.

Strep, daily shots of penicillin. Yes, I believed I could handle that. I had missed the first few days of school, but I was not too concerned as my first two years of college had bolstered me with good grades. Still, this critical Junior year would be much more demanding; I was facing decisive pre-dental classes, such as organic chemistry, that were designed to weed out the weaker students, and I knew I could not afford to miss much more school.

I took my penicillin shots, but I was not better, and after another 10-day course of sulfa antibiotics I was still sick. A tonsillectomy was the only treatment left, according to the ear, nose and throat surgeon. Six weeks of missed classes later, it became crystal clear that there was no way I would ever catch up. And that is when I started to panic.

"As you know," I explained to my professor, "I have been ill and fallen way behind, and I have also recently lost a close friend. I'm hoping you will let me stay in my classes – at the very least, to sit in on them. You understand, I must stay enrolled full time, so I won't lose my college draft deferment and be sent overseas to Korea." One by one I met with each professor, desperate for just a little bit of sympathy and understanding of my predicament.

"Well, son, I guess we could give you some kind of pass/fail grade," said one professor.

"I'll let you sit in, but you won't be able to take the exam," said another.

"Just do the best you can, that's all I can tell you," offered a third.

"What's so terrible about going to fight in Ko-rrhea?" That last southern-born professor pronounced it just like *diarrhea*, which I was about to have on the spot if someone did not cut me a little slack.

When I finally saw my grades, I knew my dream of becoming a dentist was over.

In German, the word *Traum* means dream. Add an *a* to the end, and you get the English word *trauma*, the destroyer of dreams.

I had allowed myself to dream just a little. A little river of hope had started to trickle, and then to flow. That I could make it here and become an American and be a success and leave sadness and heartbreak behind. The river had just dried up and I felt like all that was left behind were stones and dirt.

This felt like a final blow. And while it felt terribly unfair, on another level I also believed it was fair. After all, I was receiving just punishment for my sin of being alive when so many people I loved had died. Yes, it was terribly unfair, and thoroughly deserved. Could both things be true?

I knew instinctively I had to go on living, but I honestly did not know how. For a while I became a zombie, just breathing, walking, eating. But it was the fear of being sent to Korea that ultimately woke me up from my trance, giving me some purpose to continue, to not drop out of school, to find another path. And another thought kept me going: *I must take care of my mother. It is still up to me to fight for our existence in this land of exile.*

I felt like I was starting over. What was my next move? Someone suggested I try podiatry school, a common path for pre-med and pre-dental rejects. But when I tried to visualize a life of corns and bunions and yellowed toenails thickened by fungus, I shuddered and shrank away.

I tried applying to pharmacy school after a member of my house plan, Larry Nessman, got into the Long Island College of Pharmacy in Brooklyn. The Dean allowed Larry to transfer all his NYU credits and add just one additional year of pharmacy school. It seemed like a pretty good deal. But when it came time for my interview, the Dean briefly looked at my transcript and said, "You look like an erratic student. If you wait one year to be admitted, I'll let you in with three additional years of pharmacy school. It's my best offer."

Three additional years! I was reasonably sure my grades were at least as good as Larry's. Why was I getting a rotten deal? Was it my foreign accent? I honestly did not know.

I felt lost, aimless. Forget a graduate degree; now I just wanted to leave college with any skill that could land me a job. My New Hampshire friend, Sid Aliber, suggested accounting. That was his major. "Wait, Sid." I cringed. "Isn't there math involved? It's not my strong suit."

"There's math, but it's simple numeracy, Jack. Nothing fancy. Well within your reach."

So I quickly decided then and there, I would major in accounting, and minor in chemistry and history, my true passion. I would still be three credits short by graduation and would have to do an extra semester, but at least I would be graduating before I was 40.

How I hated accounting! I rejected it before I had even begun. My heart was screaming "I DO NOT BELONG HERE." I felt like I was being left back all over again. It was another failure. How could I embrace it as my future?

Just as I was entering my senior year, my mother developed an acute case of debilitating spinal arthritis. She was bedridden and unable to work and I had to take an after-school job as a file clerk to support us. I derived some perverse comfort from this new calamity. It was the proof I needed that I could never have gone to dental school. After all, it was up to me to support my mother.

It was around this time that Anita and Lou started talking about moving. We had all become accustomed to our life in upper Manhattan – Mutti and I in our roach-filled Washington Heights hovel, and my sister in her once-luxurious Harlem hideaway. Lou and I had been sharing a heap of a car, and I visited the twins whenever I could between studying and work. But Anita had to look toward the future. The twins were toddlers now, and soon headed to school. It was time for Anita to look for a better neighborhood.

"I heard about a new development going up in Flushing, Queens," she announced as she laid out her plans to my mother and me. "There are affordable, newly built apartments within walking distance of the schools. And the neighborhood feels almost suburban, with private homes interspersed among the new buildings. You two should look at Flushing as well. We can all move together."

Flushing? Well, it was certainly not an auspicious name. Who would choose to live in a town named after a plumbing function? And Queens? Where the heck was that? But we would never have considered not staying together. Not after Germany. Not after being divided by war. No, we would do everything as one unit, glued together by blood, fear, and desperation. If Anita was going to move, so were we.

That was the reason why we made the fastest, most spontaneous decision of our lives. We bought a one-bedroom apartment, sight unseen – construction not even completed – in the Kissena Co-op, located in a town whose name sounded like a sewer. It cost 650 dollars to own the whole thing, and it would be the first time in our arduous journey that we would not be heading west.

In the fall of 1953, having still not graduated, I started the very last add-on semester I needed to finish my accounting degree. I had yet to have any job experience at an accounting firm, and having made no social or professional connections while in school, I missed my opportunity to be placed at a bona fide CPA firm. The only opening the school placement office could find was with a solo practitioner.

I met Mr. Mintz for the first time on the corner of 42nd Street and Sixth Avenue. The little accountant in the wrinkled tan raincoat gave me a brusque handshake and we started walking, his worn-out, overstuffed leather attaché swinging from his arm as we completed a 14-block racewalk down Sixth Avenue. On the way downtown, he explained his work philosophy to me: "Don't you ever forget, Jack. In accounting, time is money."

I thought we were headed to his office, but instead we stepped into a luncheonette on 28th Street. Were we going to have coffee while I learned the ropes? Apparently not. We sat at the counter on adjacent swiveling stools upholstered with ripped red vinyl and waited for our first client, the owner of the luncheonette. Mr. Mintz then pulled a thick cardboard case filled with documents out of his unruly briefcase, turned to me, and simply said, "Here, Jack, start bookkeeping."

Soon there were papers and green lined ledgers spread out in front of us and I worked continuously adding up numbers. Hours passed until we finally broke for lunch. I was happily eating my egg salad sandwich when I caught Mr. Mintz staring at me. Impatiently, he tapped on his watch with his index finger. His message was clear; he meant finish – and fast. I wolfed down the remains of my sandwich, and started working again, while Mr. Mintz repeated, "Time is money, time is money." He sounded exactly like a parrot.

All afternoon I did the bookkeeping, while Mr. Mintz now stood behind me, casting a shadow over my journals. I realized he wanted more speed out of me. I had to add up numbers both fast and accurately. No, not simply fast... this was virtual speed adding, and I had to become a human calculator. I raced through my bookkeeping, adding numbers in my head, until the clock struck 6. Then I shook Mr. Mintz' small, sweaty hand, and made plans to meet him again the next day.

The human calculating went on like that for months. And while Mr. Mintz might have thought "time was money," he was awfully bad at paying *me* on time. After a while, I realized, if I were going to ever learn real accounting, and be paid for it, I would have to find employment at a legitimate accounting firm.

At the end of the year, I found a job at Simonoff, Peyser, and Citrin, one of the top Jewish CPA firms in New York. Yes, a *Jewish* CPA firm, for the firms were segregated like country clubs, and my nose fit right in. As the busy tax season got under way in January, I started working my tail off, not only during the day, but on weeknights and Saturdays, too, until I felt sure I had impressed my bosses with my industriousness. In late-April, one of the partners called me into his office, and I walked in, prepared to receive my commendation.

"Jack, you did a great job for us during tax season, and we can't thank you enough."

"Well, I really enjoy working here."

"Yes, Jack and we love you! But I'm afraid we must let you go. The tax season rush is over, and we just don't need you anymore. Lots of luck to you, son."

And just like the gift-wrapping help at holiday season, I was fired.

By early 1954, the conflict in the Korean War had ended, but the Cold War was in full bloom. Communism had taken a firm and frightening foothold and the draft was still in full swing. Young men who had deferred could still be called up until age 35, and no one felt secure.

With this anxiety in the back of my mind, I went to my semi-annual draft board appearance. I was now classified as 3H – a hardship deferment – because of my widowed, now disabled mother.

"So you're a rehhf-you-gee," drawled one of the six civilian interviewees. The southern gentleman eyed me suspiciously. I was a full-fledged US citizen, but my German accent and 10-lettered last name containing only two vowels made me very much a foreigner in his eyes. As he slowly drawled out his questions, it seemed to me they were mainly rhetorical. "So as a rehhf-you-gee, son, don't yuh feel yuh owe your country ss*suhvice*?"

"Sir, my mother's health has been an impediment to my ability to serve," I began, feeling I needed to justify my deferment. And then I put my foot in my mouth, where it became lodged there like American corn between my German teeth.

"I feel a great deal of patriotism for this country, sir. In fact, I feel I owe my very life to the United States."

Okay, maybe I was overcompensating. But like a wind-up toy, I kept on going. "If I may add, sir, my sister is planning to move to Queens, and my mother and I are going to move near them, just as soon as construction on our apartment has been finished."

My motormouth kept revving as I proved my national loyalty and boundless patriotism. "As soon as we are living near each other, my sister will be able to take care of my mother. And then, sir, I will be free to serve my country!"

I ended that soliloquy with a bang and sealed my fate. I was reclassified as I-A. I was going to be drafted.

"What have you done, Jack? You will get yourself killed!" My mother had a new burst of nervous hysteria when I presented my news to her and Anita.

"I couldn't help it, Mutti. It was so intimidating. The whole thing felt like a congressional hearing. And that southern man was basically asking, 'Don't you love the country that saved you?' My honor was at stake and I felt I had to prove my intention to serve. There's nothing I can do about it now. I'll be shipping out on October 27th."

"Don't worry, both of you," Anita reassured my mother and me. "We are in a cold war, there is no combat. And consider yourself lucky, Jack. You are about to embark on one of the greatest adventures of your life."

Maybe Anita was right. We both knew it was finally time to do my service. And what was I leaving behind in New York? There was no important career, no great opportunity I was abandoning. My future seemed so intangible and my life so unplanned; like one unfortunate event after another unfolding onto a trajectory that I never had control over. Yes, Anita was correct. Going into the Army was just what I needed.

In the few months before my draft, I finally graduated from NYU. Already 24 years old, I could not wait to be done with college. I took a job with a "real" accounting firm, Alson and Brown, a swanky firm founded in the mid-1800s with the first wave of German Jewish immigrants. I bided my time, did my work and made my 50 dollars a week.

That spring, the construction on our coop in Queens was finally complete. The name Flushing, we learned, was derived from the name of the Dutch settlement of Vlishing[6]. It was known in the 1600s as the "birthplace of religious liberty in the New World." The name, in fact, was perfect.

All of us – Anita and Lou and the twins, and my mother and I – moved together from Manhattan to Queens. We lived in adjoining buildings in a new complex looking out over a courtyard. The red brick buildings lacked any elegance, but our one-bedroom apartment seemed spacious and modern compared to our Washington Heights apartment, and at least the courtyard had a few trees.

It was another step forward on our journey out of poverty, and there was not a cockroach to be found.

PART VI

THE COLD WAR

22

MAKING ME INTO A MAN

October 27, 1954, was a beautiful fall day, if a little brisk. Having carefully selected my clothes the day before, I donned a not-so-new camel's hair sports jacket, slacks, and a sports shirt. With a whistle on my lips and adventure on my mind, I headed down to lower Manhattan to the collection point for draft inductees. I wanted to look sharp for my induction, and I was confident I had pulled it off.

I arrived at Whitehall Street to find dozens of other inductees already there. They wore youthful, casual clothes – jeans and bomber jackets, cable sweaters and leather lace-up boots. They looked warm and comfortable, and not like me at all. One of them started staring at me, and then, turning to his friends, said, "Look at this one, he thinks he's here for a job interview!"

We waited and waited. "We are like cattle being slowly rounded up," I said to myself, but sort of out loud. "Hopefully not for slaughter," I added, for drama. By 8 p.m. about 100 of us inductees were put on buses headed to Fort Dix, New Jersey. It was 10 p.m. by the time we arrived, and we stood outside ready to receive our instructions and orientation. By this time, I was starting to freeze and really kicking myself for dressing to impress in European formality. Now all I wanted was a sweater.

My civilian clothes would not be worn again after that day,

however. Our very first loss of personal identity was achieved by us giving up our clothing. A large warehouse-like building housed our uniforms, and we went from station to station while soldiers eyeballed our sizes and threw standard-issue uniform items into our outstretched arms. Dress uniforms, fatigues, undergarments, long johns, hats, shoes, boots, socks, helmets, helmet liners. Eventually, the pile reached well above our heads until we could not see, and our arms ached from the weight of it. After we collected our uniforms, I was assigned to an old barracks, and I finally collapsed into a bunk bed at midnight.

It felt like only minutes later, promptly at 6 a.m., that the not-so-gentle sounds of reveille woke me from a dead sleep. A mad rush followed to dress, urinate in the open latrines, and line up outside for roll call. We made a disorderly attempt to march to the mess hall. I was starving, and I lined up with my tray while other soldiers served us breakfast. Eggs, fries, toast, sausages. Each was piled on top of the other in an ugly layered parfait. The food was greasy, hot and salty. I washed it all down with a glass of cold milk and marveled at how delicious it seemed, while the other recruits marveled at how much I seemed to enjoy it.

After breakfast, we were examined like new farm animals, our teeth and bodies inspected, our blood taken. We were given shots for typhus, typhoid, tetanus, polio, smallpox, and tuberculosis. Finally, we were given our permanent company assignments. I was nervous now, for I had never had any luck getting assigned anywhere.

"Jack Schweitzer!"

"It's Schwersenz, sir. But yes, sir!"

"264th infantry!"

I walked over to my barracks. They were brand new with tiled floors, modern heat and ventilation. Even the toilets were somewhat private. What luck! I looked up at the black, moonless sky. "Thank you," I whispered, wondering when exactly my luck would take its usual downward turn.

Our company was a hodgepodge of recruits, with 50 soldiers to a barracks. About half were 18-year-olds just out of high school, both volunteers and draftees that could barely shave and looked like just-weaned calves. About a third were the "felons." This group had gotten into run-ins with the law and were allowed to choose military service over jail time. And the remaining 20 percent were people like me – college graduates who had deferred and deferred until they just could not put off their service any longer.

We all had to first learn the US Army rules of living. I learned to make my bed with hospital corners so tight that a coin could bounce off the blanket. I stenciled my ID into my clothes, "spit shined" my patent leather dress shoes with real saliva until they shone like mirrors, and learned how to roll all my clothes into a footlocker. All of this had to be done at a feverish pace to avoid facing disciplinary action.

The job of our First Sergeant and his assistants was to "make men out of us." That seemed to be the mantra at Fort Dix. "We're gonna make MEN outta yous!" they told us repeatedly – "yous" apparently being the New Jersey plural of you. And so, we had nighttime shooting drills, marching, inspections – all under the dreaded threat of push-ups, cleaning toilets, or KP (kitchen police) duty for any transgression. It was a strategy of compliance through intimidation.

That strategy seemed to work well for the 18-year-old recruits, but not for those of us well into our twenties. We older guys found each other rather quickly. We were a cocky bunch, to be sure. We felt like our identities were well formed, and our psyches less easily influenced. When we were told that threats and intimidation were designed to prepare us for combat and protect our lives, it rang hollow. We just did not believe it.

Within a few days, I made two close friends, Bob Langer and Gunther David. Although Gunther was a German-Jewish immigrant like me, that is where our similarities ended. Gunther had a canniness for making his life easier that just was not in my DNA. Somehow, he had managed to get himself out of basic training by becoming the company clerk's typist. When the three of us got together, Gunther, Bob and I frequently shared our skepticism of the Army doctrine and debated its merits. "Whaddya think?" Bob queried. "You think all this stuff really prepares you for combat?"

Gunther was the most outspoken of us. "Of course not," he replied. "You think surprise inspections are gonna save your life? It's abuse, that's what it is. Fear of punishment is what gets you to conform. The Army is just trying to mess with your sense of identity. Individuality is a threat to the system. That's how they get you to follow them blindly into battle – no questions asked."

He had made a good argument. Total indoctrination, with no outside influences. Maybe that's why we were not allowed contact with our family for weeks after our arrival. Then, on one unusually cloudless Sunday in November, we held a small parade.

I was given the job of carrying the flag at the head of our company. We marched from our barracks to the end of the street, then turned down another block. Despite my friends' cynicism, I started to feel the excitement and pride of being in the Army. I also started to feel something else: it was the inside of my leather boot rubbing against the back of my right ankle. Somehow my sock had rolled under my foot, and I could feel a painful blister rapidly forming.

How I tried to keep from limping! I started gritting my teeth, doing everything I could think of to walk straight, while blood, serum and pus oozed out of my abraded skin (or so I imagined). How badly I wanted to look dignified. How I wanted to look like a soldier, in my US Army uniform, holding the American flag at the head of my company! I looked around and saw what all of us had become. In just three weeks, the flab and softness were already gone. Muscles had grown firm where there once had been none. We stood strong and upright, our complexions rosy from the golden outdoor light. Our uniforms were crisp, our faces solemn.

As we turned the corner, I saw with surprise that our families had all gathered to greet us. I spotted Anita and Lou right away. Lou was carrying Lorraine, her white tights and saddle shoes peeking out from under a navy wool peacoat. Ronnie stood beside them, stick thin, just like when I was a boy; but unlike me he had his father's dark olive skin and curly black hair. And next to them stood a stern looking woman with steel-gray hair. For a second I didn't realize that the woman standing there was my mother. I was searching for the woman I remembered from childhood; the tall, strong, nervous, and impatient woman who had brought us all to safety. The woman before me – an inch or so shorter, with permanent parentheses around her pursed lips, was not the image fixed in my memory. As soon as I saw her holding her pocketbook tightly in the crook of her arm like Queen Elizabeth, she instantly reverted to the Mutti of my childhood. She saw me and smiled, and with her free arm waved and waved. I had never seen her so joyful. All of them waved. They were all waving at me, the soldier with the flag, the soldier trying his best not to limp, leading the company. I was no longer a civilian. I was the proud member of the US Army.

By the fourth week of basic training, I could shoot a rifle and a Browning automatic and stab someone with a bayonet. The skill of being able to kill someone allowed me permission to go home for one day each week, and on those days, I would collapse in the comfort of my own bed in my new quiet neighborhood of Flushing, and would sleep and sleep and sleep. Then I would drag myself back to Fort Dix every Sunday night for another week of training and abuse.

Winter finally came to Fort Dix, and with it, the dreaded news: bivouac – camping without cover – would be held over Christmas week. Bivouac was tantamount to torture, but it had to be done, like getting a tooth pulled.

We were each supplied with half of a pup tent and a sleeping bag. Bob and I put our two half-tents together to create a domicile of sorts; we called it the "house of hypothermia." We immediately got to work piling soft dried leaves onto the floor and layering dirt along the edges of the tent to keep out the frigid wind and snow. In the evening, following my sergeant's instructions, I took off my outer clothes and shoved them into my sleeping bag to provide additional insulation. But I still had one more thing to do.

It was only just twilight, and Bob found me standing right outside the tent. I was wearing just my undergarments, carrying my helmet and heading out. "Where the heck are you going?" inquired Bob.

"I need to shave," I replied, as if that were obvious.

"Are you out of your mind?" Bob exclaimed. "In your boxers?"

"Well, sure, what's the big deal? I'm just going over to the officers' squad tent. It's the only place I can get hot water. You know better than anyone, Bob, that I can't skip a day of shaving. I get a two o'clock shadow, let alone a five o'clock shadow. Anyway, there is still a little bit of light out, and I have my long johns top on. I'll be fine, Bob. I'll be back before you know it."

I trudged over to the officers' tent, carrying my shaving kit, along with my helmet to use as a makeshift sink. It was all a bit cumbersome, and as I passed my single blade over my rather hairy face and tried to rinse in my helmet, the process took longer than I had estimated. When I was done, I stepped out of the officer's tent, my face as smooth as a baby's bottom, and the campground as dark as pitch.

I had forgotten how early it gets dark in December. There was not a soul in sight. Before me, I could just barely make out the faint outline of dozens upon dozens of pup tents arranged in concentric circles around the squad tent. Each tent looked like a giant turtle stranded on a beach at night.

Where the heck was my tent? I started to look for it in the darkness, but each tent looked identical to the next, without a single distinctive feature. I started to panic. How would I ever find it? I began to run, going in circles trying to find my tent, my boxers flapping in the wind, my pale bare legs freezing in the gusty December night. What row was I in? I had no idea, because there were no rows. There were no rows, no columns, and no markers of any kind. Desperately, I started to open the snaps of the tent's entrances. "Bob, is that you?" I called, each time I opened a tent.

"What the f---!"

"Get outta here!"

"Who the heck is that?" The soldiers screamed at the shameless intruder (me) who was letting a blast of icy air into their tents. In the dark I tried to remain anonymous as I woke up soldier after soldier and ran around in circles in my boxers. Three hours later, certain I was about to lose my balls to frostbite, I finally found my tent and collapsed into my sleeping bag.

At six o'clock the next morning, still not fully defrosted, I remained fast asleep right through reveille. Bob did his best to help me. "Wake up, Jack. It's time to get up! *Get up!*"

"I was not asleep," I answered sluggishly, my eyes still at half-mast. "I was just planning my next nightmare."

Bob laughed while I wearily dragged myself out of the warm sleeping bag. I quickly dressed and went to use the latrine – just a bunch of exposed holes in the ground surrounded by nothing more than chicken wire. I saw a few men grab their spades and dig their own holes away from the others hoping for a bit of privacy. I was still so frozen and exhausted that I could not even dream of working a spade. I used the latrine as is and hoped that the warm, rising steam would offer a cloudy curtain of privacy.

Hunger dwarfed my fatigue, and I eagerly awaited my favorite activity: eating. In the absence of a mess tent, a portable gas field kitchen had been wheeled out to the camp to heat our food. Pancakes were served for breakfast and they instantly chilled upon arrival. With my trembling, gloved hands, I tried clumsily to use the aluminum cutlery in our mess kits, but eventually gave up. Ditching the flimsy bent fork and the gloves, I ate the pancakes with my frozen, numb hands. They were bland, dry, and ice-cold; but I greedily stuffed the rock-solid starch into my hungry mouth.

Dinner, disappointingly, did not hold up well in the frigid winter either. The hot food turned cold just as soon as it hit the plate, and warm gravy instantly transformed into a pale mound of congealed fat. We ate it anyway, our hunger superseding the food's lack of appeal. Only the desserts seemed enticing to me because the frozen treats were in their intended frozen state. Yet, no one seemed to be eating them. As ice cream sandwiches were distributed to all the men, I did not see anyone partaking. No one, that is, except me.

"How can you eat ice cream, Jack?" Bob asked. "It's freezing out."

"I am almost sure, Bob, that eating cold foods insulates you against the cold weather. Yeah, come to think about it, I'm certain of it!"

"That's ridiculous!" Bob said. He shook his head in disbelief and handed me his ice cream sandwich.

"No, it makes sense," I insisted. "Think about it. Cold is the best insulator. Don't people live in igloos? Don't huskies – wait, maybe it's wolves – burrow in the snow for warmth? Yes, I believe I read that in a Jack London novel," I declared, as I confidently ate my ice cream sandwich followed by Bob's. Gradually, the other soldiers passed their ice cream sandwiches down the line, and, quite pleased with my cleverness, I ate theirs. Sometimes I would have two or three a night. Finally, I knew something they did not! The others watched me eat my frozen foods while my body temperature dropped by at least one or two degrees. I shivered uncontrollably as I ate my delicious dessert, unwilling to admit my foolish error and not even minding that the other soldiers were having a good laugh at my expense.

After only a few days, we were all equally wretched and freezing. I guess I was not as sturdy as I had imagined, because by midweek, I was already trying to figure out a way to shorten our misery. The holiday season offered an opportunity to get us out of bivouac. "I have an idea, Bob; it's crazy, but it might just work. With Christmas coming, maybe we could hold a charitable event on the Army's behalf and get ourselves a trip into the city."

"It's not a bad idea, Jack, but I don't know any charities."

"Don't worry about that, Bob. My old accounting firm Alson and Brown used to do charity work with the Henry Street Settlement orphanage and I have some contacts there."

"Come to think of it, I have a friend who is in the toy business. Does that help?" Bob offered. A plan was beginning to hatch.

We presented to our officers our proposal: A Christmas party for the Settlement House orphans; good public relations for the Army, and of course, nice for the children too.

The plan worked. Plucked out of bivouac, we were sent back to the barracks to begin executing the event, then packed our things and went to New York, headed for a warm and hearty Christmas party and a chance to get our picture in the paper.

We were only gone two days, but when we returned, we were treated like honored heroes. It was all high fives and back slapping. "Hey Bob, Jack-O! Helluva job! You guys still talkin' to us or are you too famous?"

"Nice job," said Gunther in private, without a hint of irony. "What gave you two the idea?"

"Don't tell anyone," I whispered back to him, "but we were just trying to get out of the cold!"

The first eight weeks of basic training finally came to an end, and I had made it through in decent shape, all bodily parts intact. One morning we were all brought together. It was time to get our next training orders. Everyone was on edge, for we had no idea where we might be sent, but I was feeling somewhat secure. I knew my foreign language skills would get me a high-level position. Perhaps I was overly confident, however, because here in the Army, nothing could be certain. One by one, the Army captain called out names and assignments. I listened for my name, or anything that sounded close to it.

"Scherez!" he finally called.

"Yes sir," I answered, at this point just assuming he meant me.

"You have top secret security clearance, with orders from Washington D.C. You are being classified as a linguist and are done with basic training."

Oh, YES, I thought smugly. Now I just had to find out what elite unit I would be sent to.

"You will be doing eight weeks of advanced infantry training, starting now," the captain continued.

Advanced infantry training? As a *linguist?* That seemed strange. "Where will that be sir, if I may ask?"

"You'll be staying right here, kid. Right here at Fort Dix."

Here at Fort Dix? Oh, no! This was going to be hell.

Yup, my luck had run out. No surprise there. I was being left back again. My friends were being sent to Army schools to become clerks, engineers, and signal corps specialists, and I was staying right here in Fort Dix for more intensive on the ground training. It was not at all what I had in mind. If I were a superstitious man, I would say that this was my punishment for getting out of bivouac. Or maybe for excessive hubris. Pride goeth before a fall, doesn't it?

This was going to be rough indeed. And lonely, too. For my new regiment was made up entirely of youngsters about 18 years of age – mostly from the South – who were fully committed to becoming US Army rangers. I had nothing in common with these kids. I said goodbye to my friends and my modern barracks and relocated to an old coal-fired World War II barracks, without a compatriot or co-conspirator in sight.

I had a new First Sergeant, too. He was a Korean war veteran. We lined up before him as he gave his first of many pep talks. This one seemed to involve a good deal of shouting.

"I have buddies who have DIED!" he yelled. "They died because they were not hardened enough in training! I will NOT let that happen to you!"

It sounded ominous. Frightening even. A spray of spittle left his lips and exploded in the air each time he screamed at us. Which one of us was he yelling at, though? We could not tell for certain, because one of his eyes was focused all the way to the right while the other eye was locked in dead ahead.

Our new sergeant had a reputation for being one of the toughest sergeants in Fort Dix. He was strict and punitive, and always seemed to be in a foul mood. That mood always was even a little worse on Mondays, when he was rumored to return from a weekend in New York on a "bender." Yes, on Mondays he seemed to have a little extra sadism for anyone he thought lacked discipline or enthusiasm. And boy, you had better immediately respond if he looked at you, with *either* of his eyes. The best I could do was keep my head down and try to be invisible. Becoming nonexistent seemed to be my best strategy for the next eight weeks.

"We're gonna make men outta you," our new sergeant promised (loudly). But that is exactly what my old sergeant had said in basic training (to be fair, my old sergeant had said "yous"). Wasn't I a man already? Perhaps he meant a superman. Or a super killer. Because here in advanced infantry we were going to learn how to use an array of automatic weapons to kill the enemy. We would learn to fire mortars and anti-tank weapons, like bazookas. We would also learn to dismantle mines. And to get into tiptop shape for the next war, we would pass through complex obstacle courses, march at speed carrying a 70-pound pack, survive a simulated nerve gas attack, and crawl 100 yards under barbed wire while machine gun fire and shells exploded on either side of us.

Every morning, we woke up at 4 a.m., and marched at quick speed for seven miles while carrying all our weapons. By the time we got to the training site, we were exhausted and drenched in sweat. Sitting patiently in the zero-degree air while slowly turning into soldier-shaped popsicles, we looked on in envy and disbelief as the rest of the unit disembarked from trucks to the training site, warm, cozy and well-rested. It seemed our morning marches were a special exercise devised by the First Sergeant just for our regiment, to improve our discipline and stamina.

Bivouac arrived in February – it would be two weeks this time. It was still the heart of winter without any charity function or holiday parties to rescue me this time. There was one bit of hope, however. If it was below 15 degrees, regulations stated that it was too cold for bivouac, and it must be cancelled. Woo-hoo! I was home free!

The sergeant gathered all of us for a meeting. "Company!" he yelled. "It is nearly zero degrees out! Now I will tell you that normally bivouac is called off in frigid weather. That's because the folks higher up than me, sitting in their toasty offices, are afraid you pansies will get frostbite. But I say NONSENSE! I have asked for an exception to be made. There will be no reprieve for my regiment! The weather does not wait for soldiers, and we soldiers will NOT wait for the weather!"

The first week of bivouac came and went without incident. My goal was simple: survive. It was my second stint, after all, and I was better prepared. I remembered to skip the evening shave and keep track of my tent location. It was bitterly cold out, but at the end of the first week, I still had all my appendages, and they were still pink. At night, I took off my outer clothes as directed, using them as insulation for my sleeping bag. I ate hot soup instead of ice cream and tried to maintain a normal body temperature and get rest whenever I could.

By the second week, soldiers began to drop off one by one. A few men got frostbite; a couple got pneumonia. We were losing men by the day as they headed to the hospital – not from combat in a foreign land, but from hypothermia in New Jersey. I feared I was on borrowed time. As each day of bivouac passed, I nervously counted my blessings, counted down the days, and counted my fingers and toes.

During that second week, even though I had tried to do everything right, I began to falter too. The cold was relentless, and I was exhausted. One day, while we were doing exercises at the firing range, I stood in the burning wind waiting for the other soldiers to finish firing. The unrelenting gusts pierced right through the fibers of my clothing, and I could feel my eyelashes and skin starting to freeze. Trying to protect myself from the harsh wind while resting my tired legs, I dragged myself to an area behind some trees and sat on the ground. The next thing I knew, I was fully prostrate on the ground and a man was standing over me.

I must have fallen asleep. My vision was still blurry and I could not make out who was standing over me. Suddenly loud yelling reverberated in my ears.

"What is this, soldier! Are you a baby? Do you need a nap! Are you a god-damn pussy?"

I perked up instantly. The Sergeant du Sade was staring me down with one of his eyes and screaming, his spittle spraying on me and freezing instantly as it landed on my exposed face. My whole body started quaking from a combination of fear and cold. "What are you, a Quaker, now? Go over there and line up with the other pussies!" the sergeant shouted.

I jumped up and trotted over to a straight line of delinquent soldiers whose worried faces heralded the approach of the Fort Dix firing squad. That's what I imagined, at least, as I took my place beside them, rifle in hand, and worriedly awaited my punishment. Our strabismus-eyed sergeant positioned himself in front of us minutes later. With his hands on his hips, he began to spew commands at us at rapid speed. "Fall to your knees, soldiers! Now fall on your elbows! Now jump up! Now knees! Elbows! Up! Knees, elbows, up!" We did this over and over, and faster and faster. I started counting at first; but past 50, I gave up counting. The ground was frozen and hard as a rock and each fall to my knees was like landing on granite. Every time I dropped to my elbows while holding my rifle, I prayed it would not accidentally go off. It would be just my rotten luck.

A few days after bivouac had ended, I awoke in my warm barracks happy to have survived. The misery was over. I lifted off the covers and sat up; but found myself unable to get out of bed. It was not the usual fatigue; something was not right. I felt exhausted and hungover, although I had not had any alcohol in weeks. And now that I thought about it, the barracks wasn't just warm, it was hot as hell.

I tumbled out of my bunk and tried to get dressed, but I could not balance on one leg; and as I hopped around, my other leg could not seem to find the pants hole. I was simply too weak to put my clothes on. At the same time, I was afraid to miss roll call, for I would be brutally punished. With no good options, I staggered out of the barracks out of uniform, still wearing my long johns, with my bare feet slipped into my boots, the laces untied. I headed over to roll call.

The First Sergeant started heading in my direction. He intercepted me, and he looked incensed. "What do you think you are doing, soldier!" he shouted, when he was almost on top of me. "You are an embarrassment to behold!"

His face was so close I could smell the alcohol on his breath. "I'm sorry, sir. But I think I am ill, sir. I'm going on sick call."

He stared at me with his left eye (I think) and said, "If you do not get hospitalized, boy, and you are sent back here, you will be punished mercilessly. Is that understood?"

It was a short drive to the base hospital. After a cursory exam I was thrilled to find out I was going to be admitted for pneumonia. *At long last, I can sink into a hospital bed and get some well-needed rest,* I thought. I soon learned that's not how hospitals worked in the Army – rest must be earned. Well, that seemed just like home. I had to first collect my hospital gear: bed linens, hospital pajamas, regulation slippers, a toothbrush kit, and a kit for shaving. I dragged myself over a mile collecting the necessary items for my stay.

Sometime in the afternoon I woke up in the pneumonia ward confused and disoriented. I had broken a sweat and was drenched. Suddenly in a panic, I looked under the sheets to make sure I had all my body parts. Arms, *check*. Toes, *check*. Male appendages, *check, check, check*.

But something was amiss. Little red spots had emerged on all those parts I was checking. I called the nurse over to look at this new rash that had suddenly appeared. She took one look under my blanket and then grabbed hold of the head of my stretcher and broke off into a run. We ran through the pneumonia ward nearly knocking over charts and IV bottles as we sped past the other patients. We finally made it into the hallway, but the nurse did not stop; she took a wide right turn while still running. I tilted so far to the right that I had to grab hold onto both sides of my hospital bed to keep from falling out. We ran all the way to the other end of the hospital. "What is it, what's the matter?" I called out to my nurse, scared out of my mind. "Where are we going? What's wrong with me?"

The nurse did not stop to answer. She was panting as she flew past the other wards, and she did not say a word. Then I saw a set of closed double doors. A sign at the top said, "Isolation Ward." We popped through the doors and only then, the gasping nurse yelled back at me, *"You... have... German... measles..."*

Well, I was not dying, or at least I didn't think so. That was a relief. But how many young men in the pneumonia ward did I infect with German measles before I was moved? In my head, I could already hear the rumors circulating: *That German recruit (the Nazi!) has spread German measles throughout the infantry!*

I spent five days in isolation; five days of rest that I sorely needed. German measles – rubella – turned out to be not nearly as serious as ordinary measles.[1] After a week, I was discharged from the hospital, recovered enough to tolerate the hefty dose of abuse that was sure to be forthcoming from my sergeant.

"Glad to have you back, son," the sergeant said, quite kindly. Illness was apparently a tolerable offense. "However, I have some unfortunate news for you." *(Aha... Here it was...)* "I'm genuinely sorry, but due to the time you missed in training while you were ill, you will not be graduating with your class."

It was a possibility I had not even considered. My company, along with my psychotic sergeant, would be going off to Germany without me. I would have to stay behind and complete two more weeks of infantry training. I was being left back again, but this time, I did not mind it one bit.

It was mid-March already, and the worst of winter had finally eased its grip. I was allowed to sleep until 6 a.m. and take a truck to the training area instead of marching on foot. Those last two weeks seemed like a holiday compared to the prior six.

Finally, I got my orders from Washington D.C. I was assigned to a military intelligence unit in Germany and would be shipping out. At last, I was done with my training and could have my own identity back. What that identity was?

At this point, I had no idea.

23

THE RETURN

How strange it felt to be going back to Germany. Frightening and at the same time, exhilarating. Back to a country that had taken everything from us. Our citizenship, our wealth, our belongings, our home, our families, our friends. And yet, and yet... I *wanted* to go back, desperately. I was not alone. Each member of my family felt a deep personal yearning to revisit the country that was once our home.

Anita would have gladly gone in my place, her memories of Berlin even more vivid and extensive than mine. Instead, she had to settle for living vicariously through me. In the brief period until I departed, she gave me a crash course in German manners and culture, concerned that I had become too Americanized.

"Remember to give up your seat on the bus. Don't put your fingers on the glass display in a store. If you meet a group of people, shake hands with everybody. Always knock before you enter a room. Don't eat until your host says "*Guten Appetit.*" Never be late, not ever. Also, Jack, and this is *very* important... never be early!"

Anita lent me 100 dollars towards the purchase of a car. Lastly, she took on the monumental task of dealing with my mother's incessant handwringing. She swore to her every day that I would return safely.

At last, it was time to depart. As I stepped up the gangplank of my ship, my stomach turned. Was it normal anxiety? Maybe. But as I looked at that huge vessel, I had an immediate flashback to my hell-voyage on the *Navemar*, where I was packed into a hold amid filth and sickness and death.

Almost as soon as we set sail, I realized this nine-day voyage would bear almost no resemblance to my prior cross-Atlantic journey. Yes, it was packed; there were thousands of soldiers on board. But we had delicious food, nightly entertainment, and plenty of bathrooms. My traumatic memories from over 13 years ago – and any lingering fears about the next chapter of my life – evaporated into the sea air.

On my second day, with astonishing luck, I ran into a familiar face. "Why Larry Nessman, it's you, my old NYU pal! How was pharmacy school?"

"Jack, I can't believe I ran into you! Pharmacy school? Well, first I hated it, then I liked it... and then – I was hooked!"

We both laughed, and then we hugged, and I found myself full of fondness and admiration, any previous jealousy on my part instantly melting away. We spent the rest of the voyage together, enjoying the upbeat mood and the on-board entertainment. We sat together and sang and hooted and applauded as we watched the delightfully silly and uplifting movie musical "Seven Brides for Seven Brothers."[1] There was a sense of mounting excitement, and enthusiasm swept through the air like a summer storm. At night, we slept in our berths in hammocks that swayed with the ship, the rocking motion lulling us to sleep. It seemed easy, oh so easy. Until our fifth day at sea.

At first, I noticed the wind had started to pick up and clouds were gathering overhead. "We've hit a gale!" Larry called out to me. Rain began, steadily at first, and within a few hours it became torrential, landing like darts onto my exposed flesh. I stayed on deck while most of the men went below. Then I watched the sea unleash its full power.

It was like nothing I have ever seen or felt. The giant waves seemed to transform into hills. The ship steadily mounted them, suddenly diving head-first into the deep valleys between. Soon the waves were no longer hills; they had grown into black mountains towering over the ship on every side. With foamy crests like caps of snow, they crashed like an avalanche onto the ship's deck. The ship rose and fell, sometimes in breathtaking pitches. My insides would rise each time the ship plunged, and with a momentary thrill I would forget to be afraid – *I am on a veritable roller coaster, this is exhilarating!* Then I would suddenly remember that we could capsize at any moment, and I would be filled with terror.

It went on for hours and hours. Then it was over, and everything was eerily calm while our seaworthy vessel continued its quiet journey. But not far from us, a Greek cargo ship had radioed for help. In the storm its cargo had shifted and one of the sailors had been injured. We diverted course to help the stricken ship. Six hours later we found the beaten boat bobbing up and down in the water with each wave, listing badly. We deployed a line across to the Greek ship with a harpoon, and using ropes and a basket, pulled the injured sailor onto our ship for medical care.

Then we were off again. Just a few days later I arrived at Bremerhaven, a fishing port on the North Sea. I planted my feet on German soil – this time as a US citizen – and waited for the Army to figure out what to do with me.

My first thought upon setting foot in Germany was that it was beautiful. It was May and the brief and sudden showers of spring had left the countryside lush and verdant.

In Bremerhaven, I was to immediately board a train to Zweibrücken. I waited in line with the other passengers as the train pulled in; then I stepped up to the car with my suitcase. Just as I was about to board, the train porter turned to me and said, "*Guten Tag.*"

Suddenly I froze. *Good day*. That's all the porter had said. It was the most innocent of greetings, yet I found myself suddenly at a loss for words. It was not that I had forgotten my German; my language skills were fine. No, it was something else. As I stared into the eyes of the German porter, I was overcome by the thought, *What if this man were a Nazi?*

How unexpectedly this feeling rose from within me. It must have been lying latent under a blanket of pseudo-security. For I harbored no animosity toward German citizens of which I was conscious. And suddenly I was standing there, imagining the porter lifting his right arm and saying "*Heil Hitler!*"

I took my seat in the train and began to look around at the other Germans sitting aboard, nonchalantly chatting with each other or quietly reading. *The woman with the green raincoat – had she been a Nazi sympathizer? Is the middle-aged man across the aisle a former war criminal? That man who was just staring at my nose; is he an antisemite?* Paranoia overwhelmed me. The only thing that made me feel safe and confident was my US Army uniform. I wore it like armor against my perceived enemies. I reminded myself that I was an American, not just a Jew, not only a victim. I knew if I waited it out, my imagined German enemies would eventually turn back into ordinary people again. It was only a matter of time.

The train took us to a spa town of Oberursel, just 16 kilometers (10 miles) outside of Frankfurt, where I had received my assignment to the US Army Northern Area Military Intelligence. It seemed a fine place to begin my intelligence service. This was the place where East German defectors were interrogated and debriefed, and some of them were recruited as "assets." I was ready to begin.

But the intelligence unit did not seem ready for me. In fact, they seemed to have no idea how to make use of me. The officers began to debate what to do with me. "I suppose we could keep him here as an interpreter," one of them said.

"I really don't think we need him," said another officer. My recommendation is that we send him to the intelligence school at Garmisch for more sophisticated training and instruction."[2] Still another officer suggested that I be assigned to a military unit in Frankfurt.

The fate of my entire military service was in their hands, and I was shaking in my Army boots. Both these last two options seemed dreadful. *More training?* I'd had enough training and was ready for service. Furthermore, assignment to a military unit would mean living with strict discipline and a classic military hierarchy, which I would have been happy to avoid.

I could feel my bad luck closing in on me, my entire military career being thrown into turmoil. At that moment, I needed a small miracle to walk through the door. Instead, Captain Kaiser walked through the door. He was a big miracle, and he entered my life, changing it forever.

What a name, *Captain Kaiser*. Literally translated, he was Captain King. This captain, this "king," arrived in civilian clothing; and despite his German-sounding name, he was a full blooded, all-American career soldier. He hailed from Brooklyn, a borough that used to be known as *King's* County. A coincidence? Perhaps. With the heaviest Brooklyn accent that I have ever heard, the captain pulled me aside and said, "Ayy Jack. Looks like these guys don't know what da heck to do widya. Now, I work at da US Military Liaison in Potsdam, over there in East Germany. And at the Mission over there, I could really use someone with skills like yours. I got five enlisted men, all German speakers, and eight officers, all Russian speakers. All of 'em's Americans, though. We haven't got a native German speaker like you. I'm tellin' you, Jack, this here's a plum assignment."

The Captain's accent was so thick, I did not understand half of what he said, but I inferred the following: A US military liaison in Potsdam. In need of a native German speaker. A plum assignment, whatever that meant. With other officers that speak German and Russian.

But Potsdam? Potsdam was in East Germany, a Soviet-occupied, communist, socialist country. It had been my dream to travel freely through Germany and visit my beloved Berlin. The captain reassured me there would be lots of opportunity to travel and ample time off. He reminded me that the city of Berlin was physically located in East Germany now that the country was split in half, and was only a 35-minute drive from Potsdam. That sealed the deal. Was I interested? Hell, yeah! What I would be doing in my position? I had absolutely no idea.

So it was decided: I would head to Potsdam to the official US Military Liaison Mission, whatever the heck that was. But first there was paperwork to do and lots of it. It seems I had to make a pitstop at an "unofficial" branch of the Mission to get all my papers in order. That branch was located in Berlin.

I boarded an overnight train to Berlin. As soon as I got off at the Banhof station, a soldier met me and whisked me away by car to Zehlendorf, one of the more luxurious parts of the city. We pulled up to a shadowy mansion. Outside the mansion, there was nothing to denote any official capacity. No American flag. No sign that said, "US Military Liaison Mission – Berlin branch." Nothing.

If not for some rather heavy German police patrol outside, the house looked entirely unremarkable. But as I stepped inside, nothing about my surroundings looked ordinary. Security was everywhere. Each room in the villa had to be accessed with a combination lock. Heavy drapes covered the walls, under which hung detailed maps and other information which appeared to be top secret.

By day's end, I understood that the villa was a covert intelligence center. Everyone who worked there was an intelligence officer, and I mean everyone – from the chauffeur to the chef to the uniformed guard outside. All of them were trained intelligence officers working for the US. There was no doubt about it – there had to be some important spying going on here.

Oh, how I wanted to stay right there! I was in Berlin. In a stunning villa. True, the villa had the dubious distinction of being the former home of Walther Funk, Hitler's finance minister. But the intrigue of this place was undeniable.

Unfortunately, I was not meant to stay. This was just a temporary stop for paperwork. Four days after my arrival in Berlin, my documents arrived. I rifled through the papers, which included a Russian identity card. Why on earth would I need one?

Just hours later, a driver came to take me to the official Mission in Potsdam. We got in his car and darted away from Berlin, headed to East Germany.

My driver and I headed eastbound, an American flag blowing haughtily from the front of a beautiful, sleek metallic blue Ford. Bouncing along the wide, vacant road, I couldn't help but notice the absence of other vehicles. No one seemed to want to head *toward* East Germany. Overgrown vegetation bordered the left embankment, and behind it ran a continuous fence. Every few hundred meters, a warning sign popped up that read "You are leaving the American sector of Berlin." Duly noted.

We continued onwards, passing signs for Lake Wannsee, now a place for recreation. In my mind, it would always remain the location of the Nazi conference where the ultimate fate of the Jews – the "final solution" – was decided.[3] I shook the thought out of my head. That was the past. The old war. This was the Cold War. Something completely different. Or was it? We bounced along as I pondered the thought.

Old War. Cold War. As I had once told my friend Teddy Jerz, there is no such thing as lasting peace. True, there was no active combat now. But the Cold War had started almost immediately after World War II. Russia and the US had been allies for no more than a minute during the war while they were both fighting the German enemy. That alliance had ended with Germany's defeat, and now we were sworn enemies again.

President Truman and Prime Minister Stalin had competing visions for a postwar world order. Stalin was trying to squelch regrowth of a potentially dangerous Germany, but the US was doing just the opposite, in the belief that a strong German democracy would help to stabilize Europe. Stalin began placing communist governments throughout Eastern Europe to protect Russia from a formidable West and another possible German threat.

We became afraid of Russia, and they were just as afraid of us. We were both playing chicken until someone withdrew, but no one did. We had become so afraid of the Russians and so afraid of communism, that we even let former Nazis into the US, presumably so we could use their brainpower. It seemed like we would do anything, even compromise all morals, to compete with Soviet military expansion.

When China eventually fell to communism in 1949, the east and west became unofficially divided by an "Iron Curtain." And when communist North Korea invaded South Korea, the US felt it had to get involved in the Korean War to halt further spread of communism in the Far East. By then, the Soviets had already acquired a nuclear bomb. So that's what had happened since World War II. Germany wasn't the enemy anymore. It was the Soviets this time, the encroachment of communism, and now the nuclear threat. There would always be some reason to be at war.

We drove on. More signs. More warnings: "You are entering the East Zone." And now we were approaching a bridge – the Glienicke Bridge.[4] On our side of the bridge, green-uniformed German customs police stood holding binoculars, sweeping the area, looking for... what, exactly? They quickly gave us a salute and raised a trestle for us to pass. There was no hesitation; we were Americans, after all. But about 50 meters down on the other side of the bridge, we were stopped by two Soviet Military Police. They each carried a stick that had a red disk on one end and a green disk on the other, as a kind of makeshift, manual traffic signal. Saluting us politely, they asked in Russian for our identity cards. Now I understood why I needed a Russian ID. After inspecting our vehicle (for humans? contraband?), they waved us on. Still not at the finish line, we had to pass the East German *Volkspolizei* [People's Police] on the other side of the bridge, for they needed to raise their trestle to let us pass. As we finally reached the other side of the bridge, a sign read: "You are in the Soviet Occupied Zone of Germany."

That bridge over the Havel River was the only crossing point between West Berlin and the rest of East Germany. Once we were over the bridge, only one and a half kilometers lay between us and Potsdam.

We bounced and bumped along the rutted road passing only an occasional military vehicle or a rundown bus. Ordinary cars and recreational vehicles were nowhere to be seen. But one thing was in abundant supply: road sign after road sign spewing communist and socialist propaganda. Slogan after slogan of nonsense. It sounded like pure drivel. "Unity of the Socialist German People and the Soviet Union." "The Friendship of the Socialist Peoples of the World." "The Struggle to Free the World of Capitalism and Fascism." "The Greatness of Walter Ulbricht."[5]

We headed further north toward the Mission compound, located in Glienecke. Just before we turned into the entrance, we passed a small guard post containing only a single East German Volkspolizei guard (VOPO) and a telephone. We drove through the iron gate along a gravel road, passing past lush gardens, until we reached a large circular driveway. The driver pulled up in front of a three-story villa sitting right at the edge of a lake.

I don't know what I expected. Perhaps some kind of military compound. Rows of barracks, or the nondescript, ugly concrete structures that had been hastily built amid the post-war rubble. But as I rode down the gravel driveway, past the wrought iron gate and through the lush foliage, I saw right away that I had imagined wrong. Somehow, I had landed in the countryside at a gorgeous lakeside mansion. If I thought the villa in Berlin was luxurious, it did not hold a candle to the property I was staring at right now. With my mouth wide open, I stepped out of the car. "What the heck is this place?" I asked my driver as I was taking it in.

"You are standing at the former home of the Crown Prince of the Hohenzollern House."

My knowledge of history suddenly kicked in and I remembered that the Hohenzollerns were the Prussian Royal family forced to abdicate at the end of World War I. Their opulent summer estate stood on the shores of the Glienicker Lake, and I was standing in it. Lush floral gardens and manicured greens graced the property. A private tennis court stood invitingly in the distance. Recreational boats, moored on the private docks, floated quietly on the soft waves of the lake, beckoning me to enjoy them just for a few hours of pleasure. Not a bad place to do my Army service. Not bad at all.

I toured the interior of the villa with the housekeeper, all the while thanking Captain Kaiser again and again under my breath and quite possibly out loud. The housekeeper showed me the main floor which had been converted to our working office and recreational space. A smaller living room had even been transformed into an ersatz movie theater. Together we ascended the wide marble staircase. The second floor had been entirely sealed off for radio and electronic communication. We reached the third floor, which housed the bedrooms, each of which had a view of the sprawling lake. The housekeeper pointed to a closed bedroom door. "This is your room," she said.

Like the royalty of the original homeowners, our property came complete with a set of servants – a cook, chambermaid, garage attendant and housekeeper. They had their own quarters in an entirely separate building on the grounds. *How lovely*, I thought, *that a staff comes with the house, their presence simply to make my life more comfortable!* Then I remembered the villa in Berlin, where all the staff were intelligence agents. Did our villa also employ a staff of spies? And if so, whose side were they working for?

I had better find out, and soon.

This was no ordinary military assignment, to be sure. There was no military discipline, no inspections, no curfew. Captain Kaiser was certainly right – this was a plum assignment. But what would I be doing here? What was the Mission? I assumed it was a type of diplomatic Mission, like an American Embassy in East Germany. I picked up my training packet and tried to read it through. It wasn't long before I was yawning. The work, quite frankly, sounded a bit boring. Officially the Mission was supposed to:

- Help find WWII soldiers who were missing in action.

- Handle Americans who were lost on the Autobahn between East and West Germany.
- Help US citizens involved in auto or air accidents in or over East Germany.
- Maintain a liaison between the US and Soviet commanders.

I tried to swallow my disappointment as I read on, my eyelids slowly growing heavy with fatigue. Just as the papers were dropping onto my chest, Captain Kaiser walked right up to me, ripped the training packet out of my hands and tossed it in the garbage. "What did you do that for?" I cried out, sitting up abruptly. "I swear, Captain, I'm reading my packet from cover to cover!"

"Son," he said in Brooklynese that I now could translate to English, "forget those papers. Rip 'em up, Jack. Whatever you are reading there is just the official version of the Mission. But that is not what we do here."

"So what is it that we do?"

"The Mission is an above board, in-uniform, spying center. That's it, plain and simple. You are now an intelligence Missionary, spying in full view of the enemy. Yes, Jack, you are a spy, but our spying is done with the enemy's permission. They are spying on us, and we are spying on them. Now do you get it?"

Frankly I did not. I couldn't fathom it. Spying in full view of the enemy? Wasn't spying an undercover, secret operation? And there was another problem too. Naively, I had bought into American propaganda that the Russians had spies that were trying to amass secrets from us, but not the other way around. I had to quickly throw out all my assumptions. Every country was spying, including the US. It was an activity that seemed to be fully sanctioned.

The Missions of all the countries – including our French and British allies – were vital for intelligence gathering. Each Mission was trying to maximize his own intelligence gathering while restricting the other side's. By the time I had gotten to the Mission, all this spying had escalated to a nerve-wracking game of cat-and-mouse, occasionally with dire or even deadly consequences.

"We must keep the Soviets from invading western Europe," Captain Kaiser continued. "We believe the Soviets have weapons superiority over us, at least in numbers. The Mission's primary objective is to track Soviet and East German troop movements, assess their weapons capabilities, and uncover any new Russian weapons or weapons defense systems. This is serious business, Jack," he explained.

"You are also to assess our 'assets,' and see if their information is any good," he continued. "East Germany is crawling with informants earning money for their inside information. They are our eyes on the ground, and we needed them to track Soviet movements and weapons." But we could not simply trust them, the Captain explained further. Any East German willing to spy for the US for money, could also be spying for someone else. They could even be double agents, taking money from us and the other side too.

It was a complicated, dangerous game, one that I was about to start playing.

"You're going to be handling a brand new 1955 Ford sedan," the chauffeur informed me. He was in charge of my driving instruction. "It's a sweet ride, but just be aware, it's been modified for our purposes." It certainly had. The car had a compass, fire extinguisher, sophisticated radio communication system, advanced suspension system and multiple spare tires designed for dangerous chases and off-road getaways.

I had told Captain Kaiser that my driving skills were pretty good, but I had kind of exaggerated. Or you could say, lied. My only experience was driving Lou's automatic shift jalopy around the city on weekends, and Sid's Model T on our occasional double dates in New Hampshire. I had a lot to learn.

First, I would have to master driving a stick shift, the only transmission available. Only then could I tackle the aggressive and evasive driving techniques I would need for surveillance and to avoid capture by the Russians or East Germans.

The chauffeur had just finished walking me through the features on the beautiful new Ford. Oddly, an American flag sat proudly perched on the front fender of this so-called spy car. The license plate held a single digit and read 'US Military Liaison Mission.'

"Seriously!" I exclaimed. "Why would we put a veritable announcement on a spying vehicle? We might as well write 'I Spy' on the license plate."

"These are not meant to be stealth cars," the chauffeur explained. "We are the 'official' intelligence, and when we drive somewhere, we want everyone to know it."

I was then sent to the electronics expert. He stood behind an array of high-end Leica, Hasselblad, and Contax D cameras, with interchangeable wide angle and telescopic lenses. "These gadgets seem better suited for James Bond than for someone like me," I said. "What is this gizmo?" I pointed to an object the size of a cigarette lighter.

"It's a Minox Minolta camera. These little beauties are brand new."

"That tiny thing is a camera?"

"Yes, but amazingly, it can photograph an 8 x 10 document. You are to have this with you at all times. Now let's see to your recording devices."

The electronics specialist handed me tie clips and a wristwatch, both imbedded with microphones. He showed me how a wire could be threaded under my clothing to a recording device the size of a tiny match box. "These tiny avant-garde tools are now part of your armamentarium of espionage, Jack. As a German speaker you might have to get an East German to talk. Just keep them talking and talking," he instructed me as he outfitted me with equipment.

"Naturally, you will have to record it. But here inside the Mission? Here, you are to assume everything is bugged. Inside the Mission, you never talk about our own activities. Never. The staff in our villa do not work for us. They are East German spies who will smile graciously as they serve your delicious dinners. Always assume the maid or the chef or even the gardener might be listening."

My crash course on espionage driving and photography lasted no more than a couple of weeks when I unexpectedly needed to put my skills to the test. I had gone out on my first surveillance assignment with two officers, and within minutes of leaving the villa gates, I saw in my rearview mirror that a BMW was tailing us. The East German VOPO guard, whose only job was to note and call in our every movement, must have telephoned Soviet headquarters. The Soviets knew we had left the grounds and now we were being followed!

The BMW stayed exactly a kilometer behind us. Every time I looked in my rear-view mirror, there he was. There was no doubt it was a military vehicle – and I was going to have to figure out a way to lose him. Suddenly a second BMW appeared. Now I had two BMWs trailing me. In truth, at that slow speed, we looked more like a motorcade than spy cars in pursuit of each other. I wracked my brain. How could I out-maneuver them on these local pockmarked, potholed roads, scattered with ducks and chickens pecking alongside us in the shoulder?

There was only one way I could think of to shake them. I made for the East German autobahn, hoping that speed would be to my advantage. For as good as BMW engineering was, I had been assured that my Ford would leave them "in the dust."

Once on the autobahn, I downshifted into third gear and revved the car up to 160 km per hour, leaving clouds of black smoke billowing out of the exhaust from the cheap Russian gas. To my relief, the engine sang, and we flew along the empty roadway. But when I looked in my rearview mirror, there were the twins – the two BMWs – still following. They remained exactly a kilometer behind. I suddenly cut my engine to 50 kilometer per hour. Instantly, they cut their engines too. Darn! I stepped on the accelerator again and cruised back to 160, and they did the same. Then I suddenly dropped back down to 50 again, and so did my trailing Beemers. I just could not shake them. It was a road battle, Ford vs. BMW, and no one was winning. I floored the Ford to 160 again and after some period, cut the engine back to 50. I did it again and again. I was going to wear them out eventually, or at least I hoped so, because I was on a straight, open road with no place to turn off. Eventually, I looked in my rearview mirror and I didn't see them trailing me. Way in the distance, I saw both cars standing still, their BMW engines smoking and overheated, their cars, dead. It had worked!

We continued to our surveillance mission at a normal speed, the danger well behind us. I was feeling rather cocky but knew better than to take the credit. "Henry Ford would be proud of us, don't you think?" I said to one of my officers. By us, I meant me, of course.

"You do know Henry Ford was a vocal antisemite, don't you?" one officer replied, putting me right back in my place. "He called labor unions a 'global Jewish conspiracy' and ran a front-page editorial every week called 'The International Jew: The World's Problem.'"[6]

"Of course I am aware of that," I replied, swallowing hard, my ego deflating quickly. I still tried to hold my ground. "Listen, history is full of countless authors, artists and composers who were antisemites," I added. "But if I avoided every genius because of their ideology, I might never read a great novel or listen to classical music again."

We did not pursue a philosophical debate about cars, geniuses, or notable antisemites. There were enough of them to go around. From that day on, we all knew I could drive like a spy and the day might come when I would need those skills to save our lives.

The Soviets had made a pact with the Allies to allow Mission officials from the four occupying countries to drive freely throughout East Germany. Despite this agreement, each month we received a map from the Soviet commander of East Germany,

Marshal Andrei Grechko.[7] The new map would indicate certain areas of East Germany that were closed off to us. We guessed that any closed-off areas must signify the very locations where training or weapons testing was taking place. Those maps seemed like invitations for surveillance and reconnaissance. The Soviets might just as well have drawn an arrow on the map and said: "Kindly head *here*."

And that is exactly what we did. One morning, map in hand, I set out on a reconnaissance mission with my supervising officer. We were aiming for one of those off-limit sites, but when we arrived, we found it blocked by a heavy metal beam. It was even more evidence: something important was going down.

"There has to be another way to circumvent the roadblock, Jack," my officer said to me. He pulled out another, more detailed map from the glove compartment, and we studied it together.

"Look over here." I had found a nearly imperceptible turn off the road on this new map. "I think it's a secondary access route."

We got back into the car and drove slowly up the road until we found the tiny turn-off. I maneuvered the car into the narrow turn and crept slowly along the almost invisible path, barely touching the gas pedal.

I drove as noiselessly as I could along the dirt road. The progress was painfully slow. Suddenly, out of nowhere, an East German VolksPolizei Officer popped out in front of us. Brandishing his revolver, he stood directly in front of us and yelled, "Stop, or I'll shoot!" in crystal-clear German.

I was scared out of my wits, but I was ready for him, having been trained for just this type of encounter. My driving instructor's voice was reverberating in my head: *cut figure eights, cross the field, then drive, drive, drive. And whatever you do, avoid capture at all costs!*

But the officer sitting next to me was pumping out entirely different instructions and I had no choice but to abide by them. "Step on it, Jack," he yelled. "Accelerate. No, don't turn, go forward. Drive straight ahead!"

"Straight ahead? Right towards him?" I screamed back at him. The German VOPO was dead ahead with his gun pointed at us, and he didn't look like he was going to budge. Either he was going to shoot us through the windshield, or I was about to mow him down.

"Go!" I followed orders and floored the gas pedal, heading straight. The East German held his ground. I'm sure he thought that I would eventually veer off. As I barreled toward him, the look on his face turned from anger to shock. He didn't even have time to fire a shot. With no place to go, he jumped on top of the car hood. As I sped away, he slid off the side of the car and rolled on the ground and I never dared to look back again.

After a few months, I had gotten the hang of it all: the driving, the espionage, and the field work. I was enjoying the risks and the danger, the car chases, the equipment. Now we were headed on a new mission to assess Soviet troop strength at various military compounds throughout greater East Germany. It would be a multiday trip visiting the poor, rural villages that dotted the countryside.

We arrived in the first village in mid-afternoon. In keeping with my training, I drove our Ford directly into the compound of the Russian commander. It was our way of announcing our arrival openly. Within minutes, military police appeared and escorted us by motorcycle to the town's one and only hotel.

I emerged from the car and surveyed my surroundings with disbelief. How had this poverty-stricken village managed to escape all signs of modernity? I couldn't fathom it. The hotel looked as though it had fallen out of another era. "The whole town looks like it has survived an apocalypse, and this sad hotel is the last building standing," I commented to one of my accompanying officers.

He laughed and agreed. "There are towns like this all over East Germany," he replied. "Better get used to it." I grabbed my satchel from the car and walked into the small hotel, hoping to rest before dinner.

After we checked in, I turned down the narrow hallway and headed towards my room. A single naked lightbulb hung from the ceiling; it produced an eerie low glow and emitted a constant buzz. I was able to find my room, and with an old-fashioned skeleton key, unlocked the door and stepped inside. The damp smell of mold immediately overwhelmed me. I placed my satchel on top of my bed and noticed on close inspection that the woolen blanket was full of holes, and the few areas without holes were covered with an array of sewn-on patches in unmatched colors. I decided to put off unpacking until later, and to wash up instead. A small sink was located in the corner of the room. My expectations already lowered, I was not surprised to find chipped, stained porcelain collecting the steady *drip, drip, drip* from the rusty faucet, and beneath the sink, leaking pipes stuffed with dirty, soaked rags. *This hotel,* I thought, *is only slightly more inviting than a prison cell.*

I could not suppress my revulsion. All I wanted to do was to run from the dank, claustrophobic room and find fresh air and human company. I decided not to rest, and went to the lobby to join the other officers who were with me on assignment. "Well, well, Jack. Welcome to East Germany," my officer said to me sarcastically, laughing as he saw the look of horror on my face.

By nightfall we were hungry and eager to get a meal. "Where would you recommend that we eat in this town?" I asked the hotel manager.

"We have a very fine restaurant here at the hotel," he suggested. "Please stay for dinner. Most guests do, and we would be happy to serve you."

The dining room was nearly as pitiful as the rest of the hotel. It had just four tables with four stained tablecloths, and we were the only diners. A few minutes after we sat at the table, the hotel manager entered the dining room. He had thrown a cloth napkin over his arm, and was dressed for his new role as waiter. He handed each of us stained paper menus. The menu was full of familiar German delicacies, and I was relieved to know that a good meal was on its way. "There's hope for this trip yet," I said to my colleagues in English. Turning to the waiter, I said in German, "I'll have a *Schnitzel.*"

The hotel manager shook his head. "*Tut mir Leid.* I am sorry. We are out of *Schnitzel.*"

"Umm, okay, I'll have the *Rouladen,*" looking forward to an old favorite: thin slices of beef rolled around bacon, pickles, and onions.

But the manager-cum-waiter shook his head again.

"*Bratwurst*?" I inquired. Surely, they must have a basic sausage.

"Sorry. All out."

Finally, I put my menu down on the table and asked, "What *do* you have here?"

"Only *Schweinfleisch,*" he answered.

Well, that made it easy, at least. We all ordered the pork knuckle and a salad. How badly I wanted to ask why he bothered to show us menus when he only had one item. But the answer was pointless, and I did not want to embarrass him.

We waited and we waited for our food. An hour passed. "How long could a salad possible take?" I asked, frustrated and hungry.

"Maybe our waiter has now transformed into the chef. That same old guy must be in the kitchen right now preparing our meal!"

We all laughed. The salad finally arrived, and I eagerly put my fork in it. As I was about to lift it to my mouth, a worm wriggled out from under a lettuce leaf onto my plate. "Look at that. Even the worm is trying to escape East Germany," I joked. "Go west, little worm. Go west!"

Our pork entrées finally came, but by then I had nearly fallen asleep at the table. Dinner had taken hours. There had, in fact, been a bona fide kitchen staff, but the workers moved with a lassitude and inefficiency that was boggling to my New York-paced mind. I had been gradually discovering this throughout East Germany. Eventually I would learn to expect nothing more from a country where everyone's jobs were chosen by "Central Planning," instead of by desire or talent, and all motivation and incentive had essentially died.

The next morning, we exited our hotel and began to walk through the small town. We noticed that some of the villagers had gathered and were gawking at us. Our arrival had apparently drawn an audience. Although we had been warned not to engage in conversation on these trips, this one time, I ignored protocol. I turned to a woman who was among the observers. "Why is there such a fuss over our arrival?" I asked.

"No one here has ever seen an American soldier," she replied. "And such a car you have! Just like a celebrity!"

I could not deny it. With our sleek car, our crisp uniforms and our movie star sunglasses, we must have looked impressive juxtaposed to the pitiful surroundings. In this environment, at least for a little while, I enjoyed our glamorous illusion. All at once, the townspeople started to hammer us with questions, but we tried to disengage, waved warmly and walked away.

Within two or three blocks we started to notice that a man was walking behind us. As we turned the corner, he did too, and we became certain that he was in pursuit. We did not look back; we kept walking, picking up the pace, but he sped up too and was closing in. By the next block we were getting nervous, for he was practically at our heels. When he was almost on top of us, we slowed, and without turning around, I hissed, "What do you want?"

In the softest voice, he stammered, "Please, gentlemen, is it p-possible for me and my family t-to stow away in the trunk of your c-car? We are d-desperate to get out of East Germany."

I stopped walking and started to turn halfway around. The movie star facade crumbled quickly, and I was brought back to earth with a swell of compassion. *We could do it, couldn't we,* I thought for just an instant? We could help someone in need, as I hoped others would have done for me. No, I quickly realized, we could not consider it. It would be a violation of the Mission. And if a stowaway was found in our car, we would all be shot. Then I thought, *what if the man's request is not even honest? How do we know he is not a plant?*

Suspicion helped rid me of any guilt caused by my inaction. Yes, of course, he could be a spy for the other side. Problem solved. Best not to engage with the locals.

We turned our eyes forward and kept on walking and we did not look back.

Once in the safety of our car, we proceeded with our mission to surveil Soviet military compounds within proximity of the village. This turned out to be shockingly easy. The compounds were surrounded by poorly constructed fences that had been hastily erected by the Russians. If we drove at low speeds, we could see right through the slats. We identified rocket launchers, the Soviet's most advanced tanks, and amphibious tanks used for river crossings. Sometimes we captured photos of bridges lying just below the water's surface that enabled equipment to cross without detection. We drove slowly past the compounds and took picture after picture.

It was rare that we came back from an assignment empty-handed. Every mission seemed to yield fruit, and we were rewarded handsomely. Not with money, but with other things of value to young people: ample time off between assignments, and sumptuous dinners hosted by the Soviet commander himself. We ate like kings and drank glass after glass of the commander's vodka as if it was pure water. It was so pleasant that I forgot the Soviets were the enemy.

Sometimes, I forgot there was any risk at all.

In those first few months, I traveled to Leipzig, Chemnitz, Dresden, Neuripin Air base, Stralsund, Rostock, Frankfurt on the Oder. We jotted down the license number and location of every military vehicle we passed and examined every epaulet and uniform to determine which type of military was in the area. Were they Air Force? Artillery? We photographed new equipment and old weapons that had undergone modification. We filmed the first Russian T-54 tank, which was the most advanced tank of the time and had been used in Korea. We shot photos of cockpits of Soviet fighter planes, and experimental air drones, and we found information about the Russian's early use of infrared for night vision. We felt like we were everywhere.

Everywhere except the one place I wanted to be from the moment I set foot in Germany – Berlin. It's not just that I was nostalgic for my former home. Berlin was also where all the action and the nightlife was, and every soldier including me wanted to be a part of it. Yes, I absolutely had to get to Berlin. But if I wanted to make it there, I was going to have to get myself a set of wheels.

I had only the 100 dollars Anita had given me, and some money I had saved up while on assignment. That was not going to get much of a car. I simply hoped for something that would *go*.

I asked the chauffeur at the Mission for his help; he seemed likely to be the most knowledgeable about cars. "No problem," he assured me. "I can get you a solid car for about 200 dollars."

I drove off with a 1935 Adler convertible – a car that was about as popular as an Edsel.[8] By the time I got the car in 1955, the Adler company was already long out of business. Even when it had been in business, it was better known for its bicycles and sewing machines than its cars. Nonetheless, it did have some novel innovations for its day, like a reserve gas tank, a gear shift on the steering wheel, front wheel drive, and a completely metal body – features that would be eventually adopted by other car companies in the years to follow.

But those crafty novelties were not enough to make the car functional. The first time I hit the brakes on that 20-year-old disaster, the car skipped so far forward that my forehead nearly hit the windshield. I solved that problem by putting sandbags in the trunk to weigh down the back of the car. The second time I drove the car, I made a sharp left turn and felt something "pop." Then the car leaned forward and tipped to the right. When I looked out the window I saw something rolling away on the road. It was my entire right front wheel! It was as if the wheels of my car were sewn onto the vehicle. And that was nearly the truth. The bolts that attached the wheels to the axel would loosen every time I shifted roughly – which was basically every time I shifted. Every 50 kilometers or so, one or the other front wheel would detach and roll away, landing somewhere between a communist propaganda road sign and a pecking chicken. It was an automotive disaster.

I was not going to be deterred. That Adler was going to get me to Berlin no matter how many wheels were attached.

The first time I drove into Berlin, I felt the way one does when visiting one's old childhood classroom. Whatever I imagined Berlin would be – whatever my expectations – it did not live up to my memories. Or maybe my memories did not live up to my expectations. Berlin had changed and so had I. One thing that had remained, that felt so familiar, was the rubble. It was everywhere. More than 10 years had passed since the war had ended and so much of the city still seemed war torn and battered.

I passed the entrance to the Tiergarten zoo. Across the street, the ruined Kaiser Wilhelm Church loomed tall and broken, a permanent memorial to the war. Yes, it was a bruised Berlin. But inside the cracks and beneath the detritus, were also signs of rebirth. Cranes lined the skyline. New construction to erase the destruction. A fresh, vibrant, modern Berlin was growing from the ash heap. The West was pouring money into this project – rebuilding the city into a showcase urban center – for it was a symbol that capitalism had prevailed over communism. No, it was not my old Berlin, but you could feel Berlin was about to be reborn; it was in the air, and it was electrifying.

At the same time, there was also a pervasive feeling of claustrophobia, for Berlin was an island sitting in the middle of East Germany. In every direction you turned, you would encounter a sign that read "You have reached the East German border" or "You have reached the Soviet Zone." It was a free island in a prison from which you could not escape.

It was a crazy place, full of contradictions. That was nothing new. Berlin had always been a city of contrasts. Old and new, liberal and fascist, war-torn and rebuilt. But never had a virtual line been drawn down the middle. Yes, that was something new, too. East and west. Socialist and capitalist. Ideological opposites. Political enemies. In just seven years an actual wall would be built to separate the unidentical twin halves. For now, citizens could still travel freely between the east and west sides of my beloved city. That freedom of travel created the perfect conditions for an exchange of information. The stage was perfectly set for spying.

Before I could really enjoy my many forays into Berlin, I had a few practical as well as sentimental matters to attend to. I wanted to contact Dr. Behne, the landlord of our building, but I was heartbroken to learn that he had died. I had only wanted to thank him for all he had done for us. Instead, I spoke with his daughter, now the landlord of 103 Schillerstrasse, who invited me for coffee and cake and an opportunity to reminisce.

There it was, in the district of Charlottenburg, the pale-yellow stucco building almost exactly as I remembered it. Many of the balconies were gone. Nonetheless, there was solace in knowing the building was still there; that like us, it too had survived. I stepped into the courtyard and there was the pear tree, still standing elegantly in its center.

I felt a pressing need to know what happened to my friends in the building, the ones who had dropped me so suddenly. "Do you possibly remember my old childhood mates, Achim and Glatze?"

"Yes, of course I remember the families. I am sorry to tell you that Achim was drafted at the end of the war and killed, and Glatze died of typhoid fever."

My mind quickly jumped from surprise, to horror, to sadness. It was extraordinary, and strange really, that after all those years of persecution, I had somehow ended up being the lucky one who had lived. But I could not say this thought made me happy.

My next visit was to my father's clothing store. Of course, the store wasn't his anymore. It had only really been ours for a moment, and yet I still walked around with my parents' pride: We had once *owned* a store.

There it stood on the corner just as I remembered it, its slightly orange-tinted glass making a triangular facade protecting the haberdashery items behind it. Men's and now women's clothing, thoughtfully positioned on stylish mannequins, adorned the window, on which the name Herzog was imprinted in bold type.

I suppose I expected a warm greeting from Mr. Herzog, the gentleman who had bought our store. I was sure he would feel an excitement in reuniting with the past, but the Mr. Herzog I met with was angry – incredibly angry. As soon as we sat down, he began a diatribe. "I am bitterly disappointed that you did not respond to the letters I wrote you," he said. "How could you have done that to me?"

I had no idea what he was talking about, but I wisely did not interrupt, and allowed Mr. Herzog to continue his rant. "I simply asked that your family send over the documents confirming the sale of the store by Mr. Klein to your father. The least you could have done was give me the courtesy of a response. How could you treat me this way when I was so fair to you?" He went on and on, repeating the story, and growing more red-faced and heated as he spoke.

I listened politely, but after his third go-around, I simply had to interrupt. "Herr Herzog. I am sorry, but we did not receive any letters from you. We also never had these sales documents. You must realize we could not take any financial papers out of Germany, and by now you know that both Siegfried and my father are deceased. Why are these papers so important? We bought the store outright from Mr. Klein and paid him fairly before he left for Argentina."

"Well, don't you know what happened? Paul Klein sued me from Argentina. He claimed you never paid him for his business, and therefore I came to own it illegitimately. Since I had no paperwork to prove the legitimate sale, my only way to settle the claim was to pay Mr. Klein 50,000 Deutschmarks."

Now I finally understood his ire. Had Mr. Klein really told Mr. Herzog that we had not paid him for the store? Was it possible he had "misremembered" our complicated deal? Or had Mr. Klein thought we had all perished and no one would be able to repudiate his claim? Feeling terribly sorry for Mr. Herzog, all I could do was explain our situation and apologize deeply. It was not the reunion I had wished for, but I hoped I had made amends with my visit and explanation.

I had just one last visit to make to people lost long ago. It was time to check on the graves of my infant brother Manfred and my grandparents. It was time to visit the dead.

I stepped into the somber Weissensee cemetery, alone but for one old caretaker. What a state of neglect and disrepair the cemetery was in! There were so few Jews left in Berlin to tend to their families' gravestones or to hold the cemetery accountable. I was here for only one reason – to reassure my mother. Weaving my way through the twisted vines to the grave sites of Ernestine, Hiller, and Manfred, I wiped the dirt off the gold lettering, and made sure that lush ivy encircled each of our loved ones' graves.

Finished with my obligations to a life long gone, I could now join my Army mates and get reacquainted with the new Berlin. There were about 10,000 American GIs in West Berlin. The Americans were well-liked by the West Germans and we socialized with the men and women. We went to bars and nightclubs, classical concerts, and dance halls. My buddies were looking for fun encounters, but I, a hopeless romantic, was looking for real love. It had to be out there somewhere.

Then the wheel of my Adler rolled off one time too many, and the car could no longer make the trip to Berlin. I had to resign myself to visiting the local bars near Potsdam. The East German young women there were quite keen to meet an American GI. If they were lucky, they could get him to buy them a drink. Some of the young ladies set their sights even higher, hoping to find a future husband who would bring them back to the US. Still others were on the East German payroll; they were intent on having an encounter with an American, after which they would be debriefed and handsomely paid. It turned out that buying an East German woman a drink could be more dangerous and complicated than one knew.

I met a lovely young East German woman at a dance. After dating a few times I felt certain she was not an informant. She was sweet and pretty and I thought, or at least imagined, that a real relationship was starting to develop.

"Jack," she said, one evening. She looked serious and I braced myself. She was either breaking up with me, or about to tell me that she wanted to get married and move to America.

"Yes, sweetheart? What's on your mind?"

"I like you a lot. Really, I do."

"And so do I."

"But if my father finds out I'm seeing a Jew... he'll absolutely kill me!"

Well, I was quite sure he would kill me first. So I decided to end it. I would have to find love some other way. And without my handy Adler, I would have to figure out another way to get to Berlin. Unless fate would figure it out for me first.

It was June of 1955, and we had received excellent new intel from one of our most trusted East German informants. "The Soviets are going to be doing river crossing exercises in their armored vehicles tomorrow," he told us. He pointed to a location on the map, which he then tapped lightly with his middle finger. "It should be happening right here."

This was just the type of exercise we usually surveilled, giving us an opportunity to photograph any new devices or equipment being used by the Soviets. We thanked our asset warmly and paid him a nice sum. The following morning we packed up our Leica cameras and binoculars and drove off on another spying mission.

By any account, it was a typical day. I drove towards the river and one of my officers rode shotgun. We parked the Ford halfway down to the riverbank, keeping it out of sight, off the road. Stepping a bit away from the car, we waited for the Soviet exercises to begin.

It was a warm day, pleasantly quiet, but for the incessant humming of summer crickets. We lazily searched the region, taking pictures here and there, while scanning the blue of the river and the surrounding shrubbery with our binoculars.

I turned my binoculars slightly, but instead of the blue water, my lenses filled with green. Camouflage green. I instantly dropped my binoculars and standing right in front of me was a Russian infantry soldier. He had appeared out of nowhere. I looked to my right. There was another one. Then I turned my head left. Another soldier. We were surrounded. "Run!" I shouted.

We both turned on a dime and ran, heading to the car with lightning speed. Barely seated in the driver's seat, I put the car in gear and floored it, closing my door as we drove off. "Drive along the river!" screamed my officer. "Over there! Drive between those trees! Go around that bush!"

I navigated along the river embankment, all manner of foliage in my path. Maneuvering between the trees, I tried to aim away from the river and up toward the road. I drove as fast as I could, steering between the obstacles. I could just begin to see the clearing of the road ahead of me. All I had to do was make it to the road, and then we would be free to drive away. Maybe 30 more meters – that's all – and we would be there. Twenty-five meters. Twenty...

Suddenly an enormous Soviet tank appeared out of nowhere. It was the size of a building, and it was aiming directly at us. I instinctively swerved to get around it but the thing was a monster. I yanked the car nearly 90 degrees to the right, and as soon as we turned, we slammed headfirst into a tree. As the car came to an abrupt stop, our bodies flew forward into the windshield, and the Russian tank, now perpendicular to us, barreled into the left rear fender of the car. The ear-splitting sound of crushed metal reverberated in my head. At that moment, I thought to myself, *we're finished.*

Our car sat steaming, crumpled like an accordion, with a tree embracing its hood and a Soviet tank kissing its trunk. I knew I was not seriously hurt, only stunned, but the seat next to me was empty – my officer was gone. Before I could register what to do next, I was suddenly being pulled roughly out of the car by a set of unknown arms. Someone pushed me facedown against what was left of our foreshortened Ford, then handcuffed my wrists behind me. A camouflaged soldier dragged me through the woods and down the embankment until I reached a Russian car. Forcing me into the backseat by my head, I found to my relief, that my officer was sitting in the seat beside me, also in handcuffs. He looked uninjured, but the expression on his face told me I should be worried.

We drove in silence. Some time passed; it seemed like hours. Then we finally stopped and guards dragged us out of the car. They walked us into a featureless building and pushed us into a bare gray room where we sat face to face with a local Soviet commander. We were in some type of interrogation room.

"Turn over your film."

It was the very first thing anyone had said to us since the crash. We had expected it, and handed our film over dutifully.

"Are you spies?" the commander asked us. *Yes of course we were.* He knew that already.

We said nothing.

"Turn over your supplies and photographic equipment."

"No," we said.

"Sign these official documents that you are spying on the Soviets."

"Absolutely not."

I was confused. Something did not make sense. We were supposed to be in a spy game with rules that everyone agreed to, and the Russians had suddenly decided not to play by those rules. By all accounts, we were not supposed to be picked up or arrested. What had gone wrong? Had we come upon something particularly sensitive?

Worse, if the Soviets suddenly decided they were no longer

playing by the rules, what would that mean for us? Interrogation? Torture? Prison? Would we simply disappear without a trace? This was not a joke anymore. This was real. Such things were known to happen and we were starting to panic.

"Call your headquarters in Potsdam," we implored the Soviet officer. "We are allowed to be here. What you are doing is against international agreement. Call them!" We asked over and over for them to call headquarters. They did not make a call as far as we knew, and they continued to hold us.

Time seemed to have slowed. I could hear each tick of the second hand on my watch. I could practically feel my facial hair growing. Huge half-moon sweat stains gathered under my armpits. No one said a word to us for hours, and we waited and waited, unsure what would happen to us.

By the late afternoon we got word that our interrogators would turn us over to Marshal Andrei Grechko's staff. *That must be good news*, we thought. The Marshal knew who we were. We had drunk his vodka (like it was water) at all those parties and receptions. And yet, as more time passed, we were not released. Had we drunk too much of Grechko's vodka, perhaps? Reality finally started to dawn on us. We had done something to make someone very unhappy. We had been captured. And somehow, we would be made to pay.

We were not sent to a Gulag. We were not "disappeared." Eventually, the Marshal gave the order to release us, but we were not entirely in the clear. The Soviets decided they would make an example of us.

Captain Kaiser gave us the uncomfortable news. "You two have been made 'persona non grata.' As such, you are no longer welcome in East Germany. The Mission filed an official protest about your capture, but unfortunately, we were not able to influence the decision. You are both going to be discharged from Potsdam and the Mission."

So that was it. I was being kicked out, just like that. Were my days of espionage over for good?

Later, Captain Kaiser pulled me aside. He threw his arm over my sagging shoulder like an older brother. "Jack," he said, "you have no idea how fortunate you are. I don't know what you boys found, but you're lucky to be alive. Every now and then, the Russians decide not to play by the rules. And when that happens, you get killed. Shot 'by accident.' Or you disappear forever. Maybe it's good that you didn't know how much danger you were really in.

"Anyway, Jack, chin up. It ain't over. You may be *officially* discharged from the mission, on paper. That is exactly what we will tell our enemies. But did you think we were just gonna get rid of you? With your language skills? And all that training? No sir-ee Bob!"

I breathed a sigh of relief. It was not all over, at least. Though what was happening next, I had yet to find out.

Days later, I was back at the clandestine, unofficial branch of the Mission at the secret Berlin villa where I had first gotten my papers. The sexy car chases, the secret missions – they were over. Now I was stationed at the inner workings of the US spying operation. There was still plenty of useful spying to be done here at Berlin Headquarters.

And where was I now? I seemed to be in some sort of communications center. Messages were being sent to and from intelligence headquarters in Heidelberg, via untapped lines. I was also standing amidst reams of classified data. All of it had to be accessed and sorted, away from the prying eyes of the Russians. Photographs taken by U-2 spy planes of Soviet equipment and soldiers. Photographs that when laid side by side and viewed with special glasses, suddenly took on three-dimensionality and revealed their secrets: weapons, planes, East German and Russian troops and rocket launch sites.

I was put in charge of the Document Center, a treasure trove of information. The center contained copies of all commission reports and debriefings, and all data was shared with the British mission.

Every document had to be logged and inventoried. Even destroyed documents needed documentation of their destruction. No, it was not cloak and dagger work, but it was important intelligence work, nonetheless.

It required continuous effort and we worked hard. Sundays were our only days of rest and leisure, except on those occasional Sundays when I had to take shifts as duty officer. On those days, I wore my fatigues, slung a .45 caliber automatic around my waist, and stood guard to prevent unauthorized entry. If that did occur, I was to set off incendiary grenades that lay hidden near file cabinets and documents in the event the building had to be abandoned and documents destroyed.

Of course, none of that ever happened, but I was trained just in case. I tried to maintain my cool veneer of espionage, but most of the time, no exciting incidents took place. I bade my time answering the occasional phone call or reading a book – sometimes lulled into a nap – while I counted down the hours until everyone returned from their day of leisure.

On one such dull Sunday afternoon, having fallen asleep with a boring book in my lap, I was jolted awake by the unexpected and somewhat urgent sound of the doorbell ringing. Grabbing hold of my .45, I cautiously answered the door, ready to protect the villa – and my country – from the enemy.

"Excuse me, is this the residence of Dr. Solomon?" the person at the door asked me.

The woman standing in front of me did not appear to be a treacherous intruder. She spoke perfect German and was the most beautiful representation of the female species I had ever seen. In that respect, I suppose, she might very well be dangerous.

I was momentarily at a loss for words in any language. "No, no," I stuttered in German, once I found my voice. "You must be mistaken. There is no Dr. Solomon here." I was not willing to let this beautiful woman go so quickly. Thinking fast on my feet, I added, "Won't you please have a seat in reception, and I will see if I can help you?"

The mystery woman carelessly pushed her platinum blonde hair back behind her right ear. "I'm so sorry to have bothered you," she replied, graciously. "I rang the two houses adjacent to yours first, but I seem to have been given the wrong address."

She took a step inside and as I held the door, I watched her long legs sashay confidently in a cocoon of a pencil skirt. I led her to reception. Had this woman been a spy, she could have walked off with all our intelligence right then and there, or maybe pulled out a camera shaped like a lipstick and started photographing. I didn't notice her do any of that. Instead, I watched her sit elegantly in a chair, and gracefully cross her legs at the ankles. We conversed awkwardly for a few minutes. "Dr. Solomon is one of the few remaining Jews in Berlin," she explained. "We are such a small community, so I am quite anxious to find him."

For about 15 minutes I tried to make conversation, dragging out our encounter any way I could think of and trying to help her find the location of the mysteriously missing Dr. Solomon.

"I do apologize, but I have some friends in the car waiting for me," she suddenly said, and she stood up.

By then I was thoroughly enchanted. Bewitched, even. This woman was beautiful, intelligent, and refined. And – if I heard correctly – she had said "Jewish community" and "we" in the same breath. I just could not miss my opportunity. Mustering up all the newly acquired confidence I had attained from espionage, I quickly blurted out, "Is there any chance we can meet one afternoon for a coffee or tea?"

Her name was Lilli Bartels[9] and she lived in Dahlem, a district in Berlin about 10 minutes from the Mission villa. By the time we met for coffee, I was already madly in love with her. And although little by little I learned the less-savory details of her complicated life, nothing could keep me from being thoroughly infatuated. I found everything about her charming. It turned out she had a little six-year-old boy, Andreas, from a prior marriage.

A son? How adorable!

She had been married not once, but twice before.

Two marriages? The sign of an optimist!

And she currently had a lover.

Wait. A *lover*?

Not just any lover. Lilli was in an ongoing relationship with Estrongo Nachama,[10] Berlin's Chief Cantor. A Jew from Salonica, concentration camp survivor, and brilliant tenor, he was credited with reviving the small surviving Jewish community of Berlin numbering about 7,000. The cantor was a talented and formidable man. And now Lilli was about to start having an affair with me. I should have seen trouble coming. It was coming at me like a moving train, and I just stood there in its path.

As anyone in love will attest to, it is easy to ignore practicalities, complications, and red lights. Even yellow ones. I decided to ignore every color light. I became temporarily color blind. I was so color blind I did not even notice that Lilli was not a natural blonde. I was mesmerized by her, never realizing, in my lovestruck state, that I did not know this woman at all. She had her secrets, many of them, and she kept them close to her heart.

All I wanted was to spend more time with this alluring woman. I had planned to take a vacation in Italy with a group of service friends. Now I modified that plan so I would leave the group in Venice and continue travelling through Italy alone with Lilli. This would give me nearly two blissful weeks of love just with her. I presented my plan to Lilli.

"Absolutely Jack. I would love to travel with you through Italy!"

"Oh Lilli, I'm in heaven!"

"Of course, we will have to bring my son Andreas..."

I swallowed hard. "Why certainly!"

"... and my aunt must also travel with us. You know that Aunt Henriette and I are inseparable."

I knew that Lilli had lost her parents when she was just a teenager and Aunt Henriette was like a mother to her. Our romantic getaway was not turning out exactly as I had imagined, but at that point I was completely under Lilli's spell. I was prepared to walk over hot coals to be with her if that's what it took. Her son, and her aunt, in Italy with us for a romantic holiday? Heck, bring the whole extended family if you must!

And yet, the vacation turned out to be truly idyllic. Lilli's aunt acted as a de facto babysitter to Andreas, leaving us free to be a romantic couple. We explored the magnificent splendor of Italy's countryside and the glorious history of its cities. Zipping around in her brand-new Volkswagen Beetle, I wondered fleetingly how Lilli could afford the adorable, peppy car when she had no obvious form of employment.[11] Then I forgot all about these petty concerns, and enjoyed driving the tiny, agile "bug" as we explored Italy's ancient towns and sipped Montepulciano in the picturesque hillsides. At night we explored each other. Each night I made love to a beautiful woman who was confident in her own sexuality, while sultry Adriatic breezes blew in through the wide-open windows of our hot and humid hotels. I guess it was true – the Army had finally made a man out of me.

When we returned to Berlin, I had a new self-assurance, a strut in my step. How long it would last, I really did not know. My confidence could disappear with one word from Lilli ending it all. But she reassured me that she wanted our relationship to continue. I was ecstatic.

Yet not everyone was happy with our continuing involvement. For weeks after our return, the well-respected cantor sent us threatening letters. He even made lewd phone calls. He seemed to have come unhinged. And then one day it stopped. We simply did not hear from him, and we assumed he had recovered from his heartbreak and had gone away for good.

We continued our blissful relationship, both of us keeping our war traumas well hidden, and showing each other only our glamorous sides. I was an American intelligence agent during the Cold War, living a dashing life in Europe with my beautiful lover.

For that brief period, we lived a life out of a spy novel, both of us in love, and both of us in denial.

Not long after we started seeing each other regularly, Lilli began using the M word. She deftly fit it into our conversations. "It would be so nice to be married!"

Then there was the F word. No, not that one. Another one.

"It would be so good for Andreas to have a father. Such stability, and so important at this tender age, don't you think?"

I could feel myself beginning to sweat. Fatherhood? I was not ready for that. I had many things of my own to sort out first. "Look, Lilli. I am madly, deeply, head over heels in love with you. But I must be completely honest. My life back home is full of uncertainty. I don't even have an established career yet. I still have coursework to finish and don't yet have my degree and I do not have suitable employment to be able to marry you and support a family."

"And how long do you think that will take, Jack?"

"I can't be certain. Maybe a year?" I told her, though in truth I had no idea.

Why was I stalling? I loved Lilli. Yes, she was six years my senior – 31 to my 25. She had a child, two prior marriages, and lived on a different continent. If these facts gave me pause, I was not conscious of it. I hesitated, anyway, blaming my own "situation" as the excuse to delay a decision. I hemmed, and I hawed, until the decision was taken out of my hands completely.

It was just two months before I was to return home, when I got called in by my superiors. The Army had received a formal complaint about me. "We have been informed that you have been illegally selling your gas ration cards."

It was nonsense. But it was also a serious and punishable offense. An investigation was begun immediately. The Army didn't know that I had a pathological tendency towards saving just about *everything*. All the while that I had been traveling around in Lilli's VW, I had been safely storing away all my gas ration cards and now I was able to produce them on the spot.

But who had made this false accusation against me, and why? It was Cantor Nachama. Still not over Lilli, he had lodged the formal complaint.

Now that I had been vindicated, I was home free. Or was I?

The investigation had uncovered a new hiccough. The Army was now aware of my relationship with Lilli, an affair that apparently raised some serious questions.

"Jack Schwaryn?"

"It's Schwersenz, but yes, sir."

"Can you please explain how it is that you are having an ongoing liaison with a German woman while you are working in US intelligence in a supposedly clandestine intelligence location?"

"Umm... I'm in love?"

The Army didn't see the beauty in our relationship. They immediately placed me on house arrest and began an investigation. I was not allowed to see Lilli until the inquiry was complete.

Idle time was my enemy. Day after day, I sat in my room staring at the gorgeous, manicured grounds of the villa, while I wracked my brain, going over things again and again. I started to imagine the worst. Was it possible that Lilli had been an "asset?" Was her little trip to the villa to find Dr. Solomon just a ruse? Had there ever even been a Dr. Solomon? Is this how she was able to support her jobless lifestyle of glamor; of cafés and restaurants and new cars? Was her aunt even a relative, or was she an asset too? My gosh, had I been "honey trapped?"[12] Once the Army had planted the seeds of suspicion, the doubts began to take root, and the absence of activities allowed my thoughts to turn into perseverations.

Of course, I knew in my heart it wasn't possible. Our relationship was genuine. And I had never told Lilli anything about my work at the Mission; of that, I was certain. I buried my doubts and reminded myself that Lilli was not just a real woman, but one who was beautiful, sensual, extraordinarily intelligent, and unique. To top it off, she wanted to marry me. Me!

Once the Army had sorted through all the evidence and letters we had saved, they were equally convinced that the complaint about the gas cards was made by a jealous lover, and that my relationship with Lilli was entirely sincere. I was cleared and my house arrest lifted.

But by the time the Army was done with us, our blissful bond had been broken.

We thought we had recovered from the house arrest and the Army insinuations, but we felt bruised. The rapture had fizzled. After being together nearly a year and a half, I suppose that was bound to happen, but as my October discharge rapidly approached, a gloom set in. We were in a relationship that neither of us wanted to end but had no idea how to continue. A dark cloud sat over us in my final two weeks in Berlin. In our last few days, we talked only of the future, filling our heads with promises. There were so many assurances, to call, to write, to wait. To not forget. "Promise me, Jack."

"I promise, Lilli. I'll send for you and Andreas, once my life and career are in order."

And truly, I thought I meant it.

24

HOMECOMING

On October 26, 1956, the Army officially discharged me, and I headed from Germany to Fort Dix, and finally to my family in Flushing. I was coming home.

Lilli was a dilemma I had to reckon with. I was stuck and indecisive and delay seemed like the best tactic. Our first call did not go well at all. "Please be patient with me," I begged. "I need to get my life in order. How can I possibly bring you here until I can give you the life you deserve?"

Lilli was no fool. She had heard me make these weak statements before and she saw right through me. "I have a son, Jack, and I am too old for doubts and hesitation. Either you make up your mind and bring me to the United States, or I am going to end things."

I did not want to lose her, but I was equally afraid to commit. I was afraid to make any decision at all, until *not* making a decision became its own kind of choice.

I did not hear from her again. I should have sensed Lilli would land on her feet, that she would end up with a life much better than any life that I could provide her.[1] But I could not know that for sure, not for years. What I carried with me was guilt about how I had ended things – our once beautiful romance novel had turned into my betrayal without a storybook ending.

And I was certain I would never experience a romance like that again.

I am a changed man. Doesn't everyone see it?

Somehow no one did. I suppose the changes were not written across me in flashing, bold neon lights. They were not on billboards in Times Square, saying, "Look at Jack, see what a man he has become since he has been in the service."

My growth was a bit more subtle. You had to see what was going on under the proverbial hood. A bit more confidence. Worldliness. Meanwhile, I had developed a problem. I had become decidedly *less* American.

After spending years of my adolescence trying to shed my German heritage, desperate to fit in like an American, I had just spent the last two years in Germany. True, I had been a proud US soldier, but in those two years, my feelings for the country of my birth had been rekindled. I had mostly spoken German, been intimate with a German girlfriend, and relearned the culture of my youth. What was I now? How did I define myself? And there was more that had changed. Anita noticed that I no longer blindly followed her advice and direction as I had always done. My newfound independence seemed to irritate her, and a new friction came between us. And when I got cocky, she had a gift for cutting me down to size.

"So you feel pretty independent now," she said to me one evening at dinner.

"Yes. I suppose I do. I am 27 already, and I have been through a lot."

"Well, let's see, Jack. Let's go over all you've been through. By my tally, over the last few years, the Army has paid you, housed you, and fed you."

"I suppose so."

"They have protected you. Provided your medical care. Isn't that correct?"

"Yes," I replied, meekly.

"Well, I certainly hope you have a plan for how to fend for yourself. Because the Army is not going to take care of you anymore."

Anita was right, of course. I had nothing. Nada. Zilch. Nil. No career, no plan. No girlfriend, even. It was high time for me to get back on track and focus on my future. And as my never-ending luck would have it, while I was in Germany, the accounting requirements had become more stringent. As it turned out, I would now need an MBA in accounting to make up the extra course work.

I put my big nose to the grindstone. As a veteran, I was able to get my junior accounting job back, and I went to night school for my MBA. I sat for my exams. In between, I tried to squeeze in some dating – a blind date here, a fix-up there – but the women seemed no more mature than teenagers to me. They all came up short. What young woman could stand a chance against Lilli? How could anyone ever be as worldly or sophisticated?

And how did I look on paper? Not great, if I had to be honest. Twenty-seven years old and still not done with school. The word loser was beginning to ring loudly in my prominent ears, and the confidence I had gained during my time in Europe was quickly ebbing.

About a year after my return, Anita's husband, Lou, began buying jewelry on consignment from the 47th Street diamond exchange and selling it privately from home. One day, a new customer – a pleasant elementary school teacher – came to Anita and Lou's apartment to make a purchase. Although she was a total stranger, that had never stopped Anita from beginning a conversation.

"I have a brother who recently got out of the service. I hope you don't mind me asking, but do you know any single young women? A teacher like you, for example, who doesn't mind being fixed up on a date?" Anita asked with typical German directness.

"Why it so happens, I do," replied the chatty customer. "There is a lovely young teacher in the classroom adjacent to mine. I could ask whether she is available and interested in being fixed up. No, I don't mind you asking one bit."

And with that there was an exchange of phone numbers and suddenly I had a blind date on a Sunday night. I would be meeting a young teacher, Roslyn Levene – a stranger who was the friend of a stranger – and my hopes were not at all high.

I drove up to the young woman's home in Bayside, Queens. Both her parents squeezed into the doorframe to meet and assess me. Her father, Jack, was tall, fair, and blond with Charlton Heston-like good looks. Her mother, Helen, was also quite tall and attractive, but with dark skin and hair that was almost black. They looked so different from each other; I could only guess what kind of strange offspring they could produce. Just then, Roslyn came down the staircase behind them. She had apparently inherited the best of both her parents: dark wavy hair, olive skin, her father's chiseled cheekbones, and a wide, inviting smile showing even, white teeth that looked like two perfect rows of Chiclets. She was beautiful – too beautiful for me, I thought. My hands started to get clammy.

Over drinks at a nondescript restaurant on Northern Boulevard, I found myself further mesmerized. Ros was beautiful, yes, but she was surprisingly natural and down to earth. And I could not deny being charmed by the mirror she reflected at me. I could see she found me interesting. She thought I was worldly; she even thought my smoking looked sophisticated. We spoke with ease, and we parted ways, assured that we wanted to see each other again.

And perhaps for the rest of our lives.

25

AMERICANA

On our second date, I took Ros to a bar on the Bowery, a street in Manhattan lined with homeless alcoholics, the mentally ill, and a handful of scantily clad prostitutes.

What could I have been thinking? Why on earth would I bring this gorgeous gem of a woman to one of the worst slums of New York? Was I subconsciously putting her through a kind of test? Making sure she would be game to try something "off the beaten track?" Reassuring myself that she would tolerate my idiosyncrasies?

Miraculously, she still wanted to go out with me. Within weeks, Ros and I were seeing each other every weekend. She met my mother, who warmed to her immediately. Yes, even my mother liked Ros. It was impossible not to fall in love with her.

The real question was how would Ros's parents feel about me? I was nervous. I felt it was imperative that they accept me. I knew from experience that some American parents were not thrilled that I was a foreigner. I did not fit the mold and they might not be able to see past it. It was time for them to get to know me.

I parked my small European sedan in their driveway. My car was about a third of the size of their American car, whose 1950s tailfins seemed just on the verge of budding. When I entered Ros's house, I apparently interrupted a conversation she and her mother, Helen, were having about the composer, Gustav Mahler. Was that staged? For me? We all shook hands, and they switched gears, moving on to a novelist I had never heard of. It was downright intimidating. I tried to jump in, but I could not get a word in edgewise. And frankly, I did not know what to say. Was Descartes next on the agenda? *A bit of Camus for you?* I was beginning to wonder if all normal American Jews spoke this way in their day-to-day conversations.

Wedged in the corner of the little living room, stood a baby grand piano, reflecting the requisite family photos of weddings and graduations off its lacquered black surface. But the piano was not there just to hold a photograph collection. Barely had I been there 10 minutes, when Ros's very pretty, younger sister Doris slid onto the bench, pushed down her crinoline dress and began to tackle a complex Chopin sonata. Now I was really starting to sweat. I knew Ros's brother David was a brilliant actuarial student. What if he came home and started discussing math? Holy mackerel, I was way out of my depth.

Sometime between the piano recital and the upcoming statistics symposium, Ros's father, whose name was also Jack, came home from work. After greeting me with a very firm, masculine "test" handshake, he made a beeline for the large wooden console radio and turned the dial until he found a station to his liking. He then poured himself a glass of Dewar's while he hummed along to the Frank Sinatra tune that was on the air. Still holding his glass of Scotch in his left hand, he grabbed Doris off the couch with his right hand and pulled her into the center of the tiny living room, leading her in a miniaturized version of a foxtrot. "Would you like a Scotch, Jack?" he called to me, straining his voice above the music while he danced. I could swear I heard a trace of an English accent. English with a touch of Brooklyn. Or Brooklyn with a touch of English. "No? How about a Snickers bar? I aaalways keep a bahg in the freezah."

He twirled Doris, then let go of her hand and shimmied backwards into the small kitchen. Elbows bent, arms beating alternately from side to side, he snapped his fingers to the syncopated music. "Fly me to the moon," he hummed, then he came back into the living room with a frozen candy bar in his hand and tossed it to me underhand. "Here you go, Jack. Ha-ha, don't break your teeth."

Soon her father tired of dancing, and he took his drink and walked over to the tan velour La-Z Boy chair. Plopping into the seat, he pulled the lever back with his free right hand until his legs were airborne, and his back was lower than his legs. Never letting go of his Scotch, he spun his glass counterclockwise. The ice cubes clacked against each other, and he sipped lazily on his drink. I turned to Ros's mother, Helen, who had barely moved an inch. She was lounging casually on the gold velveteen sofa, her legs crossed atop the wood and glass coffee table. Helen finally put her feet down on the floor, and with what seemed like heroic effort, sat upright. She raised a crystal bowl of curiously orange commas right up to my elongated nose. "Would you care for a Cheetos?" she offered.

The whole scene left me breathless. I had never seen anything like it in my entire life.

"Your parents. They're so American. And they seem so... sophisticated," I blurted out to Ros later that evening over dinner.

Ros laughed. "Oh, American? Well, I guess in a way. But no, not really. Their families are originally from Eastern Europe, just like most Jews who came at the turn of the century – you know, Poland, Russia."

"I thought your father sounded... I don't know... English?"

Ros laughed again. "Well, it's true that my father was born in England with his older brother and sister, but he left when he was three. He has been living in New York since he was a toddler, and if you hear any accent, I can assure you, it is an affectation."

"What does your father do, if you don't mind me asking?"

"He and his brother have a business together. They sell strollers. Oh, yes, and bicycles."

Bicycles. I paused, and let the irony sink in. Her father, a bicycle salesman. "And your mother? What is her background?"

Ros continued. "My mother is from the Sussman side of the family. Her own mother died when she was quite young. Stomach cancer, I think. And her father came to the United States when he was just 14 years old. The story is that he hopped on a ship all by himself. Imagine how brave he had to have been! People were certainly tougher back then. Anyhow, I was told he changed his name to William Sussman when he got to New York."

"Changed it? From what?" I asked.

"His real name was Wolf."

Over the next four or five months, I visited the house several times. There was more Beethoven, maybe some Dostoevsky too, but I refused to be intimidated. I knew classical music pretty well from the numerous bargain-priced concerts I attended while in the service. I was reasonably literate, and I worked hard to firm up a strong, masculine handshake. Although I dreaded Helen's bland American dinners, I ate them without complaint, sneaked in salt wherever I could, and felt confident I was making a good impression overall.

One evening, while Helen and I were clearing the dishes, our conversation veered towards the hitherto taboo subject of Germans and Germany. "German men are all very authoritarian," she said to me with firm conviction and not a hint of irony. "I've been told that German women are treated like human chattel in their husbands' homes," she continued, unflinchingly.

I froze and caught my breath. Her comment had taken me totally off-guard. And it was a statement, not a question, leaving no room for debate. If Helen was willing to say this to my face, what was she saying behind my back?

I suppose I should not have been shocked, even though I felt wounded and betrayed at the time. Her comment was just one of many stereotypes circulating in American culture. After the war, American Jews were denouncing everything German: German cars, German travel, German composers. They had taken up a stance and holding firmly to it, and I had heard these sentiments before, if not quite as directly.

What surprised me is that it seemed as if *our* opinion did not even matter. No one was asking the German survivors for their thoughts or input. To be sure, there would be a wide range of carefully considered feelings. But to American Jews, there was only one answer. Denounce Germany. And at that moment after dinner, when Helen made her pronouncement, I felt like she was denouncing *me*. That I was not a true American. I was not one of them and I was not welcome here.

That night, I did not bother to correct her comic book characterization of Germans. It seemed like a conflict I just could not win. I only felt lucky that Ros herself did not share these stereotypical ideas. She loved my foreignness and found me exotic and dashing. Maybe I was just her rebellion against her parents, but I was everything her family – and every boy she had ever dated – was not.

No, I was not going to fight with her parents. Because I was also not going to be deterred. Not this time. I had no ambivalence – career prospects be damned. In May, with a ring fashioned from one of the diamond rings that had been unearthed in Holland, I asked Ros to marry me.

November 23, 1958.

It was an elaborate wedding. Ros's parents had a huge circle of friends and business clients. The men wore top hats and tails, the women, long gowns and elbow-length satin gloves. Her father even hired an opera singer, and the boisterous baritone became the main event of the night, relegating us newlyweds to second place. Of the 150 people in attendance, only 20 of the guests were my own friends and family. Ros looked beautiful, and my mother looked exceedingly uncomfortable and – no surprise – did not smile for any of the photographs. But when I looked a little closer at those photos, I saw it clearly: there wasn't a smile on my mother's face because her eyes were wet with tears.

As it was so late in the fall, we planned just a short honeymoon in historic Williamsburg immediately after the wedding, saving a six-week multi-country European tour for the following summer. We took off for Virginia in my little Simca, a French car I had imported to the States. It was metallic-blue with a manual transmission. Small, swift, and agile, it was the antithesis of the muscular American cars on the road. And I didn't care one bit. Because by then I had decided, I was going to march to my own tune. I was going to be myself.

Myself. What was that? Some kind of hybrid. German by birth and still connected to my country, for those were my roots. Jewish by heritage, a legacy strengthened by the very fact of my persecution. American by transplantation; never quite fitting in, but forever striving to.

And a survivor, always a survivor.

We continued our drive south. I considered how lucky I was to be on this road with my beautiful young wife humming softly beside me. Only 23 years old and already so accomplished. A talented pianist. A lover of classical music who would well up with tears just on hearing a magnificent melody. A well-read woman who understood the depth of a novel and could expand my world in a way I never expected. I had thought Lilli was irreplaceable, but I was wrong. It was always meant to be Ros.

As I contemplated my good fortune, an unexpected late-November snowstorm blew through, dropping 12 inches of snow in just hours. Nearly out of gas and approaching nightfall, we pulled into a tiny Appalachian village in the middle of nowhere and checked into a misbegotten hotel.

"I'm so sorry Ros," I sighed, exasperated, and embarrassed, as we stepped into the forsaken lobby with its gap-toothed front desk clerk. "This is supposed to be our honeymoon and I wanted everything to be perfect."

"Oh please, Jack." Ros laughed. "If I wanted everything to be perfect, I never would have married you. Oh, don't look so offended, Jack. I had no illusions. I knew my life would be nothing like my friends' suburban lives. That was never what I wanted. Look at it this way. This is just our first adventure, and I know we will have many!"

We carried our light luggage back outside through the snow to our plain motel room. Ros checked under the bedspread for errant pubic hair and made sure the toilet flushed, and then she exclaimed, happily, "It's clean!"

Yes, I was lucky to have found Roslyn. Thoroughly unspoiled. Totally accepting of me and my imperfections. It's true, I had curiosity and spirit, and some *joie de vivre*. But what Ros saw in me was also a facade – the dashing European ex-serviceman/intelligence officer. She would learn soon enough that she married a man riddled with insecurity and doubt. We would have a long and loving marriage, and countless adventures together – trips all over the world to exotic destinations, all on a shoestring budget, of course. But I do not think she ever imagined back then that we would be moving into my mother's one bedroom apartment in Flushing. And that we would never leave Flushing, Queens, because I would be fearful of moving too far from my mother. That I would always be afraid of becoming destitute, cold, and hungry again. That I would save and save and save money, sometimes forcing us to live as if we were poor, even when we had more than enough cash in the bank.

And when we had children, our two beautiful girls, they would grow up to have successful careers and comfortable lives. We would be a tight and close family, full of love but also full of fear. I would not be able to avoid inadvertently raising them with the anxiety that I passed down to them like a genetic disease. Yes, even my American-born children would not be entirely cured of my affliction. It would take one more generation – my five grandchildren – to finally shake the stain of persecution and immigration.

They would live carefree and without suffering, never questioning whether they belonged, in an America that felt like home.

EPILOGUE/AUTHOR'S NOTE

When my father, Jack, turned 75, he began immediately chronicling his life from his vivid memories over a period of several months. Every event in this book is true as he remembered it. It was his dream to have his story known.

Jack died in 2018, just shy of his 88th birthday. By then, he had been suffering from Alzheimer's dementia for several years, and in his last few days, he spoke only in German and called for his father constantly.

The Holocaust left its stain on an entire generation, but its effects varied depending on so many factors. Anyone with a survival story to tell went through some hardship just to stay alive. Each type of suffering was unique, and quite dependent on the person's age, country of origin, family situation and particular horror story of survival. My father, Jack, was keenly aware of how lucky he was to have avoided deportation, concentration camps and death. Yet his family lived in constant terror and survived war, deprivation, persecution, humiliation, fear, separation, and death of loved ones. The Holocaust most certainly left its mark, and the trauma had an enormous impact on the rest of Jack's life.

For Jack, his experience after escaping Germany was as

important as the events during the Holocaust. Still traumatized, Jack continued to face devastating heartbreak: antisemitism, poverty, and displacement, and the loss of his beloved father and two of his closest friends. He had escaped the worst, but the suffering continued for him as well as the entire family.

But his story by no means has an unhappy ending. By all measures my father was a successful man – it just took a lot of false starts and a great deal of hard work. While his accounting career never quite took off, and he often worked two jobs to make ends meet, in 1975, he started his own business. It was his own concept – a publishing resource for CPA firms[1] – which he operated out of our Flushing apartment. My mother, Ros, and my sister and I, who were 13 and 11 at the time, all worked in the business, and we were able to live off its modest success while he continued to teach accounting at Pace University. My father worked tirelessly to create a secure future for my sister and me and ultimately took pride that he could support our careers in finance and medicine. But no quantity of success or financial security ever shook his underlying anxiety and firm belief that all could be lost at any time. As a result, we were raised in an atmosphere of unrivalled frugality that bordered on compulsion.

My Oma, Grete (pronounced Greta), remained in Flushing, living just around the corner from us in senior housing for former German-Jewish refugees. I knew her until her death when I was 15 years old. Perhaps she wasn't the "warmest and fuzziest" of grandmothers. But she was a deeply caring woman who helped my parents immensely when they really needed her. She was indeed a gifted artisan, crafting beautiful dresses, and continuing her business as a seamstress for the rest of her life. She could never be idle, and she helped my parents and us without hesitation. Her personality flaws – her anxiety and insecurity, her temper and judgments – are presented in this story with tender understanding. Undoubtedly, however, those traits contributed to the family's social isolation upon their arrival in the States, at a time when a network of support was so critical. Nonetheless, my father loved her deeply, and fully credited his family's survival to her tenacity. She died at 86 years old, shortly after developing dementia.

My aunt Anita was diagnosed with Familial Mediterranean Fever – a periodic fever syndrome – at Robert Wood Johnson Medical Center when she was in her fifties. (Based on DNA testing, our family is 100 percent Ashkenazi Jewish with no Mediterranean DNA, however her diagnosis is not in question.) She was placed on colchicine and finally had relief of her symptoms after years of distress. Sadly, she suffered from debilitating depression – often with suicidal ideation – for most of her adult life, requiring medication, hospitalization, and at one point electroconvulsive therapy. Anita became a severe diabetic and died of complications of diabetes in her late seventies. Her children, my cousins Ronald and Lorraine, are alive and well, with healthy children and grandchildren of their own.

How I wish that I had a chance to meet my grandfather, Arthur! I'm certain Jack inherited his sense of whimsy from his father whom he described in colorful detail. Arthur's struggle with declining mental health is a tragic part of this story. His depression was not understood or recognized as a disease by my father or grandmother, and this was a source of terrible shame and guilt that my father bore his entire life. They later wondered whether my grandfather Arthur might have been bipolar, or whether he inherited some undefined mental illness from his own father, Wolf Schwersenz. Now, a specific mental health syndrome of immigrants known as Ulysses syndrome, defines the severe stress, disorientation, fatigue, sadness, insomnia, and low self-esteem experienced by my grandfather.

My mother, Roslyn, stayed with Jack until he died, remaining his best friend, supporter, lover, and eventually caregiver. He was not always an easy husband, but he had great passion, enthusiasm and curiosity, and was deeply in love with her. My mother understood him, stood by him even during hard times, and loved him. She has never left Flushing. Ros is 87 and is as beautiful as ever.

ACKNOWLEDGMENTS

I am indebted to my father, Jack, for chronicling his profoundly vivid memories of his extraordinary childhood. It was a priceless gift to his family, and an invaluable legacy. I recrafted these memories into a narrative told in the first person because it is *his* story; however, for the most part, they are not Jack's words exactly as he wrote them. Some names have been altered and dialogue has been added. I tried to make the dialogue as authentic as I could, and relied on my own recollections of my grandmother, Grete (who spoke with my father daily, usually in German or heavily accented English), and my own observations of my Aunt Anita and my grandparents Helen and Jack Levene.

Some corrections have been made where my father's memory was inconsistent with historical facts and dates, or where he did not have access to information (the internet was not available when he originally wrote down his memories). These are footnoted wherever possible. In some instances, Jack's thoughts and opinions regarding appearance, gender, or nationality, might be considered insensitive by today's standards, and I deeply apologize for anything that may be found offensive to today's reader.

Some historical information about the times is provided in *American Wolf* to give the reader context to this narrative. Most of this I researched personally. However, I am neither a historian, nor an investigative journalist, and by no means is this book intended to be an authoritative historical reference.

The sacrifices made by my father, my aunt Anita, and my grandparents Grete and Arthur – to leave their home behind, come to America, and struggle to start life anew – were immeasurable.

Any little peculiarities in their personalities that are illustrated in this book are done so with the utmost love, tenderness and compassion.

There are many people I want to thank who have played some part in the creation of this book.

First, I would like to thank Liesbeth Heenk, the founder of Amsterdam Publishers, who has been pivotal in helping this book see daylight. Her mission to publish these Holocaust and World War II survival stories and get them into the hands of readers is invaluable. I recommend reading the entire collection, as each story offers a unique and fascinating insight. We are most certainly the last living generation with first-hand knowledge of the Holocaust. The AP Authors' Group has also been a wonderful source of knowledge, camaraderie, and shared experience.

For providing factual and family information, I would like to thank the following individuals:

Thank you to Noemi Arndt who shared memories of her grandfather Siegfried Arndt (written here as cousin Sigfried), her father Ludwig (Lutz), and her Great Aunt Paula Kahnemann, a brave, proud, and fearless woman who lived through many hardships of her own, including transit aboard the *St Louis*. (Any comments about her personality belong strictly to my grandmother, Grete; I have no direct knowledge of Paula's true character.)

Thank you to Helene Greenwald, my second cousin who I discovered through writing this book. Helene shared memories of her mother – my father's cousin Elsa Jacobsohn (written here as Ilse Jacobsohn) – and her dear grandparents Hedwig (Hede) and Arthur Jacobsohn who were of so much help to my family upon their arrival in New York. Helene also had a treasure trove of my own family's photos in her possession, some of which she graciously shared.

Thank you to journalist Claudia Keller, whose priceless book about Lilli and Estrongo Nachama filled in many holes in my understanding of my father's relationship with this fascinating woman.

My family has been a source of tremendous support during this long journey. First, I owe gratitude beyond words to my husband Richard who spent hours watching me write and write, and cry, and write, and cry some more, while I practically lived a story that felt as real to me as if I were experiencing it myself.

Much affection and gratitude to my sister, Nanette Jacobson, who has been a source of love, protection, and strength since I was born – she is the only person who could ever understand what it was like to have Jack as a father. Together, in our own way, we were also "survivors."

With love and thanks to my mother, Ros, for being a wonderful wife to Jack, for learning to make *Sauerbraten* and *Rouladen* just because he liked it, and for loving him and caring for him until the end of his life. I am blessed to still have her as a mother.

To my cousins, Ronald and Lorraine, I am grateful the insights they could offer about their mother, Anita, as well as priceless photographs.

I have had the good fortune of having friends and readers who have read various iterations of *American Wolf.*

Thank you to Tziporah Thall, who has been my rock and spirit guide for most of my adult life.

Thank you to the wonderful novelist Katie Sise, whose encouragement and advice were indispensable to me as a novice writer. I am indebted to her for hours of unsolicited and generous guidance.

Thank you to Dr. Nadine Keegan for her careful and thoughtful edits. Thank you to Ann Boyle, Leslie Seidman, Dr. Lisa Namerow, Dr. David Weiss, Susan Dodes, Stacy Charney and Tina Kramer for their encouragement, their edits, and for reading, even when *American Wolf* wasn't all that readable. Thank you to Neha Bar and Dr. Caroline Cho for being the spirited, deep readers that they are.

I am grateful to the current government of Germany for honorably coming to terms with the missteps of its past and restoring German citizenship to the progeny of those for whom it was revoked during the reign of Hitler. Both my sister and I have become naturalized German citizens as have all our children.

Our family is forever indebted to Ellis and Bessie Arndt, without whom we would have all perished.

I dedicate this book to the next generation: my nephews Evan and Jeremy Jacobson, and my three wonderful children, Laura, Daniel, and Andrew Birnbaum.

PHOTOS

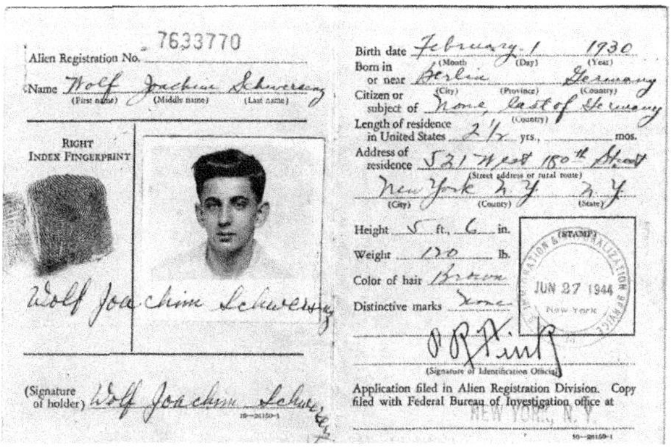

Alien Registration No. 7633770
Name Wolf Joachim Schwerin (First name) (Middle name) (Last name)
RIGHT INDEX FINGERPRINT
Wolf Joachim Schwerin
(Signature of holder) Wolf Joachim Schwerin
10—20150-1

Birth date February 1 1930 (Month) (Day) (Year)
Born in or near Berlin Germany (City) (Province) (Country)
Citizen or subject of None, last of Germany (Country)
Length of residence in United States 2½ yrs., mos.
Address of residence 521 West 180th Street (Street address or rural route)
New York N.Y. N.Y. (City) (County) (State)
Height 5 ft., 6 in.
Weight 120 lb.
Color of hair Brown
Distinctive marks None
(STAMP) IMMIGRATION & NATURALIZATION SERVICE JUN 27 1944 New York
(Signature of Identification Official)
Application filed in Alien Registration Division. Copy filed with Federal Bureau of Investigation office at NEW YORK, N.Y.
10—20150-1

Alien registration in New York, age 14. On the right, it states, Citizen of "none."

Jack, returning from Fort Dix, with his mother, Grete.

Jack (left) at sea with a friend in the US Army, heading back to Germany, 1955.

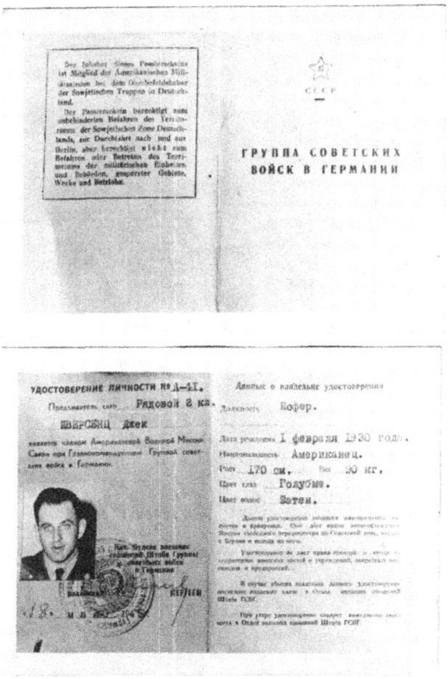

Der Inhaber dieses Passierscheins ist Mitglied der Amerikanischen Militärmission bei dem Oberbefehlshaber der Sowjetischen Truppen in Deutschland.

Der Passierschein berechtigt zum unbehinderten Befahren des Territoriums der Sowjetischen Zone Deutschlands, zur Durchfahrt nach und aus Berlin, aber berechtigt nicht zum Befahren oder Betreten des Territoriums der militärischen Einheiten und Behörden, gesperrter Gebiete, Werke und Betriebe.

СССР

ГРУППА СОВЕТСКИХ ВОЙСК В ГЕРМАНИИ

УДОСТОВЕРЕНИЕ ЛИЧНОСТИ № Д-41.

Предъявитель сего Рядовой 2 кл.

ШВЕРСЕНЦ Джек

является членом Американской Военной Миссии Связи при Главнокомандующем Группой советских войск в Германии.

Данные о владельце удостоверения

Должность Шофер.

Дата рождения 1 февраля 1930 года.

Национальность Американец.

Рост 170 см. Вес 90 кг.

Цвет глаз Голубые.

Цвет волос Шатен.

Jack's Russian Identity Card for the US Service during the Cold War.

The Mission Liaison villa in Potsdam.

The not-so-stealth Ford "spy" car.

Jack and Lilli in Italy.

East German train with soldiers: "May the friendship between people strengthen and prosper."

Russian military exercises in East Germany.

Russian soldier and tank.

On Jack's wedding day, with Roslyn, 1958.

Ronald Molatto, Grete, Roslyn, Jack, Lou Molatto, Anita, and Lorraine, 1958.

Roslyn's parents, Helen and Jack Levene, 1958.

Jack just before putting his vivid memories on paper with his daughter and author Audrey Birnbaum, 2004.

NOTES

1. For Richer or Poorer

1. The factory town of Swarsedz may have been the origin of the "Germanized" name Schwersenz.

2. Schillerstrasse, Charlottenburg

1. Paula practiced dentistry for many years and did go to a "practical" dental school; she was for some time the only practicing dentist in her town. However, she did not have advanced academic schooling or academic training as a "Doctor" of Dentistry. She later joined her husband in a very successful merchandising business, and after his death, she began her own successful store.
2. Although Wolf referred to his first cousin in his memoirs as Ilse Jacobsohn, family and genealogy records show the correct spelling of her name to be Elsa M. Jacobsohn, daughter of Hedwig and Arthur Jacobsohn.
3. Although Wolf could not remember his uncle's name, records from Yad Vashem show it to be Alfred Herrmann, born 2/25/1889 in Schwetz (now part of Poland).

3. The Beginning of the End

1. Hermann Tietz, a Jewish merchant from Posen, began the "Department store" concept in Germany. With 10 luxury department stores in Berlin and 13,000 employees, it was the largest chain of department stores in Germany.
2. Today the term "domestic worker" would be used, however the term "maid" was not considered pejorative at the time.
3. Cousin Sigfried: not to be confused with Grete's brother *Uncle* Siegfried, the spelling of Sigfried has been slightly modified.
4. The Plischkes were not able to leave for America until 1939 on the Belgian ship *Alex van Opstal*, a ship that was torpedoed later that year and was the first naval casualty of WWII.
5. Both Kolberg and Kohlberg exist in Germany, but neither is on the Baltic; however the Polish city of Kolobrzeg on the Baltic is known for its spas, and this may be where Wolf went.

4. Juden Verboten

1. The Jewish Symphony was allowed by the Nazi regime, who exploited it as propaganda: proof that Jews were not being mistreated.
2. Now Ethiopia and Eritrea.

5. Letters and Lines and Boarders

1. Wolf described the content of the letter in his memoirs; it is written here for literary purposes only.
2. The British were trying to appease the Arabs by strictly limiting Jewish immigration. A formal policy known as the White Paper was signed by the British in 1939, limiting Jewish immigration to Palestine to 75,000 people over a period of five years.
3. Eugenic theory first proposed in 1883 by Sir Francis Galton piggybacked on Darwinian theories with ideas on how to genetically "improve" a race and rid itself of unwanted traits.
4. German secret police.
5. Genealogy research has determined that Grete was referring to David and Rosalie Jeruchem (née Oppel), originally of Lobsenz, whose address in Berlin was 4 Leibnitzstrasse.

7. Walking on Broken Glass

1. Herschel Grynszpan, a 17-year-old Polish Jew who had been living in France, learned that the Nazis had exiled his parents to Poland from Hanover, Germany. In retaliation, on November 7, 1938, he shot Ernst vom Rath, a German diplomat in Paris. Joseph Goebbels, the Nazi minister for propaganda, used the assassination to rile Hitler's supporters into an antisemitic frenzy.
2. Now Croatia.
3. How they smuggled their way out was never fully explained, but in 1939 Paula and her son Arthur were aboard the *St. Louis* which left from Hamburg carrying nearly 1,000 Jews destined for Cuba and was denied entry upon arrival. The US would not allow its passengers entry, and the ship turned around with no choice but to bring its passengers back to Germany. After desperate pleas, several European countries (Britain, France, Belgium, the Netherlands) each allowed several hundred passengers entry. Paula did eventually emigrate to the United States with her daughters Meta and Ilse, and her grandchildren, Klaus, and Evelyn. Well over 200 passengers that were returned to Europe perished in the Holocaust.

8. Minus One

1. Anita's exact transportation route is unknown, but this was a typical transportation route from continental Europe to London in that year.
2. A person considered racially or socially inferior.

9. Victor, Victorious

1. Over 17,000 Jews fled to Shanghai, the majority after Kristallnacht. Until 1939, no visas were required. Most lived in poverty upon arrival in the equivalent of refugee camps/group shelters.
2. Breckenridge Long, the Assistant Secretary of State in charge of the Visa Department, wrote in an inter-department memo: "We can...effectively stop for a... period of indefinite length the number of immigrants into the United States... by simply advising our consuls to put every obstacle in the way... and to resort to various administrative devices which would postpone and postpone and postpone the granting of the visas." (judiciary.house.gov)
3. Wolf is most likely referring to the Reichsvertretung der Deutschen Juden (Reich Representation of German Jews) established in September 1933 by women organizers. Its headquarters were in Charlottenburg, Berlin, on Kantstrasse.
4. Although Wolf recalled the departure date as June 10, it is more likely that their ticket was for some time later in June, in the few days or weeks after Italy declared war on France and Britain.

12. Preparations

1. Wolf's writings did not give the classmate a specific name; he is just referred to as a "classmate." For dramatic purposes he is referred to as "Karl Ludwig" here.

14. Across the Atlantic

1. About $10,000 in today's dollars.
2. Some descriptions of the *Navemar* have been obtained from direct newspaper clippings and historical records, enhancing Wolf's otherwise vivid descriptions with further factual information.
3. According to historical and newspaper records, the *Navemar*'s departure was delayed in the Lisbon port while nearly 250 people with expired visas waited desperately while the American consulate in Lisbon worked to have their US visas extended. A monumental effort to gather personnel to issue the documents was undertaken for this purpose. Over 40 consuls participated in the effort. An American Jewish refugee committee even sent cash to Lisbon to purchase typewriters to process the massive paperwork in time.
4. A severe and systemic form of Salmonella food poisoning. The cause of the dysentery was never established. Wolf's family was convinced that it was the

oxen, whereas other passengers thought it might have been a seafood meal several days earlier.

5. The question of mutiny did arise, but it came entirely from the ship's crew who were distraught by the ship's conditions and went on a cleaning strike. Many of the crew eventually abandoned the ship before it arrived at its final port.
6. There was one official doctor on board the *Navemar*. However, passengers on board the ship who were physicians and nurses did their best to care for the sick during the voyage, at risk to their own personal safety, often treating up to 200 sick passengers each day.
7. The event was sponsored by the ladies of the Imperial Order of the Daughters of the Empire and the Bermuda Women's Auxiliary Force, according to "The Nevermore at Bermuda," by Dr. Edward Harris, *The Royal Gazette,* October 6, 2012.
8. Reports vary but there may have been up to 100 children on the ship, still a small percentage of the total passenger figures. The youngest was 10 weeks old, and many may have been an inappropriate age for a swimming trip such as Wolf described.
9. There were six deaths aboard the *Navemar*, and a seventh upon arrival. About 60 percent of the passengers developed dysentery. Upon docking, 35 ill passengers were taken to Ellis Island for quarantine in addition to those removed in Bermuda. A lawsuit was filed against the Navemar for the unsafe and unsanitary conditions, the response to which was a discontinuation of any further ticket sales on any ships to Jews. The *Navemar* was the last ship to make a transatlantic rescue voyage with a large number of Jews. The *Navemar* was sunk by an Italian submarine (*Barbarigo*) off the coast of Portugal in January of 1942.

15. No Instruction Manual

1. Landmark "five and dime" chain store.
2. Bessie Arndt née Hirsch was a former Rockette's dancer.

16. Extermination

1. Irma and Siegfried Jacob's date of death is listed as November 25, 1941 in Kovno, in the Holocaust Memorial database. Most Jews on the Berlin transports were shot upon arrival at their destinations.
2. Jack (Wolf) did not have access to the Holocaust database and never knew exactly what happened to his friends and relatives.
3. Holocaust records show the death of one Heinz Bernd Spiegel, born March 10, 1928, murdered in Auschwitz on October 28, 1944, after being transferred from Theresienstadt concentration camp the day before. Records show Ella Hammer to be on a transport to Riga on October 19, 1942, and murdered in Riga on October 22, likely upon arrival.

20. Found and Lost

1. Jack was unable to recall the code name used and Bakker is used here as a placeholder.
2. Now Greece.

21. New Beginnings, Same Old Endings

1. Worth about $250,000 today.
2. Revered concert pianist who left Nazi Germany in 1939.
3. Jack did not know the first name of the notorious Mr. Kissel, and more information about him is unavailable.
4. Bella V. Dodd did carry the dubious distinction of being the country's top communist in the late 1940s. She was a teacher, lawyer, and labor union activist. She was expelled from the Communist party in 1949, continued to practice law, and went on to denounce communism, testifying against party members to the US. She joined the Catholic church in 1952 and made an unsuccessful run for US Congress in 1968.
5. Jack misremembered the boy's name as Mike, but numerous news articles list the boy as Elliot Zemek, of Brooklyn, NY.
6. Originally named Vlissingen.

22. Making me into a Man

1. Rubella, or German measles, is very serious to pregnant women as it carries great risks to the developing fetus, but for most adults it is a mild, albeit highly contagious, infection.

23. The Return

1. 1954 comedy-musical with Howard Keel, set in the 1850s Oregon.
2. After WWII, the US took over various hotels and recreational facilities and used them as training or recreational facilities for US servicemen.
3. The "final solution," i.e., the plan to send all Jews east to extermination camps, was decided at a Nazi meeting at Lake Wannsee in 1942.
4. The Glienecke Bridge (noted in the 2015 Spielberg film "Bridge of Spies") was a common location for spy exchanges during the Cold War.
5. The leader of East Germany at the time.
6. Ford used his status as one of America's most trusted business leaders to systematically spread conspiracy theories about Jews. His diatribes against Jews in his own publication were so well known that he was complimented by name in Hitler's *Mein Kampf*.
7. Marshal Andrei Grechko was a former Russian WWII hero who would one day become the Marshal of the Soviet Union.

8. The Edsel was a heavily marketed/hyped Ford brand that did not live up to expectations and was scrapped after just two years on the market.
9. (née Schlochauer).
10. Keller, Claudia. *Lilli und Estrongo Nachama. Zwei Solisten – Ein Paar.* Hentrich & Hentrich 2018.
11. Jack did not know that Lilli used a "compensation pension" from the German government to fund many of her expenses (Keller, Claudia).
12. Jack's relationship with Lilli was investigated and cleared. He did not ever really suspect her of being an asset, despite suspicions raised by the Army about their relationship.

24. Homecoming

1. Lilli rekindled her relationship with the cantor, which led to a marriage and partnership that lasted until his death. Their contribution to the restoration and growth of the Jewish community of Berlin was monumental. Nachama would go on to lead a rich and storied life as a cantor, opera singer, and humanitarian. He would adopt Andreas who would become a rabbi, a leader in the Jewish community, an author and scholar.

Epilogue/Author's note

1. The business Jack created was Building Blocks for CPA Firms, and the publication was CPA-Client Communications.

ABOUT THE AUTHOR

Audrey Birnbaum is a physician specializing in pediatric gastroenterology. Her father's moving story of escaping the Nazis inspired her to write her first non-medical book, American Wolf. Audrey lives with her husband north of New York City. She has three grown children and is currently working on a novel.

AMSTERDAM PUBLISHERS HOLOCAUST LIBRARY

The series **Holocaust Survivor Memoirs World War II** consists of the following autobiographies of survivors:

Outcry. Holocaust Memoirs, by Manny Steinberg

Hank Brodt Holocaust Memoirs. A Candle and a Promise, by Deborah Donnelly

The Dead Years. Holocaust Memoirs, by Joseph Schupack

Rescued from the Ashes. The Diary of Leokadia Schmidt, Survivor of the Warsaw Ghetto, by Leokadia Schmidt

My Lvov. Holocaust Memoir of a twelve-year-old Girl, by Janina Hescheles

Remembering Ravensbrück. From Holocaust to Healing, by Natalie Hess

Wolf. A Story of Hate, by Zeev Scheinwald with Ella Scheinwald

Save my Children. An Astonishing Tale of Survival and its Unlikely Hero, by Leon Kleiner with Edwin Stepp

Holocaust Memoirs of a Bergen-Belsen Survivor & Classmate of Anne Frank, by Nanette Blitz Konig

Defiant German - Defiant Jew. A Holocaust Memoir from inside the Third Reich, by Walter Leopold with Les Leopold

In a Land of Forest and Darkness. The Holocaust Story of two Jewish Partisans, by Sara Lustigman Omelinski

Holocaust Memories. Annihilation and Survival in Slovakia, by Paul Davidovits

From Auschwitz with Love. The Inspiring Memoir of Two Sisters' Survival, Devotion and Triumph Told by Manci Grunberger Beran & Ruth Grunberger Mermelstein, by Daniel Seymour

Remetz. Resistance Fighter and Survivor of the Warsaw Ghetto, by Jan Yohay Remetz

My March Through Hell. A Young Girl's Terrifying Journey to Survival, by Halina Kleiner with Edwin Stepp

Roman's Journey, by Roman Halter

Beyond Borders. Escaping the Holocaust and Fighting the Nazis. 1938-1948, by Rudi Haymann

The Engineers. A memoir of survival through World War II in Poland and Hungary, by Henry Reiss

Memoirs by Elmar Rivosh, Sculptor (1906-1967). Riga Ghetto and Beyond, by Elmar Rivosh

The series **Holocaust Survivor True Stories** consists of the following biographies:

Among the Reeds. The true story of how a family survived the Holocaust, by Tammy Bottner

A Holocaust Memoir of Love & Resilience. Mama's Survival from Lithuania to America, by Ettie Zilber

Living among the Dead. My Grandmother's Holocaust Survival Story of Love and Strength, by Adena Bernstein Astrowsky

Heart Songs. A Holocaust Memoir, by Barbara Gilford

Shoes of the Shoah. The Tomorrow of Yesterday, by Dorothy Pierce

Hidden in Berlin. A Holocaust Memoir, by Evelyn Joseph Grossman

Separated Together. The Incredible True WWII Story of Soulmates Stranded an Ocean Apart, by Kenneth P. Price, Ph.D.

The Man Across the River. The incredible story of one man's will to survive the Holocaust, by Zvi Wiesenfeld

If Anyone Calls, Tell Them I Died. A Memoir, by Emanuel (Manu) Rosen

The House on Thrömerstrasse. A Story of Rebirth and Renewal in the Wake of the Holocaust, by Ron Vincent

Dancing with my Father. His hidden past. Her quest for truth. How Nazi Vienna shaped a family's identity, by Jo Sorochinsky

The Story Keeper. Weaving the Threads of Time and Memory - A Memoir, by Fred Feldman

Krisia's Silence. The Girl who was not on Schindler's List, by Ronny Hein

Defying Death on the Danube. A Holocaust Survival Story, by Debbie J. Callahan with Henry Stern

A Doorway to Heroism. A decorated German-Jewish Soldier who became an American Hero, by Rabbi W. Jack Romberg

The Shoemaker's Son. The Life of a Holocaust Resister, by Laura Beth Bakst

The Redhead of Auschwitz. A True Story, by Nechama Birnbaum

Land of Many Bridges. My Father's Story, by Bela Ruth Samuel Tenenholtz

Creating Beauty from the Abyss. The Amazing Story of Sam Herciger, Auschwitz Survivor and Artist, by Lesley Ann Richardson

On Sunny Days We Sang. A Holocaust Story of Survival and Resilience, by Jeannette Grunhaus de Gelman

Painful Joy. A Holocaust Family Memoir, by Max J. Friedman

I Give You My Heart. A True Story of Courage and Survival, by Wendy Holden

In the Time of Madmen, by Mark A. Prelas

Monsters and Miracles. Horror, Heroes and the Holocaust, by Ira Wesley Kitmacher

Flower of Vlora. Growing up Jewish in Communist Albania, by Anna Kohen

Aftermath: Coming of Age on Three Continents. A Memoir, by Annette Libeskind Berkovits

Not a real Enemy. The True Story of a Hungarian Jewish Man's Fight for Freedom, by Robert Wolf

Zaidy's War. Four Armies, Three Continents, Two Brothers. One Man's Impossible Story of Endurance, by Martin Bodek

The Glassmaker's Son. Looking for the World my Father left behind in Nazi Germany, by Peter Kupfer

The Apprentice of Buchenwald. The True Story of the Teenage Boy Who Sabotaged Hitler's War Machine, by Oren Schneider

Good for a Single Journey, by Helen Joyce

Burying the Ghosts. She escaped Nazi Germany only to have her life torn apart by the woman she saved from the camps: her mother, by Sonia Case

American Wolf. From Nazi Refugee to American Spy. A True Story, by Audrey Birnbaum

Bipolar Refugee. A Saga of Survival and Resilience, by Peter Wiesner

In the Wake of Madness. My Family's Escape from the Nazis, by Bettie Lennett Denny

Before the Beginning and After the End, by Hymie Anisman

Malka Owsiany recounts, by Mark Turkow (editor)

I Will Give Them an Everlasting Name. Jacksonville's Stories of the Holocaust, by Samuel P. Cox

The series **Jewish Children in the Holocaust** consists of the following autobiographies of Jewish children hidden during WWII in the Netherlands:

Searching for Home. The Impact of WWII on a Hidden Child, by Joseph Gosler

See You Tonight and Promise to be a Good Boy! War memories, by Salo Muller

Sounds from Silence. Reflections of a Child Holocaust Survivor, Psychiatrist and Teacher, by Robert Krell

Sabine's Odyssey. A Hidden Child and her Dutch Rescuers, by Agnes Schipper

The Journey of a Hidden Child, by Harry Pila and Robin Black

The series **New Jewish Fiction** consists of the following novels, written by Jewish authors. All novels are set in the time during or after the Holocaust.

The Corset Maker. A Novel, by Annette Libeskind Berkovits

Escaping the Whale. The Holocaust is over. But is it ever over for the next generation? by Ruth Rotkowitz

When the Music Stopped. Willy Rosen's Holocaust, by Casey Hayes

Hands of Gold. One Man's Quest to Find the Silver Lining in Misfortune, by Roni Robbins

The Girl Who Counted Numbers. A Novel, by Roslyn Bernstein

There was a garden in Nuremberg. A Novel, by Navina Michal Clemerson

The Butterfly and the Axe, by Omer Bartov

To Live Another Day. A Novel, by Elizabeth Rosenberg

A Worthy Life. Based on a True Story, by Dahlia Moore

The Right to Happiness & Other Stories. Holocaust reverberations upon survivors and their children, by Helen Schary Motro

The series **Holocaust Heritage** consists of the following memoirs by 2G:

The Cello Still Sings. A Generational Story of the Holocaust and of the Transformative Power of Music, by Janet Horvath

The Fire and the Bonfire. A Journey into Memory, by Ardyn Halter

The Silk Factory: Finding Threads of My Family's True Holocaust Story, by Michael Hickins

Hidden in Plain Sight. A Journey into Memory and Place, by Julie Brill

Winter Light. The Memoir of a Child of Holocaust Survivors, by Grace Feuerverger

Hiding in Holland, by Shulamit Reinharz

Stumbling Stones, by Joanna Rosenthall

The series **Holocaust Books for Young Adults** consists of the following novels, based on true stories:

The Boy behind the Door. How Salomon Kool Escaped the Nazis. Inspired by a True Story, by David Tabatsky

Running for Shelter. A True Story, by Suzette Sheft

The Precious Few. An Inspirational Saga of Courage based on True Stories, by David Twain with Art Twain

The Sun will Shine on You again one Day, by Cynthia Monsour

The series **WWII Historical Fiction** consists of the following novels, some of which are based on true stories:

Mendelevski's Box. A Heartwarming and Heartbreaking Jewish Survivor's Story, by Roger Swindells

A Quiet Genocide. The Untold Holocaust of Disabled Children in WWII Germany, by Glenn Bryant

The Knife-Edge Path, by Patrick T. Leahy

Brave Face. The Inspiring WWII Memoir of a Dutch/German Child, by I. Caroline Crocker and Meta A. Evenbly

When We Had Wings. The Gripping Story of an Orphan in Janusz Korczak's Orphanage. A Historical Novel, by Tami Shem-Tov

Jacob's Courage. Romance and Survival amidst the Horrors of War, by Charles S. Weinblatt

A Semblance of Justice, by Wolf Holles

Between Shadows and Light, by Jordan Steven Sher

Made in United States
North Haven, CT
23 December 2023

46467840R00253